# WHEELS
# OF
# FORTUNE

# WHEELS OF FORTUNE

## The History of Speculation from Scandal to Respectability

## Charles R. Geisst

John Wiley & Sons, Inc.

*For Margaret and Meg*

# Contents

# Acknowledgments

I WANT TO THANK JEANNE GLASSER AT JOHN WILEY & Sons for overseeing the book from beginning to end. Special thanks also to Ingram Pinn for designing the illustration opposite the title page depicting Richard Nixon and Harold Wilson berating the infamous gnomes of Zurich for speculating in the currency markets. Without the gnomes, the financial futures markets would have a much different history.

# Introduction

O N A DARK NIGHT IN CHICAGO IN THE LATE NINE-
teenth century, an old man was accosted by several
ruffians intent on robbing him. When they discovered that he was none other than Old Hutch, a legendary pit trader on the Chicago Board of Trade (CBOT),
they ran off, leaving him with his money and bragging rights
forever. Such was the power of commodities traders in the
nineteenth century. They and the exchanges where they plied
their trade were sources of legend and loathing.

Almost from the very beginning, the markets have been
called every imaginable name, from gambling dens to vital centers of commerce. They have been decried as having no economic value, yet praised as valuable marketing mechanisms.
After 150 years, their place in financial markets is vital and still
disputed. The commodities futures markets invite a wide
panoply of interpretation—from being the home of Satan
himself to the cathedrals of the messiahs of business, depending upon one's point of view. Certainly, there has been no
shortage of opinion.

How these simple markets could evoke such deep emotions

frames their history since their inception. The constant turmoil surrounding futures trading since it began in St. Louis and Chicago before the Civil War is a vital part of its history. Any market relying on the open-outcry system of trading, where traders communicate with each other by voice and hand signals in a trading area, or *pit,* is bound to come under criticism. It seems an unlikely place for serious economic functions to be performed. Critics contend that pit trading is for gamblers who stack the odds in their favor. They are neither buying nor selling on fundamentals but using collusion and manipulation to earn their living. Nineteenth- and twentieth-century farmers used this argument without fail but never succeeded in convincing legislators to alter or abolish futures trading. (They did come close, however.)

When the markets first developed, good intentions were quickly swept away by the urge to trade. The original commodity contracts were nothing more than *when-arrive* contracts, meaning that a trader would pay another trader a specific price established in the present for a future delivery. There was no intention to trade them once they were created. However, speculative elements soon took over as it became clear that dynamic speculative markets were much more interesting—and profitable—than static forward markets. Contracts began trading on a futures basis within a few years. Almost immediately, cries of foul were heard, mostly from farmers who realized that their cash prices were vacillating as a result. More conservative elements in the business community also decried open-outcry futures trading, believing that the commodities markets were becoming as bastardized as the stock markets, which were already well-known for bear raids and corners before the Civil War.

The history of the futures and derivatives markets is full of misunderstandings and false assumptions. Over the years, doubts have lingered, although the fundamentals of the markets are extremely simple and, in fact, based upon concepts that users and suppliers of commodities understand well. Simplicity can be a mixed blessing, however; the mechanics may be straightforward, but the applications may be highly sophisticated—even nightmarish. It is no wonder that nineteenth-century farmers proclaimed ignorance of the markets, and it is of even less wonder that financial experts were confused by the problems encountered by Orange County, California, during the early 1990s, when they tried to sort out the mess in its derivatives portfolio.

A futures contract is a contract to either buy or sell a specific amount of a commodity at a specific price for a distinguishable period of time. After the contract expires on a standard date within a month, it becomes worthless, so it has a useful but limited life for traders. Within its lifespan, the futures price will fluctuate, depending upon the volatility of the commodity itself. Farmers, anticipating a crop, would sell contracts short at a predetermined price and deliver their crop when it is ready for the marketplace. Processors of the commodity would similarly lock in a price by buying contracts and taking delivery. Price uncertainty is removed in the process. Whatever happens to prices after the trades is of no consequence, for the deals are done at a specified price.

This simple selling (going short) or buying (going long) indicates that both parties engage in hedging, the fundamental reason that futures markets were established. During a contract's life, however, prices on the underlying commodity (cash prices) will continue to vacillate. The earliest traders saw opportunity in this vacillation. If they could buy or sell contracts again, rather than take delivery, they could make a profit without being bothered with the eventual physical delivery of the commodity itself. Buying or selling wheat futures for a profit was certainly better than having to take delivery of the wheat and then disposing of it in the cash market. Hence, futures trading became popular almost immediately.

When the urge to trade exploded in the markets, a whole new world of market mechanics and chicanery was born. Traders soon recognized that cash prices and futures prices moved quickly in tandem and could be manipulated for personal gain. However, the tricks were not easy to execute. One of the first market operations to be mounted was known as a *corner*. A trader attempted to corner the existing supply of a cash commodity and then force the seller of the futures contract to settle at the trader's price to fulfill the seller's obligation. By buying more wheat contracts than actual wheat in supply, prices would rise precipitously, often wiping out those who sold the contracts. When the seller realizes that no wheat to deliver can be found, that seller will be at the mercy of the longs who exacted their financial revenge. The commodity will have been cornered and the shorts will have been routed.

One of the first masters of this art of deception and hoarding was Benjamin Hutchinson, or Old Hutch, of Chicago. He ruined dozens of floor traders during his years in the pits and was damaged more than once himself. His reputation became so fearsome that even premature reports of his death sent wheat prices gyrating. Despite his harsh method of dealing with fellow traders, Hutchinson constantly denied that wheat corners were possible. Time and again he maintained that there were simply too many amber waves of grain in the Midwest to assume that any mere mortal could actually corner the market in wheat. Of course, that was usually a signal that a corner indeed was being mounted, and other traders would scurry to join the operation or run for cover.

Futures trading became the signature of cowboy capitalism. The possibilities were endless, there were no boundaries, and the rules of the game only seemed to be made up along the way. The longs and the shorts stood opposite each other to have a shoot-out of sorts, with the stronger, more dexterous surviving. Farmers objected to the futures exchanges because of these myths and the amounts of money said to be made in corners and bear raids, both exact opposites. When the corner and the bear raid were combined in the same operation by a particularly clever pit trader, it became very difficult to tell what exactly was happening. Normally, traders used the cash markets and the futures markets in tandem to mount a corner. Bewildered farmers responded by asking state legislators to shut the exchanges.

Oddly, the first attempts at closing the markets were the best and only chance for farmers to accomplish that objective. By the beginning of the twentieth century, the markets were well established, and although suggestions that they be abolished occasionally were made, they were never seriously entertained. However, regulation at the federal level was slow in coming. The first attempt to regulate the markets came in the 1920s, with legislation aimed at grain trading. In 1936, it was expanded to all futures trading in the Commodity Exchange Act, the futures markets' equivalent of the Securities Exchange Act of 1934. The exchanges barely noticed, though; they were accustomed to having their own way for so many years that they took little notice of the law, and attempts to enforce it were rarely effective. Cowboy capitalism did not recognize a sheriff without a loaded gun.

One of the central issues in the futures history is determining whether the sheriff has power to control the markets. In the early 1970s, a major turning point in futures history came when options on common stock were introduced along with financial futures. Contracts on financial instruments opened the markets to more participants than at any other time and ensured their success. Unfortunately for the commodities act, there was nothing in it about nonagricultural futures, and the new markets grew rapidly with no effective regulator until the Commodity Futures Trading Commission (CFTC) was created in 1974.

After the futures exchanges introduced financial futures, the markets began to achieve the respectability that had been lacking for decades. Now they were able to offer futures contracts on bonds, money market instruments, and stock index futures, as well as options on common stock, which were also developed in the early 1970s. The ironic part of this was that these were contracts on underlying instruments traded in New York rather than in Chicago. The cash market—the market for the securities themselves—was found elsewhere, which, oddly, gave the derivatives markets more legitimacy. The prices made on the derivatives were based solely on the cash instruments and investor demand. When the futures markets traded only agricultural contracts, prices actually were trusted less, because the cash prices were made under the same exchange roof. Having futures and cash prices made in the same locale often gave rise to corners and bear raids. Separating the two gave the markets greater credibility.

Only when greater trust was achieved could the true function of the futures markets be realized. If all of the various functions of the markets could be summarized in one term, it would be *price discovery*. The true price of any commodity is the cash price, assuming that it incorporates the factors that influence its futures prices. If the price of widgets is $1.00 cash and 97 cents for delivery in six months, then the futures price would reflect market factors and conditions as well as the cost of storing the commodity for the length of the futures contract. Only by comparing the cash and futures prices can one determine whether the cash price is reflective of true value or an aberration in point of time.

The traditional futures markets became swamped by financial innovation during the 1980s and 1990s with the arrival of the swaps market. When banks began making markets for swapping interest rates, currencies, and commodities, the derivatives markets became much more sophisticated and technical. Market risk also began to shift from exchange-related products to these new contracts, which were designer over-the-counter (OTC) contracts between banks and corporate customers. The public had never heard of them until scandal erupted—first in the London borough of Hammersmith and Fulham, then in Orange County, California, and in Connecticut at a hedge fund called Long-Term Capital Management. By the time the public and the press realized these scandals, the financial system had already been groaning under the strains imposed by cowboy traders who threw prudence and sensible risk management to the wind.

Throughout their history, the derivatives markets have often been associated with gambling. Much of the public resentment against the futures markets in Chicago during the nineteenth century was due to the activities of pit traders on the CBOT, which were likened to casting enormous bets on the prices of staples like wheat and corn. The markets were originally developed to serve as marketing mechanisms for agricultural products, but they soon took on an aura of a giant casino where the croupiers dealt for themselves first. The characterization has lingered for years despite the best attempts of the markets to project a sounder economic image, but terms and techniques still seem to perpetuate the gambling analogy. A familiar contemporary tool for evaluating bond risk under different economic scenarios is called *Monte Carlo simulation,* which inadvertently gives the impression that financial markets are nothing more than gambling casinos.

If any part of that analogy is true, the futures markets are most responsible for conveying it. By the mid- to late 1980s, the futures markets were keen to give the impression that they had finally come of age and were as full-fledged as the securities markets. Then, an FBI investigation into the practices of floor traders was divulged in Chicago, providing the markets with their once-a-decade dose of scandal and recriminations. The fiasco revealed what has been known about the markets for years: They appear to be inured to public opinion, claiming that their functions are limited and difficult for outsiders to fathom. In this respect, they are correct; trading in the pits has befuddled more than one outside observer over the years.

In some cases, it is unfair to compare the futures markets and their derivative brethren to the securities markets. Retail investors do not flock to futures as they do to the stock market. Their only real object of fascination is the options markets, where calls and puts on stocks can be traded for a fraction of a securities' value. The OTC derivatives markets are purely institutional, so they have a limited purpose for the average investor. They remain hedging markets, where institutions and corporations lay off risk by swapping or trading futures. The inevitable scandals arise, as they do in every market, but in hedging markets, they always somehow seem to be larger than any other.

Being one step removed from the public does not mean that the markets should not play by the same set of rules as the securities markets. Regulation of the financial markets proceeded at a very slow pace in the first half of the twentieth century, and regulation in commodities trading was the slowest of all. As long as trading was confined to agricultural commodities, the relative lack of regulation worked reasonably well. However, when crises occurred, the lack of regulator muscle became apparent. During the great bear raid of the early 1930s, regulators could not identify and prosecute a single perpetrator of apparent price manipulation in grains because of vagaries in existing laws. The one strong reaction against alleged price manipulation came over 20 years later, when Congress actually banned trading in onion futures in one of the more unusual chapters in futures market history. For the most part, though, attempts at regulating the markets were ad hoc until the CFTC was created in 1974.

Even the markets' equivalent of the Securities and Exchange Commission (SEC) had a hard time becoming accepted. By the time the CFTC was created, the CBOT had been trading for over 125 years, and the exchange took a distinctly wait-and-see attitude toward the new body. Part of the problem was that the exchanges set high-flying goals for themselves, and the trading methods they developed over the years were always designed to ensure their survival. Being private exchanges, the only way to expand their activities was to admit new members, or *locals*, who would facilitate more activity on the trading floors. They certainly knew more about pit trading than the new regulatory commission, and they were not about to enforce stringent rules concerning trading that were imposed by those they considered amateurs.

Although the financial services industry in general is one of the most regulated, the futures and derivatives markets are the least regulated in the sector. Part of the problem in regulating derivatives stems from their very nature. The contracts are nothing more than trading positions that bind buyers and sellers. Most traders never take possession of the actual commodity involved, closing positions before they expire. As a result, possession normally is not involved as it is in a securities transaction. A contract has a short life, regardless of whether it is an option or a future. While the actual amount of money in a derivatives transaction may exceed a securities transaction, most professional traders profit or lose on the margins of a deal's price. They never hold a position long enough to suffer serious losses on the position unless they deal in enormous quantities. Moreover, if they are hedgers, the matter of winning or losing becomes academic as long as the hedge protects an asset.

This short-term nature of derivatives trading gives the entire industry a gambling casino environment. In the nineteenth century, farmers fulminated about wildly vacillating prices that could affect their crops. If farmers were not sophisticated, hedging would be impossible, and they were at the mercy of traders' prices. A century later, institutional customers complained about receiving suspect prices from the Chicago exchanges. Traders routinely dealt for themselves before dealing for customers through a practice called *front running*. As a result, they would profit regardless of the price executed for the customer.

The futures and derivatives markets have had more than their share of scandal over the years. The fiascoes have given the markets their cowboy nature. On balance, the scandals do not outnumber those in other markets but always seem to be more outlandish than others. The markets remain relatively simple and somewhat cliquish, so when a trading scandal erupts, it always seems to strengthen the hand of the markets' critics, many of whom vividly remember the last scandal. However, during a scandal—especially of the kind that occurred in the 1980s and the 1990s—more than one observer is left wondering how such relatively simple markets can create such a monumental mess.

Although the markets have become sophisticated over the years, some of their practices never seem to change materially. The derivatives markets are unique, for they provide simple but far-reaching hedging and speculative functions yet resist the efforts of outsiders and regulators to fathom their secrets. They remain the best examples of American market capitalism—Social Darwinist environments, ingenuously proclaiming their ability to provide clean, fair markets. Until the next scandal breaks.

# CHAPTER 1

# A TALE OF THE PITS

T HE CIVIL WAR WAS A CRUCIBLE FOR AMERICAN ATTI-tudes toward life, liberty, and the pursuit of money. The wrenching conflict tore at the very fiber of American life and caused a rapid transformation in views about accumulating wealth. Before the war, in what later would seem like a halcyon period, savings and frugality were heralded as traditional American virtues. During the war, a wave of general speculation in gold and stocks swept the country as the news of bloody battles filled the daily newspapers.

Oddly, the speculation came at the same time that Americans were also doing sensible financial planning. Before the war, only about $5 million of life insurance was outstanding; by 1865, that amount jumped to about $700 million. Clearly, the risk of war, as well as the trend toward increasing urbanization, created a need to pass wealth to the next generation independent of the traditional method of willing land ownership. Americans had always been speculative, but before the war, their speculation had been confined to lottery tickets and real estate transactions. The war brought with it, however, an unprecedented speculative binge in commodities and gold. Bucket shops sprang up around the country, fueling the fire even more. These gambling parlors gave the average citizen the impression that he or she could speculate in stocks and commodities like a professional. The average person on the street was goaded by stories of wealth and fortune created on the exchanges, and professional traders, inspired by even grander notions, believed that they could actually corner the entire supply of grain or gold if they possessed an iron will and enough speculative nerve. Clearly, the United States was on the verge of a great revolution in its attitudes and pastimes.

Lotteries proliferated after the war, especially in the South, where state legislatures were in desperate need of funds. Almost from the beginning, opponents of lotteries lobbied for abolishing them, calling them immoral and capable of debauching the average citizen. The futures markets, however, were on a slightly higher level. Their development during the nineteenth century in the shadow of Wall Street was a mixed blessing. These new markets had the dubious distinction of being equated with the tradition of manipulation and greed for which Wall Street was already well-known. Before the Civil War, dealing with stocks and other intangibles was not considered a respectable vocation; the traders themselves were considered to be on the edge of proper society. When the futures markets were developed, the public naturally looked askance at them and the people who traded them; however, it knew that if these new markets could succeed, their place in American economic life would be assured for generations to come.

Although the markets did succeed, their development was subject to chance. Just as the price of wheat or corn was subject to demand as affected by factors beyond one's control—climate fluctuations and insect infestations, for example—the futures markets were subject to public skepticism, internal dissension, and various external factors, all beyond their control. Unlike the stock markets, the futures markets never commanded the widespread respect that the New York Stock Exchange (NYSE) begrudgingly earned over the years. To Easterners, the markets were the places where "hicks" traded agricultural commodities basic to everyday life. Even in their own backyards, the markets were seen as suspect places where predatory "city slicker" speculators took advantage of farmers who were not organized well enough to fight back. There were actually attempts made during the nineteenth century to outlaw futures trading at both the state and national level. The futures markets had crippling legislation passed against them, but they still managed to survive.

The introduction of futures markets in Chicago in the late 1840s certainly witnessed both the highs and lows of financial life. From the beginning, the economic value of futures was never seriously doubted, but those who traded them and their motives were constantly questioned. The nineteenth-century public vaguely understood what took place on the stock exchanges but had little time for the prima donnas who were their best known bulls and bears. Buying and selling railroad shares was a legitimate activity to most observers, but when a trader such as Jacob Little or Daniel Drew cornered stock by buying all of the available supply or plunged it by selling it short (forcing its price down, ruining the "longs" or buyers), the overtly speculative nature of the market rose to the surface. Adding insult to injury, the corners and the plungers both seemed to do quite well financially, while the average investor never seemed to get ahead of the game. The markets appeared rigged in favor of the professional trader.

However shoddy the NYSE's early reputation might have been, the Chicago Board of Trade would suffer an even worse opprobrium; it would endure legal challenges and hostile state legislatures that made the stock exchanges' problems pale by comparison. The futures markets had another unpredictable foe that did not trouble the stock exchanges, located mostly in the East. In the Midwest, dealing in futures markets inspired widespread cynicism even among believers because of that region's strong, ingrained Calvinistic work ethic. Profit gained by trading intangibles was considered immoral; only real sweat and labor should be rewarded. How could one claim to be working when that person only shouted orders for buying and selling wheat on an exchange? The one who should be rewarded was the farmer whose sweat and toil brought the wheat to market. There was something inherently wrong in dealing with contracts rather than the real commodity itself. That strong Midwestern ethic would dog the futures markets for years.

The irrepressible force of westward expansion would push futures markets into the spotlight. As the country continued to grow, farms and cities began to develop west of the Mississippi River. Chicago became the gateway to this vast area, almost entirely devoted to agriculture. The railroads made Chicago a central hub, and by the time the Civil War began, the city was the main food supplier for the Union army and, along with St. Louis, a major terminus. The agricultural industry developed quickly, embracing farmers, millers, processors, warehousemen, and the marketers. It was from this last group that the futures markets developed. Trading grain futures on the exchanges was seen as a step in the marketing process of getting grains into the hands of consumers. Like their eastern stock exchange counterparts, futures traders claimed that their trading served a valid economic function. Without it, the farmers would be left with unsold crops and, even worse, potential economic ruin if prices suddenly changed during a crop season.

Experience proved otherwise, at least as far as farmers were concerned. Their crop prices were out of their control because they were in the hands of a small group of professional traders who manipulated prices on the futures exchanges for their own benefit. Making matters worse were the railroads, which forced the farmers to pay high charges for getting their harvested crops to the markets. The noble profession of farming was being drained of its vitality by unscrupulous middlemen who capitalized on farmers' isolation and economic ignorance. The whole economic process of farming needed to be returned to its rural origins. City folk, schooled in the ways of speculation and exploitation, had the farmers in a vulnerable position, a situation which only legislation could redress. The country was moving westward too quickly, however, and the argument fell on deaf ears. America was on the move, and the markets were necessary for its economic development. The rural America so fondly recalled by Alexis de Tocqueville was rapidly giving way to the new America of the railroad baron and the grain plunger. But even progress could not halt the controversy surrounding the true nature of futures trading. When combined with the stridency of the antimonopolist movement and the reforms suggested by Populists and Grangers, the issue of futures trading proved to be one of the more combustible of the post–Civil War era.

## FINE YOUNG CANNIBALS

As Chicago and other Midwest cities began to grow, they developed chambers of commerce and other local organizations to cater to the business community. Locals gathered at these places to dine, share contacts, conduct business, or simply socialize. As early as 1836, in St. Louis a merchants' exchange was developed where all of the sundry commodities that traded on the quay alongside the Mississippi River were organized into a central marketplace. In 1856, Kansas City merchants organized a board of trade to buy and sell commodities in an orderly fashion. In Chicago, a similar sort of meeting place known as the Chicago Board of Trade (CBOT) officially opened in 1848 to less-than-resounding popularity. In the same year, railroads and telegraphs reached the city, and the stock-yards were opened. Not many in the business community showed much interest in the board; most were too busy contending with the city's explosive growth.

The farming business was in the throes of its own revolution that was quickly changing the face of the city. In the 1830s, Cyrus McCormick developed the reaper, the first device that could cut grain mechanically rather than by hand. After a trip to the Midwest, McCormick realized that his device was more suited to the wide, flat plains of the breadbasket states than it was to the rougher, hilly terrain of western Virginia, where he had been doing sporadic business with his new contraption. In 1848, he relocated his business to Chicago and started producing improved reapers. Within a couple of years, the time needed to harvest an acre of wheat was cut in half. When combined with the constant expansion of farmland, wheat and other grains flowed through Chicago at a rapid pace.

Although local businesspeople initially ignored the CBOT, the increased demand for wheat during the Civil War began to change their opinions about the organization. The CBOT quickly developed into the marketing arm of the wheat industry. Since Chicago was the nexus of this quickly emerging breadbasket, it seemed a natural location for a futures market, and the CBOT seemed the logical place to house it. Futures trading was an old form of arranging crops and other basic commodities for delayed, or future, delivery. It had been used in Japan and England with some degree of success, and the New York markets had traded some commodities futures as well. Originally, the trading was known as *when-arrived* trading, in which a buyer purchased a contract for a farmer's grain crop to be delivered at a date in the near future. The price was agreed to on a specific date, and the contract was binding. If the price subsequently declined, the buyer would still be obligated to make the purchase, and if the crop failed, the farmer would remain bound to make delivery of the grain at the agreed-to price even if it had to be purchased elsewhere.

In this simple market, the chain of supply and demand was relatively stable. However, without futures trading, significant price risk was present. Buyers and sellers would have to rely upon the cash (or physicals) market with all of its vagaries and price risk. In the futures markets, uncertainty was removed. Buyers would know the price ahead of time, and sellers could rest more easily than if they had to suffer market conditions at the time of harvest and shipment. But what seemed like an excellent idea for both farmers and users of their products was constantly shrouded in ambiguity and quarrelling about the proper role of futures in everyday American life. How was it possible that such a sound economic idea could invite such heated, disparate opinions?

Between 1854 and 1864, the amount of wheat shipped from the Midwest more than quadrupled, and beef and other grains developed rapidly as well, quickly becoming a source of contention among critics of the distributors, whom many labeled war profiteers. As a result, futures trading developed at a fast pace. Problems concerning standard contract size, quality of grains involved, and delivery procedures were ironed out quickly, and acceptable futures contracts, mostly for wheat, became part of the grain marketing system. Farmers could sell their crops at a standard date in the near future; buyers could decide which crops they needed and settle on a price that was made on the exchange—technically in the *pits* where the contracts traded. The CBOT built its first pits, octagonal in shape, after the Civil War to accommodate traders. The pits were slightly concave areas on the CBOT floor where traders congregated and traded, using an open-outcry system to be heard. The system was up and running quickly. One standard feature of the market was not adhered to, however, even from the beginning. To be a true futures market, the seller had to deliver the commodity and the buyer had to pay and take delivery. Yet, only a tiny fraction of contracts ever went through the delivery process. Most were traded actively before they expired and were then closed out, meaning that standard contracts were bought back that had been sold or contracts were sold that had been bought. These floor traders were not thinking of delivery; they were thinking only of speculating in the commodity.[1]

The nascent futures markets attracted speculators to the pits, where a seat could be bought quite reasonably in the years prior to the Civil War. These traders wanted no part of a physical commodity; they were interested only in selling at a price higher than that at which they had purchased contracts. Equally, they were also avid short sellers: They would sell contracts and later purchase them back at a lower price, profiting from the price drop. These floor traders became the backbone—and the bane—of the CBOT. Its rules and guidelines were written only for serious hedging purposes. Farmers sold and buyers, usually food processors, purchased grains and produce. The CBOT's bylaws and organization did not admit to speculative traders operating in the pits, although there was no way to actually prohibit their actions. Being recognized by the laws of Illinois as a "board" gave the CBOT the unique ability to set its own regulations and adjudicate its own internal problems, its decisions having the same weight as a court of law. Clearly, the CBOT could have expelled these traders, but what would have been the point? In futures parlance, these traders were the "locals" and added needed liquidity to the exchange floor, but their activities were not officially recognized.

Without the speculators, the exchange would have been a sleepy place. The traders, however, gave it verve and a somewhat tawdry reputation that became an integral part of Chicago folklore. While clearly quick on their feet, the traders were not the most serious-minded businesspeople; in fact, they would not even be regarded as businesspeople in the conventional sense. They shared a reputation for bloody-mindedness, for conniving, and for a robust sense of humor that matched their counterparts on the NYSE, with whom they were often compared. They clearly were not ambassadors for their profession. In 1875, the CBOT played host to the king of Hawaii, who visited the exchange floor during a tour of the city. As the king was introduced, the traders cheered him wildly, but before he could speak, they broke out with a rendition of "The King of the Cannibals," a popular song of the day. The mayor then attempted to introduce him, but flubbed it when he began the introduction by saying, "I have the honor of escorting into your midst the king of the Can . . ." Obviously, the king did not appreciate the humor and stalked out of the exchange; meanwhile, the traders continued by staging a "native" dance on the floor.[2] Their reputation was already building.

Other exchanges developed in New York as the CBOT was enduring its growing pains. One was the New York Produce Exchange, which opened in 1862 to help supply Union army forces. Another was the New York Cotton Exchange, which opened in 1870 and started taking business away from New Orleans, the traditional home of cotton along with Charleston. As a result, New Orleans opened its own cotton exchange a few years later. New York's exchange attracted many Southern merchants who previously dealt cotton in New Orleans and other cities in the South. Some of these merchants, including Lehman Brothers, later became well-known Wall Street investment banks. New York and New Orleans would compete with Liverpool, in Britain, where a cotton exchange for both physicals and futures had been established in the early 1830s. The exchange played a vital role in Britain's development during the Industrial Revolution and provided jobs in manufacturing and in importing and trading. The Liverpool exchange also was seen as a place where young traders could make a quick killing. Americans were attracted to this exchange, as the magazine *Harper's* noted, "each keeping a keen eye to the requirements of his own particular mercantile connection." The Liverpool exchange tried to imbue into merchants the long-standing motto of the London Stock Exchange: that a man's word was his bond. "A sense of honor which is derived wholly from social considerations of their common interest will prevent even an individual rogue from breaking his word on the Exchange Flags," the magazine added. "They are unanimous at least in this."[3] The American exchanges were a bit more liberal in their interpretation.

Throughout their early years, all of the exchanges emphasized their economic functions over the speculative. Futures traders tried, unsuccessfully, to contrast themselves favorably with the odious traders whom they claimed inhabited the NYSE—the notorious short sellers and large buyers who arranged corners to capture most of the existing supply of a particular stock. These sharp operators had already become part of American stock market legend; their antics were known to a good part of the reading public through the newspapers and the occasional book chronicling their activities. They and many other traders made their reputations on the floor of the NYSE. They were both admired and hated by commentators, as well as by other traders. It did not take long for the CBOT to develop its own legendary trader, Benjamin P. Hutchinson, who equaled any of the short sellers and large buyers in their techniques and ruthlessness.

Hutchinson, born in Massachusetts in 1829, went to work while in his mid-teens as an apprentice in a shoe store, earning a salary of $20 per year. An ambitious young man who grew to be six-and-a-half-feet tall, he hated his first experience working for someone else and waited for the opportunity to strike out on his own. Within a year, he opened his own shoe store next to his former employer and began to prosper, soon moving his operation to a larger town with better prospects. At the age of 20, he appeared poised for reasonable success as a local merchant. He soon married, and in 1857, as he was on his way toward becoming a successful manufacturer and seller of boots and shoes, the financial crisis called the "Western blizzard" struck with full force. The crisis began with Western banks and then blew east; the NYSE suffered badly. The economic depression that soon followed ruined Hutchinson's business, forcing him to reconsider his prospects. At age 28, he made a fateful decision. He packed his wife and his belongings and moved to the Midwest, heeding the traditional Horace Greeley advice. The reputation of the CBOT was about to change, because the migrant brought with him certain skills that the CBOT traders did not possess.

After setting himself up in his adopted city of Chicago, Hutchinson naturally gravitated toward the CBOT and the wheat pits. The heavy war demand for wheat would ensure the future of the pits. Hutchinson, however, was not attracted to the marketing of wheat, only to speculation. In keeping with its original charter, the CBOT itself discouraged speculation, but discouraging frequent buying and selling in the pits was risky for the overall market because it did provide liquidity for true hedgers. As a result, speculators flourished. They bought and sold contracts constantly, attempting to make a few pennies per bushel. This activity became known as *scalping* and was something for which the exchanges became renowned. The floor traders began a cycle of trading patterns that the public could not understand. Instead of marketing wheat, they appeared to be gambling, attempting to anticipate short-term price movements or even to create them. Critics failed to make the distinction that what the buyer of a futures contract did purchase was an asset—albeit a short-term one—that allowed the buyer to take possession of a commodity if desired. Gambling was simply rolling the dice for a potential payout or loss. Ordinarily, hedgers who sold or bought represented the opposite ends of a trade; now, however, they were nowhere to be seen. Trading patterns appeared to be going in "rings," disappearing into the ether rather than resulting in a single contract between the two end parties.

Speculation became the bane of the early futures markets. The basic notion of exactly how futures markets were able to help producers and processors was not totally clear in the minds of many in the agrarian Midwest. As far as the agrarians were concerned, anyone other than a real producer or user was a gambler. Cries of speculation and gambling were leveled at the dozens of exchanges—large and small—that were growing up not only in Chicago but in St. Louis, Minneapolis, New Orleans, Milwaukee, New York, and Kansas City. They were not idle cries but set off a wave of antifutures emotions that continued until the end of the nineteenth century. The *Chicago Tribune* lamented that the CBOT was not training young men with useful skills, that "business as at present conducted is training our young men to be gamblers rather than merchants."[4] Most commentators hoped that speculation in the pits would be only a phase in the city's development.

## WHISTLING DIXIE

As the CBOT developed, the market for gold futures in New York became the speculator's market of choice. The price of gold reflected the fortunes of the Civil War and became the most speculative market yet witnessed in the nineteenth century. The traders' behavior became so repugnant to politicians and commentators that many began to doubt the patriotism of the marketplace in general. The reaction led to the first futures legislation ever passed.

In late December 1861, New York banks suspended specie payments, eliminating the gold standard in favor of newly created greenbacks. Two weeks later, in January 1862, the Gold

Room at the NYSE was established. The standard for gold trading was the $20 Double Eagle gold coin, and it was quoted as a premium of its face value. At first glance, the market appeared of be a true commodity market, for gold was the only item traded and was quoted for next-day delivery. Almost immediately, however, a market for *delayed* delivery sprang up. Prices were made either for cash or for a specific time period. For instance, *buyer or seller three* meant the number of days that the trader had to deliver. The organized gold market looked like a legitimate investors' market, but margin trading and delayed deliveries appeared almost immediately, as they had in Chicago. In the event that the exchange could not handle a special order, it could be taken to the Coal Hole at 23 William Street. This was an unofficial exchange, established by traders who did not join the NYSE. True to its name, it was a dark, dingy basement where traders carried out slick deals that even the new exchange would not countenance.

Speculation ran rampant during the Civil War. All sorts of investors began trading in gold, and not all were professionals. Tradespeople, shop clerks, and businesspeople were all buying and selling with great abandon, often for as little as 10 percent down on the full price. Soon, actual users of gold were joined by the speculating public. The game became the same one that was developing in Chicago: "longs" would watch the price rise and then settle with the "shorts" who could not cover their positions for delivery. Vast amounts of cash changed hands; brokers charged $12.50 commission for each $10,000 traded and could easily earn several thousand dollars per day simply by brokering orders. As the war progressed, the price continued to rise.

In 1862, when the Gold Room opened, the price was quoted between 102 and 133 (2 to 33 percent of $20 par, meaning $20.40 to $26.60). By 1864, the price spiraled to 220 from about 157. The price rose and fell on news from the war front. Union victories raised the price; Confederate victories drove it down. But it only took about a month for the NYSE to recognize that the Gold Room was so speculative that its traders could be described as lacking patriotism. In a typical display of solidarity with the Union cause, traders would whistle "John Brown's Body" when Union forces scored a victory but switch to "Dixie" when Confederate forces emerged victorious. News of the traders' behavior infuriated Abraham Lincoln, who asked a colleague, "What do you think of those fellows in Wall Street who are gambling in gold at such a time as this? For my part I wish every one of them had his devilish head shot off."[5]

The NYSE obliged by banishing the traders a month later, in February 1862. The outcasts resumed trading at the Coal Hole, where they remained for a year before moving to and occupying Gilpin's News Room at the corner of William Street and Exchange Place. A board was placed outside on the sidewalk so that passersby could see the posted price of gold. For $25, a trader would be admitted to the floor of the exchange, which one contemporary kindly described as pandemonium at its best. Prices ran up and down on a daily basis, and the price of the commodity became even more volatile. Gilpin's News Room became the new Gold Room, and speculation was as rampant as before. Salmon Chase, Lincoln's treasury secretary, visited the room and was so infuriated by what he saw that he urged Congress to pass a new bill in June 1864 called the Gold Bill. This bill made delayed deliveries unlawful; all trades had to be settled within 24 hours. As soon as the bill became law, Gilpin's News Room was closed and the market moved to traders' offices and street corners.

There was the matter of settling claims. Once a trade was done, certificates were transferred from sellers to buyers. Lacking a clearinghouse of any sort, the details of transactions, along with certificates of ownership, were put into large canvas bags and carried around town by boys acting as deliverymen. Often, these messengers were attacked and robbed on the street. Running became a more effective way of making deliveries; hence "runner" became a popular nickname for the messengers. More than one of these messengers occasionally disappeared with the bag, for the certificates could be redeemed by anyone. The integrity of the unofficial market was now clearly in doubt.

The reputation of Gilpin's News Room became so bad that traders organized to form the New York Gold Exchange in October 1864. Trading became more orderly and improved over the older system. The Bank of New York lent a hand and its long-established credibility by creating a clearinghouse system in which gold would not have to be delivered against a purchase or sale. Gold certificates, similar to the older, "hotter" variety, were established, each bearing the bank's imprint. By now, the market had clearly become more organized, but its speculative nature shadowed it nevertheless. Congress soon landed a bombshell that for years would reverberate over the markets: It proposed a tax on all sales of gold, leveling half of 1 percent as a form of sales tax. Traders objected vehemently, and the tax was abolished after several years, but its point had been made. Tax on commodities trading proved sobering for the markets.

In summer 1865, the gold certificates of the Bank of New York fell under a cloud when it was discovered that many of them delivered in the months after the Civil War ended were forged. As a result, the exchange established the New York Gold Exchange Bank to act as its clearinghouse, replacing the certificate system and giving the market a new credibility that had been seriously lacking. However, an unforeseen element would surface several years later when Jay Gould and his cohorts began to manipulate the price of gold. With the new markets and clearinghouse system in place, it was now easier to speculate on a large scale because of the relative ease to trade and settle gold. Organized attempts to run the price up or down actually were simplified. Even apparent reforms could not cure the exchange's reputation for wild gambling and speculation.

Nevertheless, the Gold Exchange made its debut under the auspices of the NYSE. The gold traders fell under the watchful eye of the gold committee, which oversaw their actions. Several of the committee members were well-known exchange members and had well-established names; among them were Henry Clews, Dunning Duer, and E. B. Ketchum, who traded gold with the young Pierpont Morgan for his family bank's overseas accounts. The organizational changes put the Gold Exchange on a par with the CBOT, which during the Civil War moved ahead rapidly with its own internal developments.

The gold corner mounted by Jay Gould and his cohorts in 1869 became the best known market operation of its day. It also served as a model for others to follow in Chicago. Cornering operations were nothing new on the stock exchange, but an attempt to run up the price of gold, the precious metal serving as the basis of the nation's money, was the most audacious operation ever attempted. At the time, Gould's firm on Wall Street—Smith, Gould & Martin—began to buy gold at increasing prices in an obvious attempt to run its price. Part of the strategy involved the lack of government intervention. If the Treasury released any of the gold stock from Fort Knox, the price would fall immediately. Gould, however, seemed sure that intervention would not take place, and the price rose to almost 160. One of his cohorts in the operation was Abel Corbin, President Ulysses S. Grant's son-in-law. Most insiders assumed that Gould used Corbin to keep Grant from ordering an intervention. Finally, the president was persuaded to intervene, and a selling panic quickly followed. Gould already was in the process of liquidating his positions, however, and when the smoke cleared, he was rumored to have netted over $10 million on the operation.

The gold corner enhanced Gould's already slick reputation for audacity, but it did little for Grant's developing reputation for venality. In 1870, Congress convened the gold panic investigation, hearing testimony from all the principals involved. In 1871, Charles Francis Adams and his brother Henry also joined the fray with a muckraking book entitled *Chapters of Erie and Other Essays,* which discussed the gold corner and other Gould operations. The Gold Exchange closed in 1879, when the government authorized specie payments to resume. Despite all the publicity and economic repercussions of the gold corner, the technique was still viewed as a legitimate market operation to be employed by anyone with enough nerve and available resources. The Chicago traders proved that they had ample supplies of both.

## CURBS AND CORRIDORS

Almost from the beginning, the futures markets did little to actually promote the marketing of commodities. The actual marketing took place among grain elevator operators and warehousemen, who often used the markets to ensure a steady supply of physical commodities for delivery. The markets were instead places where prices could be hedged or speculated. Only 3 percent or less of contracts were actually delivered as stipulated. The number of futures contracts traded as a percentage of actual wheat produced was extremely high. The trading became known as *wind wheat*—contracts that represented nothing but air. Almost all were closed before expiration, ending the buyer's or seller's liability. The "rings" created by the maze of trader activities confused and infuriated many on the outside who were not quite sure what occurred in the pits. Yet another trader activity proved to be the straw that almost broke the proverbial camel's back.

Clearly in violation of board rules, CBOT traders began

trading options on futures contracts. They would arrange very short term options—as short as one day—with other traders who allowed them to buy or sell depending on the direction in which they thought the commodity price was moving. The option would then give them the right to trade a futures contract. Options to buy, or *calls*, and options to sell, or *puts*, were very common among the traders and had potential to seriously impact exchange prices. Options in Chicago, however, were not referred to as calls or puts, as they were in the stock markets; they were referred to as *privileges*, and traders were engaged in *privilege trading*. The very notion smacked of monopoly and oligopoly. Unfortunately, in a region heavily influenced by the Grange movement with its strong antimonopoly sentiments, the very hint of the term *privilege* as practiced on an exclusive board of trade was almost too much for the Populists who began to use the CBOT as a rallying point for their political platforms.

Pit traders had already developed their reputations by the end of the Civil War. Hutchinson bought a seat on the CBOT for $10 a year before the war began and began actively trading, noting that the price of wheat was affected by the price of gold. So, he studied gold and traded wheat on the trends that he detected in the precious metal. The price of both commodities rose almost uninterruptedly. Hutchinson cornered as many wheat contracts as he could afford and then began selling them quietly as other traders clamored for more. When the price of wheat finally reached its high, Hutchinson had the temerity to sell even more contracts short. When the price of wheat declined, he covered them and made a small fortune. The entire operation had already become familiar, but Hutchinson's reliance on outside economic data was new. When one of the floor traders pursued him on the CBOT floor, imploring him to explain how he knew that prices would fall, the usually taciturn Hutchinson simply turned to him and snapped, "Gold! And war!"

That operation alone earned Hutchinson the familiar nickname "Old Hutch." He quickly became a legend in his own time, assuming a hallowed reputation like that of Jay Gould or Daniel Drew. In 1866, another physical corner only enhanced his stature. Again running counter to popular traders' opinion, Hutchinson bought all of the physical wheat in the Chicago warehouses and then all of the call options that other traders would sell him. The shortage in wheat began to make itself apparent as the delivery day for the contracts approached, and all the traders who were short had to bow before him as he settled their contracts at great profit to himself. He made well over a million dollars on the corner. But Hutchinson saw himself in a different light. As far as he was concerned, he was just an old country boy in the right place at the right time.

When confronted with the idea that his actions in the pits might be unethical, Hutchinson had a simple reply. "Ethics, the word has a curious rattle," he responded. "Its meaning is hardly known in business today. Yet no one has accused me of violating any laws . . . what I have done may likewise be tried by anyone who wishes to risk his fortune. The field is open to all." Then, in a clear shot at Wall Street stock manipulators, he continued by saying, "I have issued no spurious stock certificates, stolen no railroads, joined in no gold conspiracy. For a study of such type ethics, I would respectfully invite your attention to the gentlemen of Wall Street."[6]

Farmers who suffered through the highs and lows of fluctuating wheat prices did not see the distinction quite so clearly. Speculation in the CBOT pits coincided with a larger problem brewing in the Midwest that challenged the practices of pit trading in futures contracts. Investors in the East may have fretted over losing money in bad stock deals, but their losses did not necessarily challenge their very way of life. Farmers claimed that speculation was responsible for unstable wheat prices that could spell ruin for their livelihoods. Great fortunes were being made—and lost—in the Chicago pits, but the price of wheat on the open market began a steady decline once the Civil War ended. Naturally, the farmers blamed the pit traders for rampant speculation that was hurting their incomes. The pit traders responded, somewhat crudely, but to the point.

After the Civil War, the Grange movement began speaking for farmers throughout the Midwest. From the agrarian point of view, farmers were constantly at the mercy of others—railroads, pit traders, Wall Street bankers, and unscrupulous warehouse operators who charged too much to store farmers' crops. Their argument was simple. When the Civil War ended, the price of wheat began its long, steady decline. In 1866, for example, the price of a bushel of wheat was about $2.06 per bushel, and within 10 years, it had declined to $1.03. The decline did not stop. By the end of the century, the price stood around 50 cents per bushel. During that period, corners and bear raids were netting speculators millions in the Chicago pits while the average wheat farmer was becoming impoverished. Was that not enough proof that the CBOT and other futures exchanges were nothing more than gambling pits where immoral men toyed with the price of wheat for their own gain?

Adding insult to injury were the activities of grain transporters and warehouse workers. Railroads charged high rates to small farmers while granting rebates to large businesses, which could afford to negotiate with them. Silo operators did the same, usually working in concert with the railroads. By the time farmers sold their crops, they often already had recorded losses for the year. The noble profession of working the land was being degraded by these city slickers who cared little for the plight of the farmers.

When asked about cornering wheat in the pits, Hutchinson remarked that no man could stand in the way of the crop, which metaphorically rushed to market like a great wind. Standing in its way was useless. Wheat was the basic crop of the

Midwest, and there was too much supply of it to manipulate. In this respect, Hutchinson was perfectly correct. Since the time when McCormick introduced the reaper, the number of labor hours needed to bring in the crop had declined by 50 percent. Between 1850 and 1880, the number of farms in existence nearly quadrupled and wheat production doubled.[7] The decline in real prices was explained by a doubling in capacity and efficiency. No wonder the plight of the wheat farmer was becoming a matter of regional and national concern. The prices of many other agricultural commodities managed to register small gains during the post–Civil War period, but no major crop witnessed serious price increases. The economics of the situation did not favor the farmer, but how did the speculators manage to make small fortunes from declining crop prices?

Speculation was the culprit as far as the agrarians were concerned. Futures trading was attacked on two levels. First, there were the exchanges themselves, where less than 3 percent of all contracts were actually delivered. If the pits were not satisfying their original objective of hedging, what possible justification could there be for their continued use? Second, the matter of options, or privilege trading, became a hotly contested issue because it was widespread and had no basis in exchange rules. Traders would arrange options between themselves, usually for short periods of a day to a week. Since exchange rules actually prohibited any form of trading other than futures contracts in the pits, options deals were usually struck on the curb of the street outside the CBOT or in the corridors of the exchange itself.

Little-known outside the futures or stock exchanges, options had the distinction of being the first financial vehicle in American history to be labeled "immoral." In general, the Grange movement thought little of futures trading activities. In a familiar Grange song of the period, the lyrics were not very subtle:

There are speculators all about, you know,
  Who are sure to help each other roll the ball,
As the people they can fleece, and then take so much apiece,
  While the farmer is the man that feeds them all.[8]

The distinction made between options and futures was very simple. Essentially, futures were tolerable as long as delivery was accomplished in accordance with the contracts involved, whereas options were useless gambling instruments because they could not be used to make or take delivery of an actual commodity, only a contract on it. In today's parlance, these options were actually options *on futures contracts*, not on the actual commodities themselves. Traders liked them because they offered flexibility to buy or sell more contracts within one day or one week of the day in which a price was established. However, farmers and their representatives regarded them as useless gambling vehicles. Despite the rapidly growing economy in the 1870s and 1880s, farmers would win a temporary victory when antifutures and antioptions legislation appeared both in state legislatures and in Washington.

## PIT WARS

After Hutchinson's notable corners in the late 1860s, activities among pit traders intensified. Farming wheat was not a particularly profitable adventure, but traders were making more money in one cornering or plunging operation than most farmers made in a lifetime. The Chicago pits quickly began turning out as many famous bulls and bears as the NYSE. Occasionally, Easterners would venture to the Midwest to try their hand at cornering an agricultural commodity. Attracted to the pits were stock speculators who saw them as simple, unregulated gambling arenas with fewer rules than the stock markets.

As time passed, futures exchanges became symbols of civic

pride. St. Louis built its new Merchants Exchange in its downtown, not far from the levee, in 1874. The new edifice quickly became the most important building in the city. Developers were quick to point out that the costs incurred were neither exorbitant nor met with borrowed money. "St. Louis is emphatically not a mortgaged city," declared the local newspaper at the time of the building's inauguration, "the great pile now rising slowly from its foundations, covering two thirds of an entire block, was not undertaken at a venture, or 'trust to luck' style of business. Money, ready cash to pay for it, was in sight before a brick was removed from the old building."[9] Ironically, supporters of the exchange wanted to point out that while activity inside the building may have been speculative, the building itself was based upon sound financing. Chicago had a similar civic point of view. Activity at the CBOT was interrupted by the Chicago fire of 1871, which destroyed the CBOT's headquarters at LaSalle and Washington. All of its records were lost. After operating in temporary quarters for almost four years, a new building was opened at Jackson Boulevard and LaSalle in 1875. It, too, became a symbol of the city's capitalist ethic. The new digs inspired traders. Within several months, some of the most spectacular corners yet attempted in the markets would be attempted.

While agricultural production increased in general, the supply of wheat through Chicago vacillated during the 1870s, giving the corners an opportunity. In 1871 and again in 1876, the amount of wheat flowing through Chicago actually dropped, and the speculators who were quick enough to detect the trend made a killing. Hutchinson had already taught them the virtues of examining economic data from outside the region before speculating, but even he could not have anticipated the extent of the grandiose plans that were being hatched. In 1874, William Sturges, a CBOT trader, attempted a corner in corn futures, and in 1878, Philip D. Armour attempted a spectacular corner in wheat, as did James R. Keene, a Wall Street stock speculator who traveled to the Midwest to try his luck in the pits. These men all met with mixed results, but their operations drew the scrutiny of state legislatures, especially in Illinois.

Conservative sentiments prompted the Illinois Legislature to pass an anticornering and antioptions bill in spring 1874. However, what passed in the legislature and what occurred on the CBOT were two entirely different matters. Since the CBOT rules had the effect of law, its members did not give much notice to what occurred outside the exchange. Beginning in the summer of 1874, William "King Jack" Sturges mounted an ambitious corner in corn. He forced the prices up and sold short in an obvious attempt to convince other traders that he had failed. He then forced the prices up again, putting a classic squeeze on his fellow traders who were forced to capitulate and settle. The other traders returned the compliment and caught Sturges in a corner, but unlike them, he was unwilling to settle. The case eventually wound its way through the courts and was settled nearly five years later, after which Sturges resumed his place on the exchange. His past actions, however, cast the CBOT in a bad light. When his other corners, along with Hutchinson's corners, were considered, it was clear that the Illinois Legislature had reacted to real abuses in the market. But the issue was far from settled.

During the 1870s, another well-known speculator, who would also become one of the most notorious meat packers in the country, was also active on the futures exchanges. Philip D., or "Peedy," Armour was both a friend and foe of Hutchinson in the pits, where the two often matched wits, and fortunes, in elaborate market operations. Armour's reputation from an early age was substantial, although he was not quite the master trader that Hutchinson was. Born in Stockbridge, New York, in 1832, Armour had only a rudimentary education when he set out for California during the Gold Rush with three friends, one of whom died en route. Rather than search for gold, he decided to start his own small construction company, and he began digging trenches used by miners in their search for gold, making almost $10,000 from his efforts. He then traveled back east to visit his home in New York State, but he stopped in Milwaukee on the way, where he entered the hog-packing business. From Milwaukee, he was lured to Chicago, where he founded Armour & Co. and brought in his brothers from New York State to help operate it.

Legend had it that in 1852, as a young man, Armour walked from New York State to Chicago because he did not have enough money for trainfare. Although false, such stories were characteristic of traders who liked to surround themselves with myth and heroic deeds. At age 20, Armour was already in California digging ditches. Like Hutchinson, however, he suffered adversity before becoming a well-known pit trader. His greatest financial coup came in 1865 in a market maneuver that rivaled any of the previous 50 years. Sensing that Grant's march on Richmond would mark the end of the Civil War and, with it, the high price of provisions (pork), Armour began selling provisions short in New York at $40 per barrel. When news of Lee's surrender did come, Armour covered at $18, earning over $2 million and an instant reputation. Unlike Hutchinson, Armour put the money to work into a useful business by starting the Milwaukee hog-packing company that bore his name. "I like to turn bristles, blood, and the inside and outside of pigs and bullocks into revenue," Armour often remarked.

Armour & Co. became known as embodying the worst abuses of the meat-packing industry. Although Armour was already dead when Upton Sinclair published *The Jungle* in 1906, his name would forever be linked with the meat-packing industry in Chicago. And like many industries of the day, the meat-packing industry was concentrated in several firms that dominated it greatly, causing a Wharton School professor to remark that the five big Chicago and other Midwestern meat-packing firms were controlled mostly by New York bankers who recognized their monopoly on the industry and, as a result, sought financial alliances with the meat packers. The monopoly was so tight that "not only [do] they have a monopolistic control over the American meat industry, but have secured control, similar in purpose if not yet in extent, over the principal substitutes for meat, such as eggs, cheese, and vegetable oil products and are rapidly extending their power to cover fish and nearly every kind of foodstuff."[10] The meat trust, as it quickly became known, was by 1880 in total control of the meat-packing market. The trust was so tight that only the representatives of the five companies bothered to attend the daily livestock and meat auctions in Chicago, and the price that they agreed upon was the only price of the day. Usually, it was low. "No conspiracy is perceptible," wrote a contemporary commentator. "There is only an accidental harmony of minds."[11]

During the 1870s and 1880s, Armour was active on the futures markets, periodically arranging huge corners. In 1878, he cornered a high grade of wheat in Chicago and Milwaukee, sending the price soaring by over 10 cents per bushel. Then, he switched to corn and other grains before he again switched, this time to livestock. He cornered pork futures in the 1880s, raising the price by over 50 percent in two months before cashing out for a reputed profit of $4 million in four months.

The effect that this market activity had on farmers was staggering. The worst results were on those farmers who were in the process of delivering their crops when a speculator mounted a pit operation. One 1872 operation in oat futures was combined with manipulation at the warehouses, catching the attention of the *Chicago Tribune*, which described the situation: "A man in Illinois sold 15,000 bushels of his own oats on the Chicago market before the corner started, at 38 cents a bushel to be delivered in June. A blockade of the railroad and warehouse facilities made it impossible for him to make the actual delivery, and he was forced to buy from the manipulators at 43 cents to settle his contract. When his oats reached market, after the corner ended, they sold for 31 cents a bushel. So, he lost 12 cents a bushel on his own oats."[12] After the affair, the newspaper suggested that the CBOT dedicate a new building that it was about to open to the "suppression of gambling."

Operations of that sort not only helped to strengthen farmers' fears about the markets but also continued to attract speculators, not all of whom were locals. James R. Keene, a well-known New York speculator, eyed Chicago with envy and decided that he could make a killing on the faraway exchange, much as he had done on the NYSE by operating manipulative pools. Keene was an established speculator and organizer of stock market pools who decided to become king of the wheat pits after hearing of Hutchinson's reputation. Keene was born in England but raised in California, where he tried his hand at all of the traditional Western occupations while he was still in his teens. He had been a muleskinner, a cowboy, and newspaper editor before he bought a seat on the San Francisco Mining Exchange, where he had already dabbled in gold. His intention was to corner wheat in the same fashion that Jay Gould had attempted to corner gold in 1869. He began wheat dealing in fall 1878 with money raised from a pool of New York investors. With a $5 million war chest, Keene began buying up wheat and was close to cornering the market within a few months. Then, suddenly, his brokers received sell orders via telegram and sold many of his positions before he could apply the final squeeze to the opposition pit traders. The brokers dumped 3 million bushels before Keene intervened, claiming that it was not he who sent the sell order. Perplexed, the brokers bought the positions back and continued buying another 11 million bushels on his orders. It then became apparent that Hutchinson had been selling him all the wheat he wanted, because there was actually a surplus of wheat in the area. However, the origin of the sell order remained a mystery.

Keene, among others, suspected Hutchinson of sending the telegram, but the source was to be found in New York, in the likeliest of places. One of Keene's major past antagonists had been the redoubtable Jay Gould, master speculator and perhaps the most hated man in America, for his involvement in the gold corner had caused a recession in 1873. Gould had diversified from railroads, where he earned his unenviable reputation, and was now a major investor in Western Union, which he had seized in a spectacular bear raid shortly before. A colleague of Gould informed him that Keene was overextended in the Chicago wheat market and that the time was ripe to destroy him. Gould was in an advantageous position to send an anonymous telegram, and before long, the wave of selling in Chicago made Keene's creditors and bankers nervous. By the time his creditors had finished with him, Keene was in the words of Matthew Josephson, "shorn, like the veriest lamb, of seven millions and turned adrift, a bankrupt. It was a grievous lesson."[13] Undaunted, Keene's attention again turned to New York, where he concentrated on NYSE stocks and later became the master market maker in U.S. Steel at J. P. Morgan's request. Even in his later years, his sharp reputation followed him. Bernard Baruch said in the 1930s that "under the SEC's regulations, Keene's methods in making a market are no loner permitted."

Like Hutchinson, Gould recognized the link between gold and commodities prices. A year after his famous gold corner, he was called to testify before a Congressional hearing investigating the corner and its effect on gold. When asked about his ramping of gold, Gould replied in terms that the wheat traders well understood: "I went in with a view of putting gold up. At the time, the fact was established that we had an immense harvest and that there was going to be a large surplus of breadstuffs, either to rot or be exported . . . I found that with gold at [a premium of one hundred] 40 or 45, Americans would supply the English market with breadstuffs; but that it would require gold to be at that price to equalize our high price labor . . . with gold below 40 we could not export but with gold above 45 we would get the trade."[14] Arguing that he was helping exports did not necessarily convince Congress that his motives were patriotic, but it did illustrate that Gould, like Hutchinson, was aware of the factors that made the prices of commodities and precious metals move in tandem.

Keene returned to New York, where he soon resumed speculating in stocks—all the wiser for having dealt with Gould and Hutchinson. He became known as the "Silver Fox" of Wall Street and participated in many pools later organized by J. P. Morgan to prop up the price of stocks in which the legendary banker had an interest. However, his interest in Chicago futures demonstrated the reputation and vulnerability of the futures markets during the first three decades of their existence. The general reputation of the markets for creating wildly vacillating prices only made the Grangers and other critics skeptical about their usefulness. Moreover, the markets were not the only culprit in the cross hairs of the reform movement.

Chicago became the center of the country's breadbasket, and almost all wheat and corn passed through the city on its way to market. The warehousemen also made a fast killing by charging a couple of cents per bushel in storage charges regardless of whether they actually stored the grain. This served to increase prices, although farmers were left with the bill, cutting into their already meager profit margins. This rapacious attitude did little to help the grain marketing system.

Redress for the beleaguered farmers was left to the courts. One Illinois warehouseman named Munn was charged with violating a state law for operating a warehouse without a license. At issue was the matter of excess charges plus the fact that much of the wheat stored in his warehouses came from out of state and was in transit. The Grange movement contended that the railroads and the operators were interfering in interstate commerce and that Illinois had the right to fine Munn in the absence of any meaningful federal laws regulating interstate commerce. The Illinois courts agreed. Munn appealed his conviction to the Supreme Court, which in 1877 found against him in the celebrated case *Munn v. Illinois*. The decision was the first meaningful one made by the court in years concerning interstate commerce. The *Chicago Tribune* put the warehousemen into perspective when it stated that "the name of a Chicago warehouseman has become a synonym with that of a pirate in the agricultural districts and there has been ample justification thereof."[15]

The Grange movement would have little to sing about in the years that followed. The Munn decision effectively was rolled back in 1886 by another Supreme Court case, *Wabash Railway Co. v. Illinois,* which stated that states could not regulate railways that simply passed through their jurisdiction. The uproar caused by that decision prompted Congress to pass the Interstate Commerce Act the following year, establishing the Interstate Commerce Commission as the regulator of the railroads. The battle against the railroads and the warehousemen became detached from the separate but equally compelling case against the futures exchanges as time wore on. From the farmers' point of view, however, they were being held hostage by enemies on several fronts—Eastern speculators who ran the railroads, warehouses, and exchange pits. The result was a combination of wildly fluctuating prices and additional charges, adding to their woes. The legislatures were the only recourse available, so the battle against the exchanges was pursued in state capitals and, eventually, in Washington.

## A DROP IN THE BUCKET

Adding to the exchanges' woes were the infamous bucket shops of the nineteenth century. Already well-known in the New York stock and gold markets, bucket shop operators naturally took to LaSalle Street as they did to Wall Street. The first bucket shops appeared in Chicago in the mid-1870s. For only a few dollars, the small investor could play the market like Keene and Hutchinson. The bucket shop was nothing more than a betting parlor where a few dollars would allow the average man in the street to assume a "position" in stocks or futures.

Bucket shops charged their investors only a small fraction of the price of a stock or futures contract. The futures markets themselves required only a small fraction of the value of a contract to be deposited in cash for a trader to open a position. Naturally, that trader was responsible for the entire amount of gain or loss that followed, but the enormous leverage offered by the small margins was very appealing. Bucket shop customers were under the impression that they were offered the same sort of leverage when, in fact, they were only making a bet on the market's direction. Bucket shop operators were neither members of the exchanges nor qualified brokers; they simply ran betting shops where money was taken and (sometimes) paid back when there was a profit.

Bucket shop operators were nettlesome pests. The CBOT finally had to ban them from the exchange floor, where they would wander about to check out the price action before taking bets. Since only pit traders were allowed on the exchange floor, the CBOT thought that the bucket shop operators would sully its reputation. The streets adjoining LaSalle were adorned with bucket shops, and there were many more spread around the country. Oddly, they formed the first retail body of brokers, although they were independent and could assume a variety of forms and levels of sophistication. Nevertheless, they were all bogus, and more than one was known to disappear if the bets moved against it. Returning customer money on a net basis was not part of their "service." In the absence of what are known today as retail brokers, bucket shop operators did a brisk business despite the risks and the shadowy figures among them.

By the latter part of the nineteenth century, the CBOT and the bucket shop operators were at war. Many operators witnessed the success of pit traders and decided to follow in their footsteps, taking a few shortcuts along the way. One of the most notorious was William Rodman Hennig, a bucket shop operator who in 1894 appeared in Chicago from places unknown with a few thousand dollars in his pocket. Within a year of his arrival, he opened a bucket shop under the grand name of the Equitable Produce and Stock Exchange, located in the basement of the Grand Pacific Hotel. He leased private telephone and telegraph wires and set himself up into what appeared to be a miniature exchange with all the trappings. He was soon doing a brisk business and moved his exchange to more spacious quarters, changing its name to the Consolidated Produce and Stock Exchange of Chicago.

Having established a headquarters, he then produced official-looking literature to announce his business. Advertising appeared, announcing the purpose of the new business. "The Consolidated Produce and Stock Exchange," it began, "is so organized that stocks, securities of all kinds, and grain and provisions may be dealt in and handled on the floor of its exchange hall by and between members under rules, regulations, and by-laws of the most approved character." The new expanded operation opened for business in late May 1896; however, the last part of the ad's sentence attracted attention because several months earlier Hennig and his partners, as well as all of their employees, had been indicted by a Chicago grand jury for operating a bucket shop and violating gambling laws.

Legal distractions did not bother bucket shop operators in the least. Hennig hired a dozen young men to act as traders and shout orders among themselves on his exchange's floor. Visitors to his offices were given the impression that they were in a legitimate broker's office when, in fact, the entire operation was a well-designed fraud. Hennig, though, did not lack for customers, either before or after his indictment. The straw that broke the camel's back was a letter that he sent to a CBOT official in July 1896 pledging $1,000 for the CBOT's bucket shop fund so that the legitimate exchange would succeed in its effort "to break up the bucket shop element in this city, as well as to suppress the illegal traffic in privileges."[16] The CBOT official to whom Hennig adressed the letter was the same official who had brought charges against him on behalf of the CBOT several months before.

Infuriated, the official, John Hill, again began a drive that eventually saw Hennig and his accomplices indicted and successfully prosecuted in 1898 after several police raids to gather evidence. Bucket shop operators were encouraged by some of the divided court decisions made in the past and constantly flew in the face of the CBOT until they were challenged. As a result of the Hennig prosecution, the number of bucket shops began to decline and would decline even more after the turn of the new century. But the damage they did to small, uneducated speculators was considerable. A Chicago newspaper succinctly summed up the plight of the bucket shop investor when it stated that "the bucket shop victim is a hopeful wretch. He pursues his hollow object with the devotion an opium eater has for his drug. But he rarely gains it. Sometimes he wins a small sum, and the proprietor always knows he will come back with it. When he wins a large amount the keeper evades settlement . . . in the long run, practically speaking, it is impossible to win because the keeper won't allow it." The paper concluded that bucket shop operators were "among the most heartless, rapacious and cruel harpies that prey upon the deluded poor."[17]

The exchanges wanted rid of them and muckrakers ranted against them, but somehow the bucket shops managed to find a place in the odd ideological battle that waged in the nineteenth century between Populists and the business community. The world of the Populists was one of rhetoric and appeals to emotions. Policy positions often were not based on fact and often played to a very basic regional instinct that consciously sought to set agrarian interests in the South and Midwest against those in the East. Conspiracy was often at the center of their arguments. An extremely popular book that circulated in the Midwest during the late 1880s was *Seven Financial Conspiracies That Have Enslaved the American People*, written by S. (Sarah) E. V. Emery. In its discussion of conspiracies, many based on the manipulation of gold by Eastern bankers, the book attempted to show how the average agrarian was at the mercy of the Wall Street crowd that cared only for money, not products. The subtitle of the book rang especially true in criticisms of futures, but the refrain became standard in Populist rhetoric: *How the Producers Have Been Robbed by the Non-Producers Through Evil Legislation*. Facts and figures were of little use in these sorts of attacks. Implying that Easterners were at the heart of the problem played well in the heartland.[18]

Bucket shops benefited from this general sort of public relations because they were seen as a challenge to the futures market monopoly in the distribution system. The fact that they were nothing more than gambling casinos did not seem to matter; as far as Populists were concerned, bucket shops provided alternatives to the predatory pit traders and gave the little person a chance to make a buck. Adding insult to injury, some CBOT members often took orders from individuals on behalf of bucket shops, moonlighting for a few extra dollars. As far as the person on the street was concerned, bucket shops looked legitimate, and there were times when the small bettor actually won. Bucket shops posted securities and commodities prices on blackboards in their windows, usually showing prices on fictitious trades. The more sophisticated shops actually employed ticker tapes and telegraphs, or at least led their customers to believe that they did. The telegraph became the shops' battleground with the CBOT in its attempt to reassert its authority over the markets.

The CBOT asserted that any telegraph company holding space on its trading floor should be prohibited from supplying information to bucket shop operators. Such a task was not easy, for bucket shop operators constantly infiltrated the floor of the exchange, seeking tips and prices. The bucket shops responded by going to court. Unfortunately, the courts were never of the same mind, often confusing the operations of the CBOT with those of the shops. Finally, the issue wound its way to an Illinois legislative committee, which sent a delegation to the CBOT. After some extremely conflicting and confusing testimony, the committee concluded that when comparing the CBOT with the bucket shops, "one is legitimate as the other, and the business of one as honorable as the other." Even worse for the exchange, the *Chicago Tribune* concluded that by attacking the shops, the CBOT was attempting "to do away with its rivals."[19] After 35 years of existence, the CBOT was looked upon as little more than a betting parlor, serving manipulators. Because it was deemed a necessary evil, it was felt that no reason existed for the person on the street to not be allowed in on the action as well.

Liked or not, bucket shops remained on both LaSalle Street and Wall Street. They were a problem that state governments were not able to control. Controlling the activities of traders on exchanges and bucket brokers was not something that could be effectively controlled by the government during the nineteenth century. The best that states could do was pass local laws and hope that traders and exchanges would fall in line. Even after 1874, the Illinois antioption law remained vague and rarely enforced. But on the federal level, prospects were better for fighting the sorts of injustices that agrarians felt they had suffered. Futures exchanges and options trading became part of a larger issue that began to boil over after 1890. Antifutures and antioptions laws became integrally intertwined with the larger economic issue of the day. They were included in the silver question that dominated political discussions, especially during the presidential election of 1896.

In the late nineteenth century, the argument about the nature of futures exchanges was still as heated as it was during the Civil War. The old pit traders maintained that what they did was risky but still refused to recognize a larger role for the markets. Hutchinson's son Charles followed his father to the CBOT and was elected president in 1888. He made a speech on the occasion in which he claimed that the CBOT was a significant benefit for the farmer, even going as far as claiming that the institution was philanthropic. When he had heard his son's remarks, Hutchinson turned to a fellow board member on the floor and said, "Did you hear what Charlie said? Charlie said we were philanthropists! Why bless my buttons, we're gamblers. You're a gambler and I'm a gambler." But he later added a note of realism: "Even farmers can say a good word for a speculator, if he happens to be working in their favor."[20]

Despite the fact that the newer breed of CBOT member saw a wider role for the exchanges, the old guard was still up to its customary tricks. In 1888, the CBOT received a shock when rumor reached the floor that Old Hutch was dead. Traders paused in shock, wondering what to do. Shortly, they began selling wheat in droves, driving down the price. Hutchinson had been the central figure in wheat selling, and holding long positions was quickly determined to be imprudent. It was time to sell before the entire market collapsed. True to form, the reports of his demise proved premature: Hutchinson was very much alive but hospitalized after falling down a flight of stairs. Many sellers were quick to react to the rumor, however, and lost in the process. Most traders wished that he had not recovered so soon, for within a year he mounted another spectacular wheat corner, driving the price up temporarily by almost 50 cents per bushel.

## LEGISLATE AND SPECULATE

By the 1890s, Populists began to unite to formally oppose futures exchanges. A move was made to pass an antioption and antifutures market law in Washington for rescuing farmers from the clutches of speculators. To extirpate speculators was a difficult matter, however; the exchanges were now well established, so legislating them out of existence was probably impossible. At the center of the exchanges was scalping. It was felt that if scalping could be reduced, the exchanges would return to the purpose for which they were created—to provide buyers and sellers with guaranteed prices.

To reduce the amount of speculation, a proposal was devised that would tax the sale of grains or cotton futures contracts when the seller did not actually own the commodity. The proposal got its impetus from the sales tax on gold passed during the Civil War. It was acknowledged that the tax would quickly reduce the amount of short selling in the markets. But after 40 years of trading, it was not universally clear whether it was a good idea. All speculation led to increased liquidity on the pit floors, and while that may have helped the plungers and the corners, it also aided hedging real positions. More specific laws, such as the antioption law of Illinois, had proved fruitless in the battle, so taxation appeared to be a viable alternative to reduce pit gambling.

By the early 1890s, several minor antifutures bills had already reached Congress, but they had never gotten out of committee conferences. Then, in 1892, a bill sponsored by Representative William H. Hatch of Missouri and Senator William Washburn of Minnesota crystallized many of the earlier attempts. The Hatch bill began making the rounds of various Congressional committees and stirred heated debate on both sides of the issue. A 10 percent tax was its centerpiece, eliciting comments from farmers, food processors, and futures traders. Testimony poured in from both detractors and supporters, and the bill managed to touch every sensitive nerve. Charles A. Pillsbury, the nation's largest miller of wheat and other grains, supported the bill, knowing that it would hinder the pit traders whom he blamed for erratic prices and economic uncertainty. Others were not as certain. During the Civil War, gold speculation had been rampant in New York before Secretary of the Treasury Salmon Chase banned gold futures trading by speculators in 1864. The prohibition was ephemeral, however, and trading resumed shortly thereafter. What was the point in banning a practice if market forces would unite to defeat the ban in short order?

A clever defense of the futures exchanges came from those who waved the specter of the British in the face of the opposition. These individuals claimed that if futures trading dried up as a result of the Hatch bill, the markets would shift to Britain. Liverpool already had the world's largest grain futures market, and it would take decades for Chicago to supersede Liverpool's market in size and importance. Did antifutures forces want to give the British a backdoor entry to one of America's vital markets? This was clever; the British were in favor of the gold standard, whereas Midwesterners and Populists favored a dual-metal standard of gold and silver. Because the British were the largest foreign investors in America at the time, they had created some enmity in agrarian regions by being absentee landlords. Claiming that the Hatch bill might actually help line their pockets even more seemed appealing.

The bill went for a vote in 1893. It passed the House by 167 votes to 46 and the Senate by 40 votes to 29. The geographical breakdown of the voting followed what was expected of the various regions. It was opposed only in the House and the Senate by the Middle Atlantic states and southern New England—and then only by the narrowest of margins. The rest of the country favored it by a resounding "yea" vote in both houses. The final vote revealed that over 80 percent of Congress had voted for the bill.[21]

Yet, the Hatch bill never became law. Proposed amendments were never added, and the bill died a slow death after Congress adjourned. The issue was, in fact, never raised again after Congress recessed. It became apparent that agrarian opposition to futures trading was still as strong as ever but the legislation would not see the light of day. Then, a severe recession followed a stock market panic, leading to J. P. Morgan's famous rescue of the U.S. Treasury by helping to sell it a gold-backed bond. In 1893, Congress repealed the Sherman Silver Act of 1890, and the country returned to a gold-only standard. These two events were much more momentous than anti-futures legislation, eclipsing the Hatch bill. Also, the Populist influence began to wane even before the presidential campaign of William Jennings Bryan against William McKinley in 1896. Against this political backdrop, pit traders had little to restrain them in their dreams of corners and manipulation.

The Hatch bill did contain several lessons for posterity. One futures market would be regulated during World War I, and the failure of the bill proved an invaluable lesson to future regulators. It did underscore the fear of short selling, however. The process was vital to the markets, but it ran against the grain of conservative thought throughout most of the nineteenth century. How could someone sell something he did not own with the intent of buying it back at a later time for a profit? As far as critics were concerned, it was only an excuse for forcing prices down to make a profit. There had been several vain attempts to curtail the practice, dating as far back as the War of 1812 in New York, but all proved futile. The Hatch bill was nothing more than an anti–short selling bill in disguise, with its proposed 10 percent tax a warning to traders not to sell something that they did not own.

Lotteries, the one popular form of gambling, were also in legislative trouble at the end of the nineteenth century. The many state lotteries that had begun since the Civil War were constantly attacked by critics on grounds of being immoral, leading to their gradual abolition during the 1880s and 1890s. The one exception was the Louisiana lottery, the most successful in the country in the latter half of the nineteenth century. A private company was granted the right to operate in Louisiana, and its lottery was enormously successful. When it first began operation in 1868, the lottery held lavish ceremonies whenever drawings were made. The lottery's organizers hired Confederate General P. G. Beauregard to preside over the drawings and they managed to pay handsome dividends in many years to the lottery's investors. Its tickets were sold nationwide, becoming even more popular as many states banned their own lotteries. In 1899, however, the national antilottery movement finally ensnared it. Congress passed a law that prohibited the use of public mail service for selling lottery tickets, effectively putting an end to Louisiana's lottery operation. By the time the law was passed, 42 of the existing 44 states at the time had already banned lotteries, and the ban effectively ended the practice of selling tickets via the mail.[22]

The ingenuity of lottery operators continued, however. Many of the tickets sold in the United States were from foreign lotteries and their operators simply avoided the public mail by using private courier services to deliver the tickets across state lines. Then, finally, Congress put an end to that practice as well, and the issue wound its way to the Supreme Court. In *Champion v. Ames* (1903), the court ruled that Congress indeed had the right to prohibit the transport of lottery tickets by means other than that of the U.S. mail. The *New York Times*, taking note of the decision, queried whether "the right to 'regulate' includes the right to prohibit commerce in articles deemed prejudicial to the public health or morals."[23] The court apparently thought it did. Moreover, supporters of national securities legislation thought that the law would help them in their quest to impose regulations on the stock exchanges, but the law was not applied to securities dealings.

Much of the furor surrounding lotteries was as practical as it was moral. Besides believing that gambling was unconstructive, leading to idleness and debauchery, many were opposed to them simply because they were ripe with fraud. Often, ticket holders were defrauded when too many tickets were sold or when the potential payout was exaggerated. State legislators frequently were bribed so that the lotteries could obtain favorable legislation and were continued to be bribed so that the lotteries could continue operating. The Louisiana Legislature became as well-known for corruption as the New York Legislature had been during the Tammany Hall days, and the bill introduced during Benjamin Harrison's presidency to deny the use of public mail service to lotteries was meant to be an effective antidote to the fraud. In many ways, the opposition to lotteries was framed in a similar fashion to the opposition to futures markets, and it certainly was more successful.

While Washington was busy with economic affairs, the traders again were having their way in the pits. Another massive corner was organized in 1897 by Joseph Leiter, a newcomer to pit trading. Leiter was one of the new breed of floor traders who saw opportunity in the Chicago pits. Born in Chicago in 1868 to real estate magnate Levi Z. Leiter, he attended Harvard before returning home to Chicago. His father entrusted him with a million dollars, hoping that the young man would manage his real estate holdings. But Leiter had other ideas and headed straight for the CBOT, where he had already decided he would make his own fortune. He was a bit of a fish out of water, because the pits were not accustomed to college-educated traders.

Leiter's plan was to corner the supply of wheat, emulating Hutchinson in the process. He did not keep his ambition a secret. "Mind you, he is a bright boy," remarked the old trader, "but it can't be done again. The market is too big, too immense." Nonetheless, Leiter proceeded with abandon, and after several false starts, he finally made some money in the pits and began to mount his corner—the largest operation of its sort to date. The syndicate that he formed to pursue the operation cornered nearly 16 million bushels at a time when world reserves of the grain were running low. In addition, he planned to corner wheat in December, when the supply was naturally short because of the winter season. It appeared that Leiter had successfully cornered December wheat, but then the plot thickened.[24]

While Leiter's syndicate was buying all of the contracts available, Philip D. Armour and his agents had been selling. Suddenly, traders were not sure that the market had been cornered successfully, especially if Armour was involved. In a classic confrontation of liar's poker, Armour asked Leiter face to face what he had in mind. Leiter laughed at him, telling him that he would force him to settle the contracts at a great loss. Armour became so infuriated by the upstart that he went away and devised a method to break the arrogant young man rather than capitulate to him. He ordered his agents to send all available wheat through Duluth, Minnesota, to be forwarded to Chicago. He then hired adventurous sailors who were willing to sail the Great Lakes in the dead of winter to deliver the wheat.

He even hired tugboats to break the ice on the lakes so that the boats would arrive before the delivery date of his contracts. To the astonishment of all, he delivered his wheat on time, breaking Leiter's corner in the process. Leiter profited but not by the amount originally hoped for.

As a result of the corner, the price of wheat rose 24 cents a bushel to $1.09. Leiter then cornered May wheat with the profits he made from the Armour deal, and the price shot up to $1.85 per bushel. But Leiter became too greedy. Not knowing enough about agriculture, he continued his new corner into the summer months, when a record crop followed. A surfeit of wheat flowed into Chicago, and his positions collapsed. What had been a $7 million paper profit in May disintegrated into a $9 million loss, absorbed by his father. Ever the gentleman, Armour sent Leiter a photograph of himself, inscribed "with best regards," after the escapade ended.

Leiter learned a lesson from the affair, and the family fortune was reduced about 9 percent. He went on to become a typical heir to a family fortune of the period, dabbling in horse racing, philanthropy, and other acceptable sporting and social pastimes. He maintained a liquor vault at his Washington, D.C., home, which robbers once raided of $300,000 worth of liquor and wines. When he died in 1931, a local newspaper eulogized him as "cut in the pattern of the daring visionaries who built a titanic Chicago out of a mud flat pioneer village."[25] He was best remembered, though, for the attempted wheat corner, perhaps a lesson that getting out early with a smaller-than-anticipated profit is better than no profit at all.

Leiter did have one success, but probably not of the sort that he envisaged. Farmers were elated over the increase in the price of wheat caused by his corners, and many made handsome profits by supplying Armour. In this case, the wild speculation worked in their favor. Criticism of the speculators was nowhere to be found, but the quiet would not last for long. The

Progressive movement was gaining strength and would prove to be a more significant adversary than the Populists. Conspiracy theories would give way to more cogent arguments about what ailed America, although a clear break with the Populist past was not possible. The idea that speculators and rapacious Easterners dominated the futures markets would continue. Old notions died hard in the heartland, where anyone who was not a farmer was viewed with suspicion.

Armour did not confine his speculation to the futures pits in the 1890s. He also was active on Wall Street, where his tips were known to move the prices of railroad stocks, especially those operating around Chicago. Speculating in more than one market was relatively common before the turn of the century as communications improved and were faster than ever before. In late 1893, Armour was talking up the price of the St. Paul & Duluth Railroad, which, like many other railroad shares, was not faring well in the market. A local Wall Street newspaper reported that "he declares he is as firm a believer in the stock as he ever was and has been buying it on the way down." The stock retreated from a high of $80 per share and was currently around $27 when he started bulling it. "He swears that there is no human power that can prevent it from advancing again to the high prices at which it sold years ago," the newspaper added.[26] As it turned out, the opposite was true, and Armour lost a sizable amount on the trades.

The days of the megalomaniac corners and massive bear raids appeared to be waning but still managed to survive the nineteenth century. Ironically, Hutchinson's career came to an end with another ambitious corner. In 1889, he was lured into believing that a massive corner in wheat and corn could still be accomplished, and he ventured millions to prove himself once again. However, after reading the markets correctly for years, he overestimated the demand for the two commodities and paid a heavy price. The prices did not respond to his massive buying efforts, as international financial developments began to take their toll on commodities prices. In 1890, the British banking house Baring Brothers failed, putting a serious damper on foreign—especially British—investment and speculation in the American markets. As gold began to flow out of the United States, depressing the price of wheat and corn, Hutchinson refused to read the market signals and continued to purchase contracts. Hutchinson was the same trader who, years before, had unraveled the connection between gold and grain prices, but he misread the situation in 1890 and suffered heavy losses as a result.

Within a year, Hutchinson's fortune and reputation were broken. The last attempt at a corner lost him $2 million in July corn, causing him to retreat from the pits permanently. After his personal debacle, Hutchinson secretly decamped to a small office near Wall Street, living anonymously for months before being accidentally discovered by a visiting Chicago businessman. Although he eschewed the pits, he still needed to be near the action, and Wall Street seemed like a natural place to hide. But he had lost his market touch and was growing too old to influence the markets. Although he occasionally was seen in the galleries of the CBOT following his retirement, he never again traded on the floor of the CBOT. He spent his last years alone at a retirement home in rural Wisconsin but not forgotten in the pits where his legend lived on.

Hutchinson died in 1899, marking the end of a half-century of grandiose speculation. Younger traders were eager to take his place as the king of the wheat pit on the CBOT. These larger-than-life characters immediately stepped forward to assume his mantle. The idea of cornering the entire wheat supply of the United States held its allure, although agricultural production continued to increase and the supply of most agricultural commodities appeared too large to corner. That would not, however, stop speculation on the exchanges. In the years preceding World War I, different exchanges would begin to regulate themselves with greater efficiency and integrity. The Supreme Court helped define the markets' role in several important rulings early in the new century. For better or worse, the futures markets did leave their mark on society. In the late 1890s, a play called *Other People's Money* started a run in New York, starring Hennessy Leroyle, a well-known period comic actor. Leroyle played the role of the king of the wheat pit, who just happened to bear a strong likeness to Joseph Leiter. Louis Brandeis would later use the same title in a book that he wrote to excoriate those bankers who exploited the public during the heyday of the Progressive Era.

## *NOTES*

1. *Standard* meant that the contracts did not vary on the exchanges listing them. It did not imply a nationwide standard by any means. Contracts in Chicago could not be mixed with contracts in St. Louis or Kansas City. If a contract had been bought on an exchange, it needed to be sold on that exchange only, and vice versa.
2. Jonathan Lurie, *The Chicago Board of Trade 1859–1905* (Urbana: University of Illinois Press, 1979), pp. 30–31.
3. *Harper's Weekly*, September 5, 1874.
4. *Chicago Tribune*, September 15, 1865.
5. Kinahan Cornwallis, *The Gold Room* (New York: A. S. Barnes & Co., 1879), p. 7.
6. Edward J. Dies, *The Plunger: A Tale of the Wheat Pit* (New York: Covici-Fried, 1929), p. 50.
7. U.S. Department of Commerce, *Historical Statistics of the United States: Colonial Times to 1957*, pp. 278–297.
8. James L. Orr, ed., *Grange Melodies* (Philadelphia: Geo. S. Ferguson Co., 1912), p. 193.
9. *St. Louis Republican,* June 7, 1874.
10. Theodore J. Grayson, *Leaders and Periods of American Finance* (New York: John Wiley & Sons, 1932), p. 396.

11. C.E. Russell, *The Greatest Trust in the World* (Chicago: Ridgway-Thayer, 1905), p. 286.
12. Lurie, *Chicago Board of Trade*, p. 55.
13. Matthew Josephson, *The Robber Barons* (New York: Harcourt Brace, 1934), p. 208.
14. Report of the Committee on Banking and Currency. *Gold Panic Investigation*, 41st Cong., 2nd sess., Feb. 28, 1870, Rept. 32, p. 132.
15. Lurie, *Chicago Board of Trade*, p. 53.
16. John Hill, Jr., *Gold Bricks of Speculation* (Chicago: Lincoln Book Concern, 1904), p. 80.
17. *Chicago Journal*, July 16, 1898.
18. Certainly not everyone in the Midwest subscribed to the conspiracy theories. A congressman from Wisconsin, Joseph W. Babcock, refuted the assumptions made in the book as bogus before Congress seven years later. He then published a pamphlet entitled "A Populist Humbug Exposed," which outlined his position.
19. Lurie, *Chicago Board of Trade*, p. 87.
20. Dies, *The Plunger*, p. 138.
21. Cedric B. Cowing, *Populists, Plungers, and Progressives: A Social History of Stock and Commodity Speculation 1890–1936* (Princeton, NJ: Princeton University Press, 1965), p. 22.
22. George Sullivan, *By Chance a Winner: The History of Lotteries* (New York: Dodd, Mead, 1972), p. 57.
23. *New York Times*, February 24, 1903.
24. December wheat means that contracts were due for December delivery, expiring on a specific day in that month. Futures contracts traded on a quarterly basis so that a contract would become due at every season of every year, namely, December, March, June, and September.
25. *Wisconsin State Journal*, April 12, 1931.
26. *Wall Street Daily News*, December 23, 1893.

# CHAPTER 2

# FUTURES AND
# "WILD JACKASSES"

**T**HE LAST 20 YEARS OF THE NINETEENTH CENTURY WIT-nessed a constant battle for the markets in their quest for respectability. Although the federal anti-futures law was never signed, state laws against gambling did have a serious effect on the markets. Options trading was still considered gambling and more vulnerable to state laws than futures trading itself, which was considered necessary by all but a handful of the more radical agrarians. Probably the most important development for the exchanges in the waning years of the nineteenth century was the realization that they would have to police themselves more carefully and wage a more vigilant war against bucket shops. Public sentiment linked gambling to bucket shops and bucket shops to the exchanges. To destroy this perception, the exchanges would have to put the bucket shops out of business.

After the classic corners and market manipulations of the nineteenth century, the twentieth century began on a similar note of massive market operations. However, bad press and a movement toward increasing standards in the pits took center stage as bucket shops receded slightly from view. Although Progressivism was in its heyday, the myths surrounding Hutchinson and Leiter still evoked admiration from the newer generation of pit traders. Trying to corner the supply of wheat was still a goal worth achieving, even during the trust-busting presidency of Theodore Roosevelt. The largest operation mounted after the turn of the century was by the new king of the wheat pits, James A. Patten. He cornered wheat in 1902, forcing it up 34 cents per bushel. The profit on the corner was $2 million and ranked the largest of the period. Although the freewheeling days of the McKinley administration were over, market operators did not heed the warnings coming from reform-minded politicians both in Washington and in the state legislatures. Pit trading remained as freewheeling as ever. Patten became the first pit trader to attempt simultaneous corners in wheat, corn, cotton, and oats. In 1910, he became the largest corner to date in the wheat market, attempting to assume the mantle of wheat king.

Putting their own houses in order became an even greater necessity for the futures markets before World War I. The rift between farmers and industry was growing wider as disparities between farm and urban incomes became more pronounced. Rural life did not change as rapidly as life in the rest of the country, and attitudes in the farm regions also were slow to change. Futures markets were still the enemy of the farmer, although cries for the abolition of the exchanges were being replaced by a begrudging acceptance of the markets. The general price rises in agricultural commodities during World War I helped reduce the amount of shrill criticism from agrarians, but in the 1920s, the outcry would begin again with the post–World War I decline in farm prices.

The 1920s were destined to become a crucial decade for farmers and their favorite bête noire, the futures markets. Other factors also entered the equation to put the markets on the defensive again, as outlandish as they might have seemed at the time. The rise of the Ku Klux Klan in agrarian states, coincidental with Henry Ford's series of anti-Semitic articles published in his newspaper *Dearborn Independent*, cast a dark shadow over the markets and over Wall Street in general. The attacks were not against the markets directly but were more insidious because they raised the specter of anti-Semitism and a visceral distrust of finance in general. In the simple logic of the agrarian movement, bankers, Jews, and gold were all responsible for the continuing plight of the farmer. How the logic was applied or whether it made sense was of secondary importance. Markets of all sorts were responsible for impoverishing the farmer; there was no shortage of culprits. All one had to do was look to the past to see how the machinations of Wall Street and LaSalle Street had conspired to dupe the simple, independent farmer.

Public sentiment rallied around farmers with the publication of popular poet Edwin Markham's *The Man with the Hoe* in 1899. The poem, originally published in the *San Francisco Examiner*, quickly appeared in most national newspapers, making it one of the best-read of the century. Markham characterized the farmer as "plundered, profaned, and disinherited." But it was not until the futures markets became the subject of the muckrakers, just as the stock markets had been in the previous generation, that popular sentiment turned against the common enemy. Even the notorious NYSE did not suffer the bleak portrait painted by the most famous critic of pre–World War I laissez-faire commerce. Frank Norris' *The Pit* was published in 1903 and became an instant classic. The novel portrayed the business practices and personal lives of Chicago pit traders, a portrait that was not complimentary. Already known for his cynical view of the railroads expressed in *The Octopus*, Norris based his story of the pit traders on characters easily recognizable to newspaper readers. The protagonist was a character who had already made a fortune in real estate in the Chicago area, while his elder colleague was a reformed former trader originally from Massachusetts who at one time cornered wheat from Milwaukee before moving to Chicago. At one point in the book, the elder trader commented that "those fellows in the Pit don't own the wheat; never even see it. Wouldn't know what to do with it if they had it. They don't care in the least about the grain. But there are thousands upon thousands of farmers out here in Iowa and Kansas and Dakota who do, and hundreds of thousands of poor devils in Europe who care even more than the farmer," referring to the producers and users who depended almost solely upon American-grown wheat. By the turn of the century, it was clear that not only Americans but Europeans, too, had come to depend upon a reliable supply of grain from the Midwest. "If we send it [the price of wheat] up too far, the poor man in Europe suffers, the fellow who eats it. And food to the peasant on the continent is bread—not meat and potatoes." Norris made little effort to disguise Leiter and Hutchinson as the models for his characters. After years of hagiography by sympathetic writers, the book was a sobering blow to the reputations of those whose names were synonymous with futures trading.

Despite the gains made by the CBOT in fighting bucket shops and, to a lesser extent, privilege trading, general consensus existed that futures markets would not be able to correct the problems of farmers through pricing and that new institutions were needed in the public sector to assist agriculture. Beginning during the Cleveland administration and continuing into the Wilson administration, Congress created federal agencies devoted to farm finance. It was clear that farmers needed better financial institutions if they were to survive in the twentieth century. The Farm Credit System, established in 1916, was patterned after the Federal Reserve, created several years before, and was intended to make farm loans easier to obtain so that the farmers could obtain working capital as easily as industry. But the battle was an uphill one, for farmers had the odds stacked against them and continued to blame Wall Street and LaSalle Street for their problems.

By 1900, many futures exchanges already were well established or quickly on their way. The CBOT had almost 1,800 members and was the largest grain exchange in the world. Chicago already was acknowledged as the world's breadbasket. The American grain surplus quickly found its way onto the world markets, and foreign demand often had a profound impact on both spot and futures prices. But despite their growth, the exchanges as a group still suffered severe growing pains. Bucket shop operators were still present, although in declining numbers, and some commodities had spotty records for delivery and quality. Meaningful regulation, aside from a few state laws, was noticeably absent; the exchanges ran their operations their own way unless challenged by scandal. It was becoming clear, however, that the exchanges would have to make significant strides to clean themselves up and get rid of bucket shop operators, who would either have to fill the order of public sentiment or fear being killed off by a reform-minded Congress.

Traders and legislators were also aware of the attempt made in Germany in the late 1890s to curb futures trading. A law was passed that prohibited futures dealings in grains unless the names of both parties—buyers and sellers—were recorded. As of 1897, it was impossible to speculate in German grain futures, since the act effectively prohibited short selling and scalping. However, the drawbacks to the law were painfully clear, because only hedgers could use the market. Without speculators to provide liquidity on the exchange floors, only brave pit traders would buy from recognized sellers. If the market moved against them, they could be liable for providing farmers with a stable price for their harvests, in effect stabilizing the German grain crop themselves. Nobody assumed that sort of risk alone, so the German law proved ineffective at a time when agriculture was becoming more sophisticated and productive. The law was aimed at both stock and futures exchanges and did immense harm to both. Consequently, futures traders took their business to Liverpool; stock traders, too, moved some of their activities overseas to avoid the law. As a result, German commerce was hurt on both counts. American futures traders watched the German situation with keen interest, noting the shortcomings of the law and quick to repeat them at any time the occasion arose.

## "THE GREATEST OF BUCKET SHOPS"

The war between the CBOT and the bucket shops was still raging at the turn of the century, although the CBOT was gaining the upper hand. Despite the fact that telegraph services were forbidden to the bucket shop operators, the shops still managed to transmit live prices to their bettors, who thought that they were dealing with legitimate brokers. The CBOT took great precautions against releasing prices to nonmembers, but the bucket shops still posted live prices on their boards and ersatz ticker tapes—a feat that nobody could understand how the shops accomplished in the face of tight security as implemented by the exchange.

As early as 1890, Hutchinson pointed out the practice whereby a young boy, legitimately employed by the CBOT, would sit at the edge of the pits and use hand signals to convey prices from the pits to another boy, who would be perched on the roof of an adjacent building using binoculars to read the signals and passing the information downstairs to the bucket shop operators. As a result, the CBOT soaped all of its windows to stop the practice. Deprived of their cloak of legitimacy, many bucket shops closed their doors within a short time as a result. Without current prices, their pretence of operating as honest brokers crumbled in an instant. Some, though, were remarkably persistent and able to grow despite the odds.

At the turn of the century, the most powerful bucket shop operator in the country was C. C. Christie in Kansas City. He came to be an operator from the legitimate stock-and-futures brokerage business. In 1887, Missouri passed an antigambling law that forbade bucket shops, and Christie—still in his legitimate profession—addressed the Missouri Legislature on the evils of gambling operations. He told the legislature that "the bucket shop has, within a few years past, sprung from comparative inconsequence into an institution of formidable wealth and threatening proportions. There are nearly a thousand in the United States . . . having banded together they sneer at legislation. Grown rich, they scoff at antagonistic public opinion."[1] The legislators, however, already were aware that the shops used false advertising, often with enticing invitation letters to potential investors, and kept "sucker lists" of those with whom they had dealt or those who had answered their ads. The problem was a national one, and no one was certain how the gambling could be stopped.

Banding together was the real issue concerning the bucket shop operators. To stay in business, they had to ensure that their customers lost money, so they usually took opposite positions in the markets. While telling their customers to buy, they would sell short en masse, guaranteeing a loss while making money for themselves. In other words, bucket shops used customer funds to open their own contrary positions and make money. Christie's frank admission is one of the few enlightening remarks publicly made during the nineteenth century about the effects of the shops. In another of his more intriguing remarks, he stated that "and so, like any other professional gambler, the bucket shop took the $10,000,000 entrusted to it by those who played against its game, and entering the markets of the country used this tremendous financial engine to force prices downward by every available means."[2] The problem was widespread—so widespread, in fact, that Christie gave up legitimate brokering and became a bucket shop operator himself. When he did, he displayed the same arrogance he accused others of showing to the authorities.

For bucket shops to prosper, they needed access to live prices from the CBOT. However, the CBOT would have none of it, for it had already banned bucket shops from using its prices. Without those prices, the bucket shop operators could not give the appearance of true brokers. The developing battle would not be over bucket shops as such but, rather, the proprietary nature of the prices created in the CBOT pit and transmitted by Western Union wire in conjunction with the exchange. How were bucket shop operators able to remain in business when they were barred from sharing the telegraphs and the CBOT needed to soap its exchange windows? They appeared to be out of the information loop.

Christie blatantly remained in business when it appeared he had been defeated. In 1900, he was operating in Kansas City as the Christie-Street Commission Co. when the CBOT and Western Union took out an injunction against the firm, depriving it of the grain prices it desperately needed. The firm was discovered to have a pirated loop wire service provided by a legitimate broker that had been supplying the firm with prices, but the wire went quiet when the injunction was upheld in the courts. Appeals against the injunction, in both local and state courts, were to no avail, and it appeared that Christie would soon be out of business. Undaunted, he reorganized as the Christie Grain & Stock Co. but was still unable to gather legitimate price quotations, so he resorted to subterfuge. Soon, he prospered again. When the CBOT was unable to determine how Christie was managing to stay in business, it began its own investigation.

The operation was too large to have a boy on the floor of the exchange secretly transmitting prices, as in Hutchinson's time; it now relied on technology. Christie had secret transmit-ters placed in other legitimate brokers' offices that bugged all conversations, including price reporting. The CBOT, under John Hill—a member who headed the bucket shop drive and who was better known as the CBOT's Sherlock Holmes—suspected that something was amiss and hired its own telegraphy specialists to uncover the practice. Subsequently, the CBOT asked for an injunction, granted in 1902, barring Christie from using the stolen quotations. Christie naturally appealed, claiming that the information was public, not proprietary. The case made its way to the Supreme Court, but Christie found the high court to be even more formidable than local and state courts, and its decision afforded him no escape.

The appeals process was not exhausted until 1905, when the Supreme Court finally ruled on the case. The case was favorable for the CBOT on several counts. Upholding the injunction, Oliver Wendell Holmes delivered the opinion of the court, stating that the exchange and the telegraph companies did not restrain trade by restricting prices to outsiders, as Christie's lawyers had argued. The bucket shops were getting their prices from sources outside the contractual arrangements between the exchange and the telegraph carriers, and since they were not parties to the agreement, it was assumed that "they get, and intend to get, their knowledge [of prices] in a way which is wrongful. . . ." Simply put, the bucket shops had no claim on the information, since they intended to use it in a fraudulent manner. Their nature was not something the court discussed; however, the nature of the CBOT was another matter.

Unlike earlier state-court decisions of the nineteenth century, the Supreme Court had no problem with the economic functions of the exchange. Acknowledging that three-quarters of open futures contracts were never delivered, Holmes nevertheless called the CBOT "one of the great grain and provision markets of the world." He also labeled Christie as the keeper of one of the "greatest of bucket shops . . . places wherein is permitted the pretended buying and selling of grain, etc., without any intention of receiving and paying for the property so bought, or delivering the property so sold." After years of feuding, the matter of bucket shops was finally settled, at least in legal terms. Clearly aware of earlier state-court pronouncements about the CBOT, the Supreme Court addressed the problem of speculation on the CBOT, finally settling the issue of the exchange's legitimacy.

Undelivered contracts were the CBOT's weak spot among its critics, who charged it with being a mere gambling den—no more than a big, monopolistic bucket shop. The argument used by Progressives, agrarians, and the bucket shops themselves finally fell by the wayside when Holmes stated that "in a modern market, contracts are not confined to sales for immediate delivery." This one statement gave the markets the legitimacy for which they had fought desperately. The method the CBOT used of settling open contracts, known as set-offs, or ring settlement, was also vindicated, taking much wind out of critics' arguments. Using this technique, floor clerks on the exchange matched open buy-and-sell orders so that they were all closed on the final settlement day. "The fact that contracts are settled in this way by set-off," the court concluded, "and the payment of differences detracts in no degree from the good faith of the parties . . . [and] is perfectly consistent with a serious business purpose, and an intent that the contract shall mean what it says."[3] Futures markets around the country breathed a collective sigh of relief.

The court's ruling was a great victory for the CBOT and futures markets in general. It also was a personal victory for William Baker, the CBOT's long-time president—known fondly as "Bucket Shop Baker" because of his reputation as the greatest foe of the gambling dens over the years. He and other select members of the CBOT's board, including John Hill, actively pursued bucket shops since the early 1890s and successfully invoked sanctions against several pit traders for colluding with them. Also, they opposed the trading of privileges. Baker once called the trading of CBOT options "so common outside of exchange hours as to impair the good name of the association."[4] The days of trading puts and calls on the sidewalks outside the exchange were finished, a victim of the CBOT's attempt to spruce up its image.

In the Midwest, options trading remained an extracurricular activity on most of the futures exchanges. Even though Justice Holmes' ruling in the Christie case stated flatly that the exchange was not a monopoly even though it enforced rules upon its members and tried to control trading, privilege trading was still frowned upon and considered a form of gambling; it was therefore illegal in many states. In the East, however, practicality prevailed. Options were traded actively on the curb market on the streets outside the NYSE and were considered an indicator of the health of the market. In late 1893, as the market was turning down during the Panic of 1893, the local press recognized that options trading was a bellwether of the market's direction. "Often the market for stock privileges is as good an indication of the speculative sentiment as can be had on Wall Street," commented one market newspaper, adding that "the New Street brokers just now report a good demand for puts . . . judging by this would indicate that would-be purchasers of stocks are desirous of limiting their losses," meaning that they wanted to buy puts when the market declined to hedge their actual stock holdings.[5]

Despite the court victory and strict self-regulation, bucket shops continued to operate, although there were fewer of them. Some of the larger shops employed political help to ensure that they remained free from prosecution. The chairman of the CBOT's bucket shop committee, John Hill, went so far as to suggest that "notorious but rich bucket shop-keepers when employing counsel, always give the preference to the law firms of United States Senators and Representatives." They were also aided by more than one avaricious state legislator. Citing a 1903 case in Minnesota in which a bank failed after a junior employee stole funds and passed them to a bucket shop, Hill raised the question of how it was still possible for bucket shop operators to defeat an anti–bucket shop law in the Minnesota Legislature. "Can it be possible that the 'loot' from the Duluth bank aided to kill the bill?" he asked. "Some of us who have experienced the humiliation of being forced to witness the bartering of votes in law-making bodies know the answer well," he concluded, barely avoiding libel by failing to mention the names of the naysayers to the bill.[6]

By the turn of the century, futures markets had achieved a certain level of sophistication that was indeed helping to market grain and establish prices for delivery. But their critics persisted, maintaining that futures trading was gambling and ought to be prohibited. They looked at the dark side of the markets rather than the bright. What was clear was that the futures markets performed their tasks differently. Some were efficient, as was the CBOT, while others were poorly organized and less well run. Other than establishing a price on which buyers and sellers could rely, the other major contribution of futures trading was that it established a uniform grade for hedgers and speculators. Regardless of whether a trader was long or short, if delivery was expected, a particular grade of that commodity had to be delivered on physical settlement. If a market accepted too wide an array of grades of the commodity for delivery, it needed reform. The commodity with the worst track record also spawned the first national futures legislation.

## EARLY REGULATION

Remarkably, the futures exchanges remained unregulated until World War I. Regulations at the state level met with mixed results over the years, but federal regulations were noticeably absent. The futures markets were not alone in being unregulated. Regulation of the country's securities exchanges also was noticeably absent, and the NYSE, like the CBOT, was able to sidestep most serious public criticism. Ironically, the country's commodity pricing was left in the hands of exchanges that most insiders and critics recognized as being somewhat inadequate for the task. Providing foodstuffs for both American and foreign consumers was almost solely in the hands of pit traders, who still occasionally got the grand notion that they could corner the entire supply in a nineteenth-century-style pit coup. Guidelines for the trading of vital commodities were sorely needed but very slow to develop; they were developed only in response to a crisis that specifically underscored the weaknesses of the laissez-faire pit system of pit trading.

Congress passed the first federal law regulating the futures exchanges in 1915—the Cotton Futures Act. The cotton market contained many grades, or types, of cotton that could be delivered against a contract, but the prices of the grades often did not reflect differences in quality. Sometimes, low-grade cotton fetched as high a price as high-grade, a situation with the potential to deprive actual users of the types of cotton that they needed while exacting an exorbitant price for what was actually delivered. What could one expect? asked Southern cotton growers. After all, the futures market was located primarily in New York, not in New Orleans or Charleston.

Trading in cotton moved to New York after the Civil War in 1870, and developed into a large market called the Cotton Exchange. Many commodity brokers and dealers moved to New York from other parts of the country to establish a presence, enhancing New York's growing importance to the commodities business. At one point, 17 grades of cotton were considered acceptable for delivery, a situation that occasionally caused chaos among traders and hedgers. Chaos finally struck in 1906, when a major tropical storm swept through the cotton-producing states and destroyed much of the cotton crop, forcing prices to go up and making it difficult to deliver with any immediacy or assurances about quality. After complaints about the quality of deliveries and the prices on its exchange, the Cotton Exchange still refused to act to remedy the situation, and several years later a push toward legislation was begun. The provisions of the act were very technical, but they essentially required the exchange to make clear, firm prices and standardize delivery grades and procedures. Most important, perhaps, was that Congress acted when requested to clear up a messy situation involving a national market.

Reforms in cotton trading came just in time, because World War I proved to be a bonanza for futures markets. The price of cotton rose 500 percent between 1914 and 1918, while the price of corn and most grains doubled. Short sellers did not do well during those years, for prices constantly rose. Only after 1919 did prices again recede to their prewar levels. Originally, however, Americans misread the opportunity that war in Europe presented to domestic producers. The NYSE shut down operations in 1914 for several months so that the prices of its stocks would remain stable. Traders feared that British investors would dump American shares, forcing prices down. The British were the major suppliers of capital to the United States, so the fears were well founded though misguided. The Cotton Exchange and the Coffee Exchange in New York followed suit, although neither had anything to worry about. By December 1914, they all reopened, and prices were strong. The war, it seemed, was good for business.

Demand for agricultural commodities came from both home and abroad. Foodstuffs were in demand for soldiers and cotton was needed for uniforms. The futures markets were not alone in setting prices, however. The wartime food effort was coordinated in Washington by Herbert Hoover, named by

Woodrow Wilson as the country's chief food administrator. A former businessman who had already made his fortune, Hoover displayed strong skills when dealing with the European food crisis. After a stint in coordinating relief efforts for Belgium in 1914, Hoover became the "Food Czar" of Europe. He began organizing the American effort by mobilizing and conserving foodstuffs in 1917, purchasing and allocating vast quantities to war-ravaged combatants. He was so adept at the effort that a new verb, *hooverize,* entered American usage, meaning to economize and allocate scarce portions efficiently. While in Europe, Hoover helped distribute more than 20 million tons of food and millions of pounds of cotton in a massive humanitarian effort. The effort helped him develop strong opinions toward the markets that were to become evident in the 1920s and 1930s.

The war was a rocky time for the markets. As wartime demand caused the price of most grains to rise, speculation rose in suit. The press became incensed at this new outburst of speculation, claiming that it came at the expense of American lives and values. A new round of antispeculator sentiment filled both the newspapers and Congress just when it appeared that the futures exchanges had made some real gains in public acceptance. The futures markets, however, were not alone; anti–Wall Street sentiment also abounded against speculators and investment bankers in general. The U.S. Treasury kept a tight lid on its war bond–distribution process. The massive Liberty Loan bond program was launched without the underwriting efforts of Wall Street securities houses, which merely helped sell bonds for the Treasury but did not reap any unusually large fees for their efforts, as they had often done in past wars.

Strong demand for foodstuffs caused Congress to pass the Food Control Act in 1918. The prices of foods considered vital for the war effort were frozen and futures trading in them was banned. The CBOT suspended wheat futures, and the smaller

Chicago Butter & Egg Board suspended trading in its two mainstays. Trading of wheat resumed in 1920; trading of butter and eggs, in 1919. Trading of other grains on the CBOT continued as usual, and the pit traders contented themselves with limited activity. Although the traders and the CBOT were unhappy about the price freeze, the alternative would have been considerably worse. There had been talk of abolishing the exchanges or at least closing all of them for the duration of the war.

The immediate postwar years were not as bullish as many had expected. With the cessation of hostilities, European demand for American-produced goods and foodstuffs declined, leaving farmers and factories with excess capacity. The recession that followed was particularly unpleasant and somewhat contrary to the expectations developed during the war. As early as 1916, economist Irving Fisher predicted that once the wartime pent-up demand was released, prices would rise substantially and the economy would boom. As it turned out, prices did not rise to serious inflationary levels and the boom was put on hold until 1923, when the economy began to recover. In the interim, agrarians again began blaming their traditional bogeymen for the problems.

## SONS OF THE SOD

After the war ended, a severe recession occurred that delayed the rally in the economy and the markets that would occur later in the 1920s. However, charges of profiteering during the war continued, and there was still sentiment throughout the country to restrict the exchanges whenever possible. Matters were made considerably worse when Henry Ford's newspaper the *Dearborn Independent* began publishing, from 1920 to 1921, a series of highly inflammatory anti-Semitic articles entitled "The International Jew: The World's Foremost Problem."

Ford's newspaper based these articles on the "Protocols of the Elders of Zion," another series of articles purportedly uncovered in Britain during World War I. The earlier work revealed documents supposedly written by Jewish elders, showing their contempt for the rest of the world and the methods that they used to "control" it.

Ford's newspaper articles pulled few punches in attributing America's social and economic ills to Jewry. All social "problems," from bootlegging, the content of movies, the Versailles peace treaty terms, and the banking industry in general, could be attributed to a conspiracy of peripatetic international Jews who controlled the reins of power in major Western countries. Despite all of these social evils, however, Wall Street banking was at the very heart of the attack. Bankers, many of whom happened to be Jewish, were believed to be the common element of these various problems. The Versailles conference was dominated by bankers from J. P. Morgan & Co., who clearly were not Jewish, and by other members of its close syndicate of bankers, several of whom were Jewish. The article's favorite whipping boys were Otto Kahn of Kuhn Loeb & Co. in New York, and Paul Warburg, also of Kuhn Loeb and a former member of the original Federal Reserve Board. Kahn was one of New York's best known socialite bankers who made a habit of popping up at all of the proper social events of the day. Warburg, less flamboyant than Kahn, was an ardent supporter of a central bank in the years before the Fed was founded. He then served on the Federal Reserve Board.

Other Jewish bankers also had a profound impact on the country in less visible ways. The Wall Street banking houses Goldman Sachs and Lehman Brothers were responsible for bringing many of the large chain stores to market (a postwar phenomenon), a trend that had a profound effect upon American retailing and consumer-buying habits in the years before the 1929 stock market crash. Many critics of the trend blamed

Wall Street, although by "Wall Street" they meant Jews in general. The list of America's ills attributed to Jews grew quite lengthy. The heart of the matter was reflected in one particular article published in *Dearborn Independent* entitled "Jewish Power and America's Money Famine." It was felt that the power exercised by Jews over the nation's supply of money was insidious by helping deprive farmers and others outside the banking coterie of money when they needed it most. The timing of the article seemed appropriate, for the economy was in recession, credit was scarce, and commodity prices were falling rapidly. The Congressional elections of 1920 put many demagogues in office, mostly from the rural states, and the message of the article was well received in agrarian regions. The message was crude and simple but it did reflect the tenor of the times.

In the article, the logic employed to connect Jewish bankers to the gold and money problem was simple and pointed. "Where is the American gold supply?" the article asked. It then answered its own question with a paradox: "It may be in the United States, but it does not belong to the United States," meaning that it was in the hands of Jews and those who conspired with them. The part of the argument that appealed to farmers was tinted with shades of the gold issue that had been a major campaign issue of William Jennings Bryan in his 1896 presidential election. Speaking in favor of silver at the time, Bryan thundered at his opponents before the delegates at the Democratic National Convention in 1896, "You shall not crucify mankind upon a cross of gold." Picking up the popular agrarian distrust of gold and the gold standard, the article stated that "Whatever the gold in the country, the wealth is still greater. There is more wealth in the United States than there is gold in the world. One year's products of the farms of the United States exceeds in money value all the gold in the world."[7]

The rest of the anti-Semitic logic was a simple corollary. Since Jews controlled the gold supply, they controlled American money. Problems encountered by farmers were problems created by Jews and their gentile banker friends who controlled the supply of credit. Moreover, the center of the money universe was New York. "Where is the money," said the anonymous author, "it is in New York." The logic then presented "irrefutable" evidence to true believers in the Midwest and South: "Where did this money loaned in New York come from? It came from those parts of the country where money was scarcest . . . the money is in New York. Go out through the agricultural states and you will not find it. Go into the districts of silent factories and you will not find it . . . the Warburg Federal Reserve has deflated the country."[8]

The articles targeted other aspects of American life dominated by the Jewish "threat," but those articles targeting bankers and finance were to have long-lasting effects on the fortunes of the stock market and the futures market. Although their tone seemed to make the articles appropriate only for fringe groups, it was those same fringe groups who, during the 1920s, assumed power out of all proportion to their memberships and hate messages. The easy answers that the articles provided for complex questions became something of a rural rallying cry against Wall Street and LaSalle Streets at a vulnerable time for the financial centers since almost no federal legislation, except the cotton market regulations, existed to control the stock-and-futures markets. Although nobody on Wall Street and LaSalle Street ever heard of some of the rural politicians who were to make life uncomfortable for them during the 1920s and 1930s, they would soon become all too familiar with their names and firebrand ideologies that had little room for bankers, traders, and speculators.

After the war, the Progressive tradition that began with William Jennings Bryan and continued with Woodrow Wilson began to dissipate. However, a handful of reformers remained in the South and Midwest who maintained the tradition, mainly by attacking anything that affected farming or industry in their home states as having originated in New York. The intellectual range of these homeland radicals was wide. It included Senator George Norris, a Republican from Nebraska first elected in 1913, who refused to allow the Muscle Shoals, Alabama power project fall into Henry Ford's hands in the early 1920s and was one of the chief architects of the Tennessee Valley Authority, created under Franklin D. Roosevelt's first administration. Although nominally a Republican, Norris would ally himself with anyone who shared his Progressive views, making him anathema to the party faithful. His humility helped him overcome the charge of being a party traitor on more than one occasion. When asked what he would do if he inherited a million dollars, he responded, "I would like to know how it feels to walk into a restaurant and order a first-class meal without looking at prices on the menu." Next to Robert La Follette, Sr., Norris was the best known and most widely respected of the post–World War I Progressives.

Other members of the group included Fiorello LaGuardia of New York (the only member of the House included), Senators William E. Borah of Idaho, Gerald P. Nye of North Dakota, and Hiram Johnson of California. Johnson in particular was a constant thorn in the side of the Republican Party, of which he was a long-standing member. Johnson, who considered Harding, Coolidge, and (especially) Hoover somewhat wishy-washy and intellectually weak, especially in international affairs, was a former governor of California who at one time had been dubbed the "lone wolf of the Senate." So fiercely individualistic were his principles that he declined to be Warren Harding's running mate in the 1920 presidential election, even though he was told by party members that only a slim thread of life stood between the vice presidency and the top job, a not-so-oblique reference to the fact that Harding's health was in some doubt. Johnson was a great friend of Theodore Roosevelt, who held the California senator in the highest regard. For his part, Johnson did not think much of Roosevelt's successor, calling William H. Taft the most pitiful figure in American history. The fringe Republicans did not put party loyalty above principle.

Another member of the agrarian radical group was Senator Smith Brookhart of Iowa, a homespun, down-to-earth politician who saw conspiracies at every turn. Born in 1869 in Missouri, he moved to Iowa at age 10 with his family. Originally a schoolteacher, he studied law at night and passed the bar exam in 1892. A dedicated prohibitionist, he dabbled with mixed success in local politics but lost bids in both congressional and senate primaries. While seeking office, he made his living operating a small newspaper. He finally succeeded by winning election to the U.S. Senate during the severe agricultural recession in the early 1920s. An indication of his temperament was detected when he wrote to his supporter Senator Robert La Follette, Sr., describing his Republican adversaries in the primary as "a can of fish worms, all scrambling to dig in and crawl out of sight, but they all bait for the same hook—the nonpartisan league of Wall Street."[9]

Elected in 1922, Brookhart was referred to as an "economic illiterate" by the man he defeated for the Senate. His middle name was Wildman, a name that his opponents gleefully seized upon when he was running for office. A staunch opponent of finance and Wall Street, Brookhart constantly championed the economic rights of common people. Once, when finding himself seated at a Washington dinner between Otto Kahn of Kuhn Loeb & Co. and E. E. Loomis of J. P. Morgan & Co., he remarked that "I was the only one there dressed like an American citizen." His own campaign manager remarked that "on certain of his economic questions I believe him to be crazier than a whole tree full of hoot owls. I doubt whether he has any constructive ability."[10] True to his nature, he adopted the farm cause naturally and used simple ideas to further not only his own cause but that of farmers as well. Politically, he was a Republican in the Norris sense of the word—actually an independent who preferred the title of Progressive. Collectively, the group was given the unflattering nickname "Sons of the Wild Jackass" by colleague Senator George Moses of New Hampshire.

The influence of both the Ku Klux Klan and the prohibitionists in the Republican Party was loudly decried in the 1928 presidential campaign. Governor Al Smith of New York, the Democratic candidate, charged Moses with making his Roman Catholicism an issue in the election. Noting attacks made by the Ku Klux Klan and some prohibitionists, Smith told a campaign rally in New York that "Senator Moses, the eastern manager of the Hoover campaign, mailed scurrilous literature to be published in the State of Kentucky making an attack upon me because of my religious faith and incidentally upon 20 million American citizens who share that belief with me." But one of his policy problems shared with the opposition centered on farm policies. "How many people in the United States today realize that it costs the farmer from $1 to $1.72 to produce a bushel of wheat which he is compelled to sell today at much less than a dollar?"[11]

The early 1920s were a disaster for farmers and helped create a political climate that would be unfriendly to the futures exchanges in the years ahead. Having recovered from the war, European farm production increased, putting downward pressure on farm prices in the United States. Prices collapsed rapidly as a result. Between May 1920 and June 1921, prices on some commodities fell by 50 percent or more. The recession was one of the most severe in years. Farmers suffered the most. Farm income dropped dramatically and agriculture faced another crisis. Many farm foreclosures followed, and the new federally inspired farm-assistance agencies had their hands full coping with the demands for liquidity by farm credit banks around the country. Bad weather in both the Midwest and the South did not help matters. The agrarians did not blame the futures traders entirely for their plight, because they understood that prices had been higher-than-usual during the war years. However, the matter of credit for farmers was an issue that would arise during the stock market boom after 1925. Agrarians had never lost their suspicion of Wall Street and LaSalle Street after the years of political attacks and antifutures legislation.

Frustrated by the growing farm depression, the agrarians in Congress demanded action. Banding together into what would become known as the Farm Bloc, the House and Senate, prompted by the agrarians, held a conference in early 1921 to deal with the worsening economic situation. At the heart of the matter was the issue of futures regulation and the amount of credit available to farmers. The resulting five pieces of legislation were passed to alleviate the farmers' condition. Three pieces amended existing legislation to extend more—and easier—credit to farmers; the fourth piece placed regulations on packers and the stockyards; and the fifth piece was aimed squarely at the markets.

Congress reacted to the continuing problems and complaints in the markets by passing the Futures Trading Act of 1921. Immediately after the war, Congress again investigated the markets and heard testimony about regulating the markets. One person who testified was Herbert Hoover, the former food administrator and now Secretary of Commerce under Warren Harding. Hoover's views were avidly sought by committee members because of his experience with grains during the war. He was questioned at length by Representative J. N. Tincher of Kansas, a hard-liner who favored strict regulation of the futures exchanges. Hoover, however, displayed a pragmatic view toward regulation. He favored keeping the exchanges open, as they were, and allowing speculators to continue trading. He did, however, favor limiting the number of trades that a pit trader could consummate to reduce the amount of price distortions that excessive trading could cause. Otherwise, he championed the free marketplace.

Tincher and Senator Arthur Capper of Kansas sponsored the futures bill. It was fitting that two Kansans spearheaded the legislation, for it was Kansas that sponsored the first blue-sky law in securities regulation before World War I began. The new bill applied only to grains. However, one contentious section of the bill, based upon Congress' taxing authority, was struck down as unconstitutional within one year. That section originally enabled Congress to levy a tax on grain contracts for delivery and options on them. The power harkened back to the gold tax imposed during the Civil War on gold trading in New York. The Supreme Court held that applying it in the manner that the law prescribed was a misuse of congressional authority, for the tax would be used in a punitive fashion.[12] Congress, however, was not deterred in its effort to regulate the exchanges.

The law was quickly replaced with another, passed by Congress in 1922 and again limiting the freedom of the futures exchanges. This time, the language of the bill was passed so that it emphasized Congress' powers in interstate commerce, not taxation. Called the Grain Futures Act, or Capper–Tincher Act, it sought to shed some light on the esoteric corners of the markets that only insiders understood fully. The law required the exchanges to maintain adequate price records and store those records for three years. It also prohibited the dissemination of false reports regarding crop production that could affect grain prices. Traders had to report large positions in an attempt to shed more light on pit trading. Also, the law limited trading in grain futures to boards of trade that were located at cash grain terminals, where inspection of the delivered products could be made. The Secretary of Agriculture was given responsibility for overseeing the exchanges affected by the law and became their regulator. Upon signing the new bill into law, President Warren Harding stated confidently that "this law does not interfere with hedging transactions on the boards of trade. Neither does it interfere with ordinary speculation . . . however, if there should be evidence of undue manipulation, or attempts to corner the market . . . such conduct will be inquired into and promptly dealt with as required by the law."[13]

Naturally, the futures traders were not fond of the law. Constant violations of delivery methods and deliverable grades were the major factors behind it, along with price manipulation. It clearly was not the product of the Republican administration but of a diverse coalition of agrarians, Progressives, and Democrats who saw it as an opportunity to finally impose some discipline on the markets. Despite its shortcomings, the law was nevertheless the first salvo in the war, initiated unsuccessfully many times in the past, to gain some modicum of control over the futures and (indirectly) stock markets. Its supporters claimed that it was designed only to give the market more structure and provide redress in the event of manipulation.

The CBOT sued the United States, claiming that the law did not apply to it but was rebuffed by a district court. When it appealed to the Supreme Court, it was again rebuffed, but the court took the time to comment on the state of the futures markets. "Corners in grain through trading in futures have not been so frequent as they were before 1900, due . . . to the stricter rules of the Board of Trade as to futures and to the Sherman Anti-Trust Act, . . . , though they do seem to have since occurred infrequently."[14] However, the court would not let the CBOT off the hook on any technicality.

The section of the new law concerning false information that could affect prices was the part that drew the most vocal response. The *New York Times* commented that "at the time of passing the bill, the wheat market was depressed by the [agriculture] department's report of a full yield. Just now, it is raised by reports of a war [between Belgium and Germany]. Is the department to be punished if its reports are true? Who is to be punished if the war reports are false?" Clearly, the language was too vague to be implemented properly, but the paper recognized that the parts of the bill dealing with misinformation were passed because of farmers' wishes—despite the fact that after 70 years of market operation they apparently still did not fully understand the functions of the futures markets. "The farmers are seeking to 'hog-tie' the exchanges because they do not understand them," the paper concluded, using an agricultural metaphor.[15]

Although agricultural prices were flat in the late 1920s, fortunes had been made and lost after the 1920–21 recession that left a bad taste in many mouths. The sort of rumors that the Grain Futures Act attempted to curb had forced the price of wheat to $2.00 per bushel. In 1924, rumors of a worldwide wheat shortage forced prices up, and American farmers benefited because of the bumper wheat crop in the Midwest at the time. The speculating public began to buy wheat, taking the proverbial flyer when the market was already high. Then came the inevitable price declines. One commentator remarked that the "frenzy of speculation, brought on by prospects of a crisis, carried prices 25 to 30 cents too high, there was the usual thunderous outcry: Investigate the exchanges."[16] The public response was not far from the mark.

The unconstitutional part of the original 1921 Futures Trading Act effectively killed the market for options that had existed for years. There was an unusual reaction to the regulations in the Grain Futures Act. Some speculators began to withdraw from the Chicago pits, looking for greener pastures elsewhere. Even the suggestion of government regulation was too much for them. One was the best known wheat traders of the period was Arthur W. Cutten, a classic pit trader and worthy heir to the tradition of Hutchinson, Leiter, and Patten. Cutten was born in Guelph, Ontario, in 1870 and spent his teenage years as a messenger in a Chicago hardware store before finding his way to the pits. He bought a seat on the CBOT and entered the pits in 1897. The most secretive of all traders, Cutten was so laconic about his business that even his entry in *Who's Who* amounted to only two lines. All he was willing to provide was his name, place of birth, and serial number. He almost never commented about his business or trading positions. A slender man of average height, he blended into LaSalle Street perfectly, except that some recognized his prowess in the pits. From 1924 to 1926, he was reputed to have made $15 million in the corn pit. Profits of that magnitude attracted both admiration and unwanted attention.

After the two futures acts were passed, Cutten began to remove himself from the CBOT and became a major speculator in stocks. He became acknowledged as one of the top ten operators in the stock market, joining legends such as Jesse Livermore, Ben Smith, and Michael Meehan. When he began his withdrawal from the CBOT, his fortune was reputed to be around $75 million. It rose considerably during the stock market rise. He amassed huge positions in some of the stocks, such as RCA, Montgomery Ward, and U.S. Steel, that were strongly supported by the activities of investment pools during the period. His personal rivalry with Jesse Livermore demonstrated that the good old days of rank speculation were not over but only entering their latest phase.

In a strange twist, Cutten began abandoning (at least temporarily) the Chicago pits for New York while Livermore was doing exactly the opposite. Their rivalry was reminiscent of that between Leiter and Armour years before. Cutten was attracted to New York because its stock exchange was subject to less regulation than the futures markets. Livermore's attraction to Chicago was more curious. When word leaked out about Cutten's trading profits, many traders in the East began to take notice of the pits, especially since the margins were attractive and the atmosphere was still freewheeling despite the Grain Futures Act.

In 1924, Livermore began trading wheat on the CBOT in Cutten's shadow. Cutten accumulated around 20 million bushels of cash wheat at the time and controlled numerous contracts for future delivery. Livermore began accumulating as well, raising the anger of the pit trader. Cutten's massive long position, reputed to be the largest ever accumulated, began a massive spree of speculation in Chicago. Soon, everyone was buying wheat, including small investors, in a frenzy that would be seen on Wall Street a few years later. Then, in 1925 while Cutten was vacationing in Florida, the market broke and wheat prices began to fall dramatically. Friday, April 3, 1925, became Black Friday in Chicago. Wheat prices fell 16 points within a few hours in intraday trading. Rumor abounded that Livermore staged a bear raid and sold short around 5 million bushels. Cutten remained steadfast, however, and continued to buy in the wake of falling prices. His perseverance paid off shortly thereafter when he cashed out his positions for millions in profit. The entire affair was surrounded in mystery, however, and neither man would divulge exactly how the trading had affected him.

One of the effects of Chicago's Black Friday took years to be implemented. After the precipitous intraday price movements, the CBOT approved daily price limits in the pits. Each commodity was given a range in which it could trade on a daily basis. If prices slipped outside the range, trading would be shut down except for those individuals who wished to trade within the range. The limits were designed to give the market some order and allow trades to be cleared. Panic could be avoided, at least momentarily, by assurances that prices were within the range for the rest of the trading day. Even though limits were instituted to protect pit traders, it still took another 10 years for these limits to be fully implemented in October 1935.

Cutten dabbled in stocks as early as 1923, but his successes, mostly by short selling, were not large by Wall Street standards. In 1928, Livermore again shorted many stocks that Cutten was reported to be holding, but the damage was minimal. When the 1929 stock market crash occurred, Cutten's losses were a staggering $50 million on paper, although his accounts were still worth an equally staggering $100 million. Only after the crash, when action on Wall Street diminished sharply, did he return to the pits. His successes—and travails—continued well into the 1930s. Livermore committed suicide in 1940, leaving only about $10,000 in his will.

At one time, Cutten bought all of the stock of Armour many years after Armour's death. He also reportedly made a profit of $18 million in Montgomery Ward alone. The money used for the stock purchases originated in the pits. In his swan song at the CBOT, it was he who suggested that the price of wheat would rise from $1.70 to over $2.00 per bushel in late 1924, causing the market to rise strongly in the wake of Calvin Coolidge's election. His excuse for the move and the unusual public remark was that the public had no business playing in the pits, for the marketplace was full of too many pitfalls. He admitted, "If I had a son I would not let him touch it with a ten foot pole. People call themselves brokers but they are only part of that—the broke part."[17]

In 1922, Cutten suffered an indignity similar to the robbery Leiter experienced at his Washington, D.C., home. Many legendary pit traders were, in fact, victims of robbery. Hutchinson, for instance, once recalled being robbed by several thugs on the streets of Chicago who, until he told them who he was, were set to do him harm. While Hutchinson's story was probably embellished, the Cutten incident became the stuff of even more pit legend in the 1920s and 1930s.

While at home, Cutten and his wife, along with his brother and several servants, were robbed. The thieves made off with $20,000 worth of jewelry, some cash, and 25 cases of whisky from Cutten's cellar. After tying up his wife, brother, and servants, the thieves locked Cutten in a basement vault, where he almost suffocated. Locking him in the vault enraged the trader, and he vowed to find the robbers and bring them to justice. "That was an unnecessary, futile, and fiendish piece of cruelty," he fumed, "and I vowed then that I would spend every dollar at my command if necessary to put them where they belong—behind bars." With the use of private investigators, Cutten had each of the thieves hunted down and prosecuted for their crime, although it took over eight years to accomplish. The incident showed the dogged determination that made Cutten a pit legend. However, his most important battle was to be fought in a more familiar arena.

One topic that did evoke a public response from Cutten was the matter of income tax—both ordinary tax and the special tax enacted on privilege trading. In 1924, he was reputed to be the largest taxpayer in Chicago, paying the Internal Revenue Service almost $550,000. Responding angrily to the tax, he remarked, "It's nobody's business how much I make during the year, nor how I make it." The tax on privilege trading especially was galling. "The law is a brazen violation of personal rights and should be repealed," he stated unequivocally.[18] Within two years, he would be pleased.

In 1926, a case reached the Supreme Court that freed the options market from the tax cloud. A Missouri trader sued the Internal Revenue Service for the 20-cents-per-bushel tax that he had paid on options under the 1921 Futures Trading Act, claiming that the tax was unconstitutional. When the case eventually reached the Supreme Court, it became clear that the highly charged political nature of the attempts to curb the markets was becoming passé. Justice James McReynolds, writing the majority opinion of the court, upheld his claim, stating that the "imposition is a penalty and in no proper sense a tax."[19] Congress had overstepped its authority, and the law was declared unconstitutional. Although the judgment came long after the fact, and the Grain Futures Act had already been established, the markets took it as a sign that options trading among pit traders was free to proceed.

The futures markets reacted predictably. Within two days of the decision, the CBOT actively was trading puts and calls again, reacting quickly to establish a uniform set of commissions for options—with regular trading hours. When the court's ruling made it clear that Congress' power to tax did not include penalizing traders in options or futures, the door was finally open after decades of attempts by agrarians and Progressives to defeat privileges and the markets quickly developed a new generation of derivatives to aid pit traders and other large wholesale traders. As in so many other cases that would arise in the twentieth century, the markets proved themselves much more flexible and adaptable than regulators in reacting to new developments. Restricting old practices or products would simply effect new practices or products that Congress and the agencies would then have to learn at the risk of falling even further behind.

## MERC RISING

After the recession ended in 1921, agricultural prices began to fall, leaving farmers angry and frustrated. The war years had been good to them, and although prices had been frozen in some foodstuffs, they were now double what they were in 1914. The price declines were sharp, and antifutures cries again were heard from the agrarian states. In summer 1923, pressure was building on Harding to call a special session of Congress to deal with the wheat situation. The pressure was brought by

Brookhart and Senator Edwin Ladd of North Dakota. Being a free-market advocate, Harding resisted. Ladd especially was critical of the wheat speculators, whom he accused of creating the price slide. "The decline is clearly attributable to the wheat speculators," he stated. "Their object is transparent. For thirty years they successfully fought legislation that would curb their activities." In his opinion, the new futures law passed the year before did not do enough to restrain them, and selling short was their response to the new regulations. "Their system has worked very cleverly during the last three months in driving down the prices of wheat by means of heavy short selling . . . ," he stated, reviving the old agrarian bugaboo about the motives of pit traders.[20] Ladd would die within a year of making that statement, but Brookhart would revive the issue several times during the 1920s and 1930s. Every time prices declined, the agrarian radicals blamed short sellers. As far as they were concerned, market mechanics and human nature were to blame for their problems. Give speculators a speculative tool and they will destroy the economic well-being of others, all in the name of personal profit. The criticism had not changed since the 1870s, but one fact did emerge from the early 1920s. The depression that would plague the country throughout the 1930s had already begun in agriculture, and no relief was in sight.

Advances in technology and science made agriculture more efficient and productive in the 1920s. Profitability, though, was another matter. Farm incomes flattened out after 1920 and remained low for the remainder of the decade. At the time, no one saw this as a deep structural problem, and most policy makers assumed that agriculture would rebound in due course. The futures exchanges also expanded, with new markets springing up to compete with the older ones that had become established during the previous century. The impact of Prohibition added an unknown dimension to commodities prices. Ever since the Volstead Act made the manufacture of alcoholic beverages illegal, bootlegging was rampant. Much of the bootleg liquor was made from corn or from stronger industrial alcohol made from wood. Demand—at least legal demand—for many traditional commodities began to display erratic patterns, and their prices gyrated accordingly. As Al Smith noted in the 1928 presidential campaign, grain prices were higher in Winnipeg, Manitoba than they were in the United States, suggesting that manufacture had shifted north of the border and that the final product was being smuggled south of the border. Alcohol consumption was strong in the cities. Chicago and New York speakeasies thrived while Prohibition made a more serious impact in rural areas. Al Capone easily overtook Arthur Cutten as Chicago's most successful businessman, with an estimated annual income between $70 and $100 million.

In the first decade of the twentieth century, another Chicago futures exchange surfaced after two decades of relative obscurity. The Chicago Produce Exchange had grown slowly since its establishment in 1874. Like many futures exchanges, the exchange owed its growth to developments in technology. The refrigerated railway car made transportation of perishable commodities possible for the first time on a large scale. Previously, butter and eggs were produced locally on small farms and traveled only as far as nonrefrigerated transportation could carry them in as short a period of time as possible. When refrigerated cars became widely used, it was possible to market these perishables on a regional if not national basis. Hence the small, sleepy Chicago Produce Exchange was poised for a new era of growth.

The Produce Exchange never traded grains, as did the CBOT. Consequently, it remained a sleepy backwater before refrigeration became common. Lack of interest in trading produce led it to suspend trading in 1878, and the exchange remained dormant until 1882. It then began trading egg contracts. For the next decade, it acted informally, polling members concerning daily prices but never actually allowing the market-place to post trading prices derived from floor traders' dealings. Finally, in 1894, all of Chicago's butter and egg dealers joined in the Produce Exchange's activities, and prices became more uniform and reflective of market conditions. A year later, dealers organized the Produce Exchange Butter & Egg Board within the Produce Exchange. Trading was expanding quickly, and speculators were attracted to the contracts. Following the CBOT's earlier lead, the Produce Exchange then closed its floor to all but recognized traders to keep the ubiquitous bucket shop operators away from the premises.

Fortunately for the Produce Exchange, many of the CBOT's problems never spilled over onto its own floors. The idea of cornering the market was impractical because butter and eggs were too perishable to corner, having a shorter life-span than grains despite the use of refrigeration. Unfortunately, there was dissent among the butter traders on the exchange that led to a mutiny. The butter traders had long been feuding with the makers of oleomargarine about which product should take precedence on the exchange. Oleomargarine, a butter substitute, was considered a valid, deliverable grade of butter by its producers. The controversy caused great dissension within the industry, and when no solution could be found, the original butter and egg traders abandoned the Produce Exchange and founded the Chicago Butter & Egg Board in 1898. There were only a handful of members, but some of the best known firms in the produce and meat-packing businesses, including Swift and Armour, were members, which helped ensure the new exchange's success.[21] The board ceased operations in 1919 and became the Chicago Mercantile Exchange (CME) in a clear attempt to be as successful as the CBOT.

Competition between exchanges in different parts of the country began to heat up considerably in the 1920s because of the buoyant economy. In 1926, the New York Produce Exchange announced that it was opening a grain futures market to compete with the Midwest exchanges. Delivery of grain would take place in Buffalo, New York far from the delivery locations mandated by the older grain exchanges. By the late 1920s, the CBOT and the CME were trading commodities very similar to those traded in New York. The CBOT, taking a significant step toward calming fears about the integrity of its marketplace, created in 1926 the Board of Trade Clearing Corp. The separate company was organized to guarantee that all trades requiring delivery would be honored, a development that would become a requisite for all future markets. By creating a separate clearinghouse for trades, the exchange ensured that deliveries would be independent of the traders who created prices in the first place. Doing so represented a significant shift in risk for futures traders and was one of the exchange's major institutional achievements. The clearinghouse was funded by traders' subscriptions but remained otherwise independent. The fox was not completely out of the henhouse, but at least he was no longer selling admission tickets.

## DEPRIVED INDIFFERENCE?

Tensions began to develop between agrarians and the rest of the country during the 1920s as a result of farm incomes. Although the consumer boom began after 1922, farmers were not participating in it. Instead, they were contending with the normal problems of drought, plagues of insects, and vacillating prices. The United States was urbanizing rapidly, but life on the farm was much as it had been for decades. Two Americas were developing; the wealthy and the growing middle class together were much better off financially than the working class and the farmers. Wealthy and middle-class Americans were buying radios and automobiles in record numbers, while working-class Americans struggled to make ends meet and farmers were desperately clinging to their farms and their way of life. The discontent on the farm resulted in the election of demagogic politicians such as Smith Brookhart during the 1920s. Even less Populist-minded politicians in the heartland began to sound more and more like Populists as the decade progressed.

After the price fluctuations of the early 1920s, the commodities markets began a long period of weakness. From 1925 to 1929, the price of most agricultural commodities rose only slightly. The price of wheat actually declined, whereas the price of other agricultural commodities barely kept pace with inflation. The agrarians, who were very vocal in Congress and in the press when describing their plight, had a simple answer for the problem. As far as they were concerned, the stock market boom of the 1920s was siphoning money away from the agricultural sector and diverting it to New York instead. Moreover, the occasional bear raid on wheat, when prices temporarily surged, did not help.

At the same time, the stock market boom was diverting attention to Wall Street. While farmers were faced with stagnant prices, the prices of stocks began an inexorable climb. Certainly, it was not the first time that the stock market had rallied during a period of general farm malaise. Many stock purchases were being made on margin, and brokers and banks were creating loanable funds, or call money, for speculators as quickly as possible. In addition, many nonfinancial corporations were putting their cash to work in the market as well after realizing that broker loans paid twice as much interest as money market rates. Finding call money was not difficult for brokers, whose customers were clamoring for credit with which to buy stocks. However, a farmer needing a loan for new land or equipment was in dire straits because of no available cash. Resentment against bankers and Easterners began to build in the Midwest once again, on a scale not seen since the nineteenth century.

The agrarians of the 1920s were a loosely knit group, but they all had the same aim—protection of farmers from bankers and speculators. They were a disparate group considered somewhat loony by the Republican establishment. In good economic times, their message would have been virtually ignored, even though they represented a wide constituency with solid political roots who could not be ignored. Calling for the abolition of the futures exchanges sounded distinctly dated. The calls were not heeded in the nineteenth century, and there was no possibility of accomplishing such a radical task in the twentieth. That, however, did not deter the agrarians from trying. The United States rapidly was becoming urbanized, and the farmers' collective voice was becoming more and more distant. As a result, when their voice was occasionally heard, it was very shrill.

Two antifutures bills were debated in the Senate. Both were proposed by Senator Thaddeus Caraway of Arkansas, a longtime opponent of futures trading. One was a prohibitive tax on cotton futures; the other, an outright ban on futures trading of any sort. Both bills were defeated, reflecting the general public disinterest in futures markets, especially when the stock market was rising. Even the more radical members of Congress who normally sided with antifutures legislation were themselves busy with stock market matters. Brookhart of Iowa, a rabid defender of his own state's interests, was more concerned with the allocation of credit in the country than he was with futures legislation. He took his seat after the second futures bill became law, so the primary problem as he saw it, was Wall Street's influence on farmers. At one point, he actually called for the Federal Reserve to be taken over by farmers rather than continue to be controlled by bankers. The call money market in particular worried him, as it did many others who expressed interest in the financial markets. Credit to farmers fell dramatically after 1925, and the agrarians blamed Wall Street for diverting funds that otherwise could have found their way into the Farm Credit System. Brookhart proposed that the Federal Reserve increase its reserve requirement on member banks so that more reserves would be held in the regional Fed bank. He reasoned that the tighter requirement would allow fewer funds to find their way into the call money market. If the stock market bubble were to burst, the local Midwestern banks would be protected from any failures by brokers, which were bound to come. When the idea failed to muster interest, Brookhart then retreated to the time-proven method of stopping what he considered to be excessive speculation. He suggested that state banks that failed to adhere to his proposed Fed regulations be denied use of the public mail service. He declared that "unless something of this kind is done we are now headed for the greatest panic in the history of the world."[22]

Exaggerations of that sort made him look somewhat pre-scient after the 1929 stock market crash, when he became a member of the Senate committee investigating the causes of the crash. Although none of his suggestions proved successful, they clearly indicated that the traditional chasm between Wall Street and the rest of the country was as wide as ever. Part of the problem could be attributed to the fact that despite the con-tinuing public outcry against the exchanges, attitudes were beginning to soften somewhat. In 1927, when the Illinois Leg-islature began an investigation of the CBOT that revealed more shenanigans by pit traders, the public support for the CBOT was moderate, because some farmers recognized that the occasional price spikes in grain caused by the pit traders could benefit them if the timing happened to be right. While the exchange did not appeal to everyone, it was not roundly condemned by farmers as the Farm Bloc in Congress would like to have believed.

The same hostility was evident on the floor of the Senate during a debate on the role of the Fed in the stock market boom that occurred during the winter of 1929. The conservative J. Thomas Heflin of Alabama bellowed that Wall Street was the "most notorious gambling center in the universe. . . . Whereas the Louisiana lottery slew its hundreds, the New York State gambling exchanges slay their hundreds of thousands."[23] To the relief of the stock and futures exchanges, these remarks fell mostly on deaf ears. The agrarian radicals did not appear to have the necessary following to translate these ideas into meaningful legislation. Less than 10 percent of the population was engaged in farming, and three-quarters of that 10 percent were members of family-run farms. The Sons of the Wild Jackass—Heflin, Brookhart, Norris, Norbeck, and Senator William E. Borah of Idaho, as well as a few other kindred souls in the Senate—represented states with small populations whose main business was agriculture. They were out of the mainstream and, as a group, did not have a direct influence on the course of public policy. However, their unflinching defense of their constituencies from what they perceived as the Wall Street and LaSalle Street gangs did, through their consistent pressure, fuel antifutures legislation during the 1920s.

Farmers had another ally in the 1920s, one who would prove to be a more durable, respected friend than the agrarian Populists. This ally was Henry A. Wallace, born in Iowa in 1888 and graduated from Iowa State University in 1910. Upon graduation, he joined the staff of *Wallace's Farmer*, the family magazine run by his father Henry C. Wallace, who served as Secretary of Agriculture under Harding and Coolidge. The magazine was widely read in the Midwest, and the younger Wallace soon became a respected journalist and agricultural economist. He accurately predicted the price drops caused by the recession of 1920 to 1921 and succeeded his father as editor of the magazine in 1924. In 1928, he switched to the

Democratic Party out of disgust with the Republicans' infighting. He became a staunch ally of farmers after observing their plight firsthand in the 1920s.

One trend that upset Wallace the most was the farm-to-city migration during the farm crisis of the 1920s. "The great industrial system is running away with us," he wrote. "Soon we shall have four or five people living in the city to every one person living on the land. It is time for the people of the United States to stop and ask themselves just how far they want to travel along this path."[24] Wallace took up the gauntlet of inspiring farmers to stay on the land and preserve their heritage. When Franklin D. Roosevelt was elected president, he named him to be Secretary of Agriculture in 1933, a position he held until becoming Vice President in 1940.

Farm prices remained stalled, and although a few price spikes did benefit pit traders, the second half of the 1920s did not produce a stock market–like bubble. But this was not attributable to a lack of credit or a squeeze engineered from Wall Street. Small investors flocked to LaSalle Street, lured by tales of Cutten's legendary corners, and a sizable amount of retail investors' money was put into the pits, especially in the late 1920s. The farm problem clearly was overproduction. Most grains were still being produced at wartime levels 10 years after their peak. Despite the fact that prices were relatively low, production continued at a steadily increasing pace. A crash was coming in the futures markets as well as on Wall Street. The circumstances were similar, but prices remained lower in the futures markets before the rout that helped soften the blow for traders, for prices did not fall from bubble-like levels.

## PRELUDE TO DISASTER

Although agricultural prices were flat, production was strong in the 1920s, contributing to the farm problem. The exchanges all recorded increased trading volume and thus prospered, continuing to be the pride of their home cities and the Midwest rivals to the stock market. The CBOT in particular was particularly affluent and enjoyed the boom. It demolished its old headquarters built in 1885 and moved into new quarters in 1928. The old building was often described as somber, although Frank Lloyd Wright called it a "hard-faced monstrosity." The new building evoked civic pride in Chicago, and like its predecessor, it recalled war stories of days past. "Knowing nothing of trading, demand and supply, futures and hedging, [the public looks] at the stone mass that blocks LaSalle Street and [lets its imagination] run back to the days of horse-drawn cabs, of the World's Fair, of P. D. Armour and B. P. Hutchinson," one commentator wrote as the building was under construction. Fortunately for the CBOT, the building was completed by the time of the stock market crash a year later.

Late in the 1920s, the rates for call money in New York were still diverting funds that would otherwise have found their way to agriculture. The rates for margin were about 6 percent in the wholesale market and substantially higher when passed to speculators by the lenders. Of the $6.5 billion on loan in the market, about one-third was supplied by banks both in and outside of New York. The balance was supplied by corporate lenders who fueled the market boom by making easy credit available. Many companies took to speculating by putting their excess cash out for loan. Brookhart's farm credit fears were being realized, although the banks were not the main culprits. The point was still abundantly clear. Farmers could neither get a good price for their crops nor obtain credit. The stock market provided too much competition.

Part of the farmers' problems could be attributed to supply. During the year preceding the crash, the supply of wheat and other commodities increased dramatically. The Agricultural Marketing Act, created by Congress in 1929, established the

Federal Farm Board. Among its duties was to reduce speculation in commodities and control surpluses. Alexander Legge,
the chairman of International Harvester, was named chairman
of the Farm Board. The board began buying wheat to help stabilize prices. Surpluses were especially harmful to prices,
because short sellers recognized that prices would only drop in
the near future and so began selling, thereby forcing prices
down. The board, mindful of its mandate to protect farm
prices and supplies, was busy buying wheat to keep prices
steady. The inventory increased dramatically as a result. In a
dreadful case of bad timing, the amount of wheat held on
farms and in storage silos doubled from 1928 to 1929 while the
price increased by about 3 percent. Production actually
decreased during that time in what appeared to be a successful
marketing reaction to the problem of market overhang. The
same was true of other grains, but to a smaller extent.[25] The
board accumulated over 200 million bushels of wheat—about
one-third of a year's production—when demand began to fall.
When the stock market collapsed in October 1929, the markets
were long on wheat and other foodstuffs. Prices were poised for
a drop that recalled the 1920–21 recession.

Adding to the oversupply problem, several Canadian wheat
pools, designed to protect the supply and price of wheat, were
operating in the prairie provinces. These were not pools in the
manipulators' sense but rather carefully designed syndicate
groups made up of producers and marketers intent on stabilizing the price rather than leaving it solely to the futures
exchanges. Winnipeg had one of the larger grain exchanges at
the time, with significantly less regulation than the CBOT.
When the price began to drop, there was excess supply on both
sides of the border, which only added to the problem. Canadi-
ans did not trust the Winnipeg traders. When regulation was
threatened in the United States, either by the individual states
or by the federal government, many pit traders gave up their

seats in Chicago and elsewhere to take up membership on the Winnipeg exchange. Operating pools in Canada's prairie provinces were seen purely as a defensive measure by farmers and grain elevator operators who wanted to stabilize prices in the wake of tumultuous trading by pit traders.

Just before the stock market crash in October 1929, the Sons of the Wild Jackass and Otto Kahn of Kuhn Loeb & Co. again crossed paths. George Moses of New Hampshire appointed Kahn, an active Republican, to be treasurer of an important party committee. But the Farm Bloc vociferously objected to Kahn's appointment. It also objected to many of Herbert Hoover's policies and the White House power clique that controlled access to the president. In its opinion, Kahn, was just another moneyed financier with inside ties to the White House administration. As a result, Kahn declined the post. He wrote to Moses, stating that while he was "a Wall Street man, I was known to be, as indeed, I am, a liberal in politics."[26] However, because of staunch opposition from the Progressive Republicans, ostensibly because of his ties, he declined the post. A week later, Moses, addressing an audience in New Hampshire, labeled the group the "Sons of the Wild Jackass" for the first time, a term that became a household term for much of the 1930s. Rejecting ties with Wall Street financiers at the time was expedient, although the Republican Party missed Kahn's expertise at a crucial time in its history as a result.

On a lighter note, at the annual Gridiron Club roast in Washington, a skit was presented in which impersonators of the Progressive Republicans who had been opposing Hoover since 1929 appeared onstage, to the strains of Hindu music, as the Three Mahatma Gandhis—George Norris, Hiram Johnson, and Smith Brookhart. They announced to the person impersonating Senator Simeon Fess, Chairman of the Republican Party, that they had bolted from the GOP and its extreme policies, adding, "Hence we intend to overthrow you and Mr. Hoover."[27] The humor could not disguise the fact that the Farm Bloc persisted in its criticisms of mainstream Republicans, of Wall Street, and of futures markets. The agricultural recession of 1920 to 1921 proved to be a prelude of what the country would endure after October 1929. The causes were much the same—overproduction and a growing conflict about who was responsible for sorting out the mess. Unfortunately, the simple ideas of the Farm Bloc and the distance that it maintained from the mainstream kept its ideas at bay, especially since America was becoming more internationalized and urbanized. When economic conditions began to deteriorate, however, these once-outlandish ideas started to assume more of an authentic ring.

A bold move in 1929 was poised to put the CBOT in the vanguard of the financial markets. The CBOT announced that it was to commence trading in Chicago Stock Exchange (CSE)–listed stocks in early September. The move would easily make the CBOT, with its curious mix of instruments, potentially one of the largest financial markets in the country. Initially, it intended to trade in only 10 CSE stocks, planning to add more at a later date. However, the CSE demurred, and the two exchanges began trading threats of legal action over jurisdiction. The CSE thought that it should have the same right, in reverse. Would the CBOT allow the stock exchange to trade wheat if it so desired? After arguing about reciprocity and the rights of those traders who already held seats on both exchanges, the CBOT issued a statement for which it would later be sorry. In granting the same right to nonmembers, it stated strongly that "the officers of the Chicago Board of Trade, in insisting upon their right to engage in any lawful business without criticism or hindrance from *any one*, concede freely the same privileges to other organizations and individuals."[28] Refusing to recognize the agriculture department as its regulator would amount to a costly mistake in the 1930s.

The plan began slowly, extending into the mid-1930s. The opportunities for speculation in CSE-listed stocks on a loosely regulated commodities exchange were too good for some legendary NYSE traders, who began buying up relatively cheap CBOT seats. Michael Meehan and Jesse Livermore both turned up in Chicago to try their hand at trading after the experiment began, although both would be gone by the mid-1930s—either expelled or bankrupted by the aftermath of the stock market crash. The CBOT was not alone in spotting the opportunity. Other commodity futures exchanges also began trading common stocks. The Produce Exchange in New York traded locally listed stocks. On the day after the October 23, 1929 stock market crash, the exchange announced that it had successfully traded almost 14 million shares during that year alone.[29] That figure represented about two weeks of NYSE volume. While the amount of trading formed a very small portion of the NYSE and the curb market's total volume for the year, it did illustrate how trading could be conducted in an almost regulation-free environment, especially since the exchanges themselves were monitored on all but a very superficial basis. Dual trading was the allure for New York traders seeking seats on the CBOT, perhaps more so than doing the occasional commodity futures deal.

The lesson would not be lost on lawmakers who watched the actions of stock and commodities traders from the sidelines. The stock market, and the NYSE in particular, was so unregulated that it was attracting pit traders who sought more unregulated action. Cutten and others, however, were always quick to spot opportunities. In the months preceding October 1929, grain prices again dipped low. At slightly above $1.00 per bushel, wheat found some support as Arthur Cutten and other speculators were lured back to the pits from Wall Street and began buying. Their actions forced up the price to slightly over $1.30 per bushel, and farmers again could smile temporarily as they fetched a decent price for their crops—probably for the last time in what would prove to be a decade of deflated prices.

The potential for an expanded CBOT that traded stocks brought some prodigal sons home. In January 1929, a seat on the exchange sold for $45,000; by October, $58,000. Cutten bought another seat, anticipating the move toward stock trading. Ironically, the CBOT moved toward stock trading at the top of the market, acting like many of the small retail investors who had lost money over the years and joined the buying spree only when it was too late. The CBOT saved itself a good deal of grief by never seriously participating in the stock market bubble, proving once again that the wheel of fortune did not stop on its number.

Despite being flat for most of the 1920s, commodities prices suffered badly after the stock market crash occurred on October 23, 1929. The price of wheat dropped almost 12 cents per bushel—from $1.24 to $1.12—on October 25 before recovering slightly to finish the day around $1.20. Price drops of 4 to 5 cents were rare on the exchange. The *New York Times* reported, "There never has been such a wheat market as that of today outside of wartime. Chaos prevailed among the brokers in the pit and excitement ran high in LaSalle Street brokerage offices as grain quotations dropped 11 cents a bushel in a short period."[30] The intraday price movements were worse than prices at the close of the day, but the damage was substantial. When the smoked cleared temporarily, it was discovered that over 145 million bushels had traded that day. In comparison, the entire market had a hangover of about 250 million bushels that were not in firm hands. This large unsold surplus had already been keeping prices low when the crash occurred.

At first, the commodities crash was not as pronounced as the stock market crash, but it would match the latter in intensity over the next several years. Prices actually rallied slightly, and by January 1930, the price of wheat rose to $1.38 per bushel before beginning a long, sharp descent. This situation caused one of the great ironies in American history. Foodstuffs were cheap and plentiful, yet shantytowns, or "Hoovervilles," began to spring up around the country, and breadlines of the homeless and the unemployed formed in the cities. Still, the markets proceeded with their old ways as if oblivious to what was occurring on the streets outside their buildings. Stock and commodities traders were selling short, depressing prices even further and making a buck but certainly not many friends in the process. Soon, the agrarian Progressives and others would pursue the markets again, and the ensuing changes would radically alter all of the financial markets.

## NOTES

1. John Hill, Jr., *Gold Bricks of Speculation* (Chicago: Lincoln Book Concern, 1904), p. 69.
2. Ibid. The magnitude of the problem was understated. If bucket shop operators could take $10 million of customers' funds and put it into the markets at current margin rates, they would have between $100 and $500 million worth of total purchasing power with which to take opposite positions. The sheer magnitude of the money would significantly force prices down if they decided to sell short en masse.
3. *Board of Trade of City of Chicago v. Christie Grain & Stock Co.*, 198 US 236 (1905).
4. Lurie, *The Chicago Board of Trade*, p. 158.
5. *Wall Street Daily News*, December 23, 1893.
6. Hill, *Goldbricks*, pp. 493–497.
7. *Dearborn Independent*, July 1921.
8. Ibid.
9. Ray Tucker and Frederick R. Barkley, *Sons of the Wild Jackass* (Seattle: University of Washington Press, 1932, reprint 1970), p. 346.
10. Ibid., pp. 350–352.
11. *Campaign Addresses of Governor Alfred E. Smith* (Washington, DC: Democratic National Committee, 1929), pp. 301, 392.

12. *Hill v. Wallace*, 259 US 44 (1922).
13. *New York Times*, September 28, 1922.
14. *Board of Trade of City of Chicago v. Olsen*, 262 US 1 (1923).
15. *New York Times*, September 21, 1922.
16. Edward J. Dies, *The Wheat Pit* (Chicago: Argyle Press, 1925), p. 62.
17. *New York Times*, December 16, 1928.
18. Ibid.
19. *Trusler v. Crooks*, 269 US 475 (1926).
20. *New York Times*, July 22, 1923.
21. Bob Tamarkin, *The MERC: The Emergence of a Global Financial Powerhouse* (New York: HarperBusiness, 1993), p. 28.
22. Joseph Stagg Lawrence, *Wall Street and Washington* (Princeton, NJ: Princeton University Press, 1929), p. 310.
23. Cedric B. Cowing, *Populists, Plungers, and Progressives: A Social History of Stock and Commodity Speculation 1890–1936* (Princeton, NJ: Princeton University Press, 1965), p. 150.
24. *Wallace's Farmer*, March 6, 1925.
25. U.S. Department of Commerce, *Historical Statistics of the United States: Colonial Times to 1957*, pp. 296–298.
26. *New York Times*, October 30, 1929. Kahn's biographer concurred that the opposition to the appointment seemed to have stemmed from a patronage dispute, "the latest and bitterest row between President Hoover's White House coterie of political advisers and Republican Senators." See Mary Jane Matz, *The Many Lives of Otto Kahn* (New York: Macmillan, 1963), p. 217.
27. Harold Brayman, *The President Speaks Off-the-Record: Historic Evenings with America's Leaders, the Press, and Other Men of Power at Washington's Exclusive Gridiron Club* (Princeton, NJ: Dow Jones Books, 1976), p. 218.
28. Italics added. *New York Times*, September 13, 1929.
29. Based on an ad placed by the New York Produce Exchange in the *Brooklyn Daily Eagle*, October 24, 1929.
30. *New York Times*, October 25, 1929.

# CHAPTER 3

# THE GREAT BEAR HUNT

I N THE AFTERMATH OF THE 1929 STOCK MARKET crash, attitudes about the nature of American capitalism and free markets began to be questioned. For years after the Civil War, economic downturns had been accepted as part of the freewheeling nature of the economy because of a permissive business environment and the lack of a centralized banking system. Social Darwinism was the accepted philosophy in the American markets, and survivors of the predatory process were viewed as heroes. However, the severity and depth of the Great Depression proved a sobering blow to futures traders, who were still called businessmen and capitalists by even the most reputable newspapers. If this was capitalism and its rewards, then something needed to be corrected. Lawmakers were determined to respond.

Benjamin Hutchinson once remarked, somewhat ingenuously, that it was impossible to corner the wheat market because there was so much of the grain being farmed that any attempt would be lost in a "sea of wheat." The best that a pit trader could do was follow the tide. Ironically, that remark became a reasonable explanation of the problems that beset

the markets in the 1920s and 1930s. Farm production and efficiency had increased dramatically since the nineteenth century,
and wheat, as with most grains, was plentiful. However, when
demand dropped, there was little farmers could do to respond;
unlike manufacturers, they could not simply slow down the
wheat harvest. To prevent prices from collapsing, agriculture
needed a sophisticated marketing system that would release its
products to the market when demand rose and withhold it
when demand fell. Unfortunately, futures markets did not fulfill that function, and the government proved somewhat inept
as well.

The 1920s were a paradoxical period for futures markets.
After 1925, farm incomes dropped and commodities prices
remained depressed. The occasional price spikes were witnessed when large-scale traders such as Arthur Cutten decided
to move into the markets. The 1930s did not present even a
glimmer of hope for farmers. The depth of the commodity
price depression was similar to that of the stock market rout,
and little relief was on the horizon. Futures traders, however, as
with many of their stock market counterparts, found themselves behaving much as they did in the past. Government
interference in the markets presented them with opportunities
not unlike those of the past. When called upon to defend themselves, though, the traders sounded anachronistic. Their re-
sponses were a product of the past, more appropriate for a time
when future expectations were more optimistic than they were
in the early 1930s.

On the industrial side of the economy, the country had
excess capacity and little demand for products. After the stock
market crash, too little money was chasing too many goods,
most of which were suffering severe price declines. Within two
years following the crash, the prices of commodities would
become so cheap that it was uneconomical for farmers to harvest their crops, forcing them to leave them in the ground to

rot. During the early years of the Depression, farm income was less than half that of the rest of the country, and many farmers simply packed up and moved away from their homes after losing them through foreclosure or bankruptcy. The vivid descriptions of the Okies, as depicted in John Steinbeck's *The Grapes of Wrath*, who would leave behind their farms and move West to look for work, became one of the most haunting images of the Depression. Could the futures markets be blamed for their plight?

Clearly, the agrarian radicals thought they could. The old complaints about the role of speculators during periods of price declines again came to the fore with more stridency than at any other time during the twentieth century. Futures prices in the pits varied widely from the spot prices in the physical markets. In 1931, farmers' production costs were above the spot prices for many grains, and as a result, crops were left to spoil in the fields. The Farm Board, established for stabilizing prices, did not seem to know its own mind, and consequently a great deal of wild speculation occurred in the pits. The international economic situation did not help. Britain had abandoned the gold standard in September 1931, after which the international financial system was thrown into a state of confusion. The United States did not follow suit immediately, and the price of American goods—especially commodities for export— became too expensive for many foreign buyers. Temporary American ambivalence toward gold did not help the American farmer, although the pit traders naturally fed off the uncertainty.

The role of the Farm Bloc Progressives became more entrenched as the financial crisis worsened in the early 1930s. What previously had sounded like agrarian demagoguery suddenly began to take on some relevance as unemployment grew rapidly and farm prices collapsed. Was the United States the victim of an internal conspiracy, by Wall Street and the wealthy, designed to make more money for bankers and corporate executives at the expense of the working class and the farmers? Naturally, some of the Sons of the Wild Jackass thought so, and their conspiracy theories began to emerge from the shadows and assume a fresh relevance. Even in their wildest dreams, however, they could never have concocted the story that the Russians and the pit traders scripted for themselves at the beginning of the Depression.

## STALIN GOES SHORT

Revelations about market activities in September 1930 illustrate how confusing the economic situation was in the wake of the stock market and futures market crashes of October 1929. Prices fell sharply on most agricultural commodities, while trading activities increased, suggesting a great deal of short selling. If the exchanges themselves did not prohibit the practice of short selling, there was little that lawmakers could do. Attempting to invoke the Grain Futures Act proved difficult, for its language was preventative, not penal. Catching a trader in excessive trading had to be done at the time of the actual trading—a difficult if not impossible task given that the CBOT and other major exchanges were opaque at best. This did not, however, stop the debate. Long-standing discussions about the value of the futures markets were again raised, and new discussions arose about the importance of hedging and the evils of speculation. The real question that emerged from the events was simple. Were these issues genuine or was the political leadership in Washington looking for a scapegoat for the deteriorating economic situation?

The pits had been relatively quiet during World War I and the early 1920s. However, price movements after 1924 and internal developments at the CBOT that encouraged stock trading attracted a new breed of speculator in the mold of

Hutchinson and Leiter. Trading actually increased at a time when outsiders thought the pits would have been quiet. Deflated prices, caused by international gold problems, suggested that trading would be minimal. Pit traders, though, realized that declining prices were conducive for short selling. Or were they caused by massive bear raids? Cause and effect became volatile issues in the markets.

Less than a year after the stock market crash, short selling became the hot topic in Washington and on both Wall Street and LaSalle Street. Was the decline in the stock market caused by short sellers, forcing down the price of stocks that had little good news to support them? And were pit traders selling contracts short, forcing down the already depressed price of most agricultural commodities? The question was not new but the circumstances were certainly unique. If traders were indeed selling contracts short, did their greed stand in the way of their patriotism? Should the markets perform a stabilizing function rather than take advantage of deteriorating conditions? These were difficult questions with no easy answers, but there was no shortage of opinion in Washington.

The short selling controversy was opened in September 1930 by Secretary of Agriculture Arthur M. Hyde. After conferring with President Hoover, Hyde sent a telegram to CBOT President John Bunnell asking the CBOT to look into short sales by the Soviet Union, a country that Hyde maintained was forcing down the price of wheat. Bunnell responded that he would be happy to do so if Hyde provided him with specific allegations that he could investigate. Both sides were about to enter the fuzzy area of the Grain Futures Act. Who knew exactly about the positions of pit traders and their customers? Hyde hinted that he had the necessary information to prove his point but added that it was primarily the duty of the CBOT to provide disclosure of its own activities.

In his telegram, published in the *New York Times*, Hyde

pulled a few punches concerning the issue of short selling. He wrote, "These transactions by the Russian Government are not based upon even a remote possibility of delivery upon your market or in the United States and have the effect of manipulating the price downward against every farmer who has sold his wheat since these short sales were executed." The point was simple. Soviet grains and American grains were different, and the former could not be used for delivery against a Chicago contract. At the same time, the Soviets were flooding the French market with millions of eggs, which the French claimed were a danger to the public health. They feared that the eggs would be relabeled domestic and exported as if they had originated in France. In the case of wheat, the same appeared to be the case. The Soviets were leasing ships from the Italians to export wheat to Britain and the United States when the short selling operation was discovered. The export operation was then promptly canceled. Even if the wheat had been successfully exported and sold abroad, the costs of actual delivery would have been exorbitant—greater than the actual spot price—showing the CBOT short selling operation to be nothing more than a speculative short sale rather than a hedging operation. Without the intent of hedging, it appeared that the Soviets had been caught with their shorts down.

Bunnell's response, however, only threw more fuel on the fire. He responded to a flock of comment-seeking reporters with the suggestion that "you take up with the Secretary of State [the] right of Soviet Russia to transact business in the United States through its corporate agents."[1] For its part, the Soviet government pleaded innocence. Its New York agent, E. Y. Belitzky of the All-Russian Textile Syndicate, admitted that his company had sold short 5 million bushels of wheat in Chicago but claimed that the transactions were for the entire nine-month period of that year to date and represented nothing more than normal hedging operations. The CBOT average daily volume was around 50 million bushels. Wheat was not Belitzky's forte, as indicated by the name of his company. Textiles were his usual business.

Belitzky pointed out that ordinarily he was a net buyer of cotton, having purchased over $250 million worth over the past several years. Sarcastically, he noted that no one wanted to portray him as a friend of American agriculture for having purchased so much, but critics were happy to paint the Soviets as manipulators for selling short a "negligible" amount of wheat. "Recently the All-Russian Textile Syndicate received orders from its client in the Soviet Union to sell a relatively small quantity of wheat on the Chicago market," Belitzky stated, defending himself and his client. "These sales were intended as usual hedging operations and the Chicago Board of Trade would not reflect the international price in commodities if it would decline such transactions," he added with conviction.[2] But what exactly was being hedged?

The political and economic situation of the Soviet Union at the time belied the explanation. The country was in the early stages of collectivization under Stalin, and it is questionable whether farmers in protest of Stalin's plan, especially those in the Ukraine, had yet begun to destroy their crops as they were to do later, causing a severe shortage of wheat. In the years preceding 1930, there was a general surplus of wheat, so the hedging explanation did not strike a responsive chord. It appeared that the Soviet Union had an adequate surplus. At the time, however, food rationing was being practiced by the current regime, so the nature of the local market in the Soviet Union was not clear. However, it was possible that the Russians were not referring to hedging an actual delivery but to price hedging, where the short seller who possesses the commodity simply sells it short to protect the current price with no intention of delivering. This strategy would have made perfect sense amid the criticisms that the Russians faced from the Hoover administration. However, it appeared that the real target of the criticism was again the CBOT.

Smith Brookhart of Iowa gave his own interpretation of the affair with a comment that was to be reiterated many times over the next few years. "The situation presented by Secretary Hyde, if true, proves that the price of wheat is in the hands of gamblers," he commented, "and the complaint should be made against the system and not against those who use the exchanges and employ methods permitted by law."[3] The CBOT and the other futures exchanges shuddered, for this was a criticism they had endured for decades. Now, by implication, they were aiding and abetting an alien social and political system to the detriment of the American economy.

The downward price spiral for wheat was behind all of the accusations and counteraccusations. In January 1930, the spot price of wheat was about $1.38 per bushel; by September of that year, the price had collapsed to 79 cents per bushel. Clearly, short sellers were involved in the price decrease, so the Russians certainly were not alone. The *New York Times* commented that "the entire performance looks like a stupid business on part of the Russian syndicate, but at least our own government might keep its head."[4] But the pressure succeeded. Within a week of Hyde's comments, the CBOT decided to end short selling by foreign governments on the exchange. Because no one could recall another government selling short, the ban applied primarily to the Russians. All member firms of the CBOT (except one) reported their positions to the board. The CBOT absolved its traders of any wrongdoing but acknowledged that the selling was unethical and would put an end to it. When told of the CBOT's action, Hyde remarked, "I am glad to see that the Chicago Board of Trade is making an effort to protect the market of the American farmer."

The Russian claim about a simple hedging operation was also belied by statements made by Farm Board Chairman

Alexander Legge concerning wheat. In September 1930, Legge claimed that the United States had exported so much wheat to foreign countries and fed so much to livestock that it barely had enough for internal consumption. At the time, tariffs on imports pegged the price of wheat at 42 cents. The market price was so low that a market report at the time claimed that "not a bushel can leap that barrier."[5] With a short supply and a relatively low price, it was highly unlikely that the Russians were hedging rather than speculating with the help of the pit traders.

The Russian fury did not dissipate quickly. By the end of September, the ban was in place and the short selling was finished. It appeared that the Russian agent in New York had bungled the operation when it was clear to him that it was difficult to be long and short at the same time on different grades of wheat, which were not fungible. The *New York Times* concluded that "there must have been a dreary sense of amusement when the Kremlin learned of the interpretation on which the foreign wheat trade placed such bungling."[6] But the affair was far from over. While the Russians receded from view, the matter of short selling was only beginning. Politicians found a convenient hot-button issue for their public pronouncements about the markets' decline. Other issues were simmering as well. Some traders still believed that their positions did not have to be made public, even when required by the CBOT, as prescribed by the Grain Futures Act.

Arthur Cutten was one of the few traders who refused to fully disclose his positions in 1931. It was widely suspected that he, among others, had been involved with the Russian short sale, but proof of his involvement was difficult to obtain. As early as February 1930, Cutten was suspected of bearing the market. Secretary Hyde sent him a telegram at the time, stating, "It is reported to me that you have been operating on the bear side of the grain market and that these operations have contributed to the collapse of the market. I have no right or authority to suggest any course to any businessman but must in the public interest. If you could abandon such a course it would help many thousands of people in a time of distress. If the report is untrue then disregard my anxiety in the matter."[7]

Cutten's response was typical. He told Hyde that his information was incorrect and dismissed it out of hand. He did state that he had been inactive in the pits during that period. Subsequent information, however, revealed that statement to be false. Legal action against him was then begun, especially since his positions were over 500,000 bushels each, the threshold level above which positions had to be reported. Another trading firm sued the Secretary of Agriculture to prevent him from enforcing the Grain Futures Act about disclosure, claiming that it applied only to the CBOT as an institution, not to individual traders. But a federal judge upheld the act. The Grain Futures Act required all positions of that size to be reported. The Cutten case dragged on for almost five years before the Supreme Court made a final decision in 1936 that was to have wide-ranging results for the futures markets.

One transaction did become highly publicized in late 1931, only adding to Cutten's mystique. In November of that year, a spectacular long position was accumulated in the Chicago and Winnipeg exchanges, again attributed to a group led by Cutten. He had joined the Winnipeg exchange earlier in disgust at having to report his large trading positions in Chicago but moved back to Chicago within a year. Reports circulated internationally that the Russians were no longer exporting wheat, a dramatic turnaround of their position from only a year before. The spot price sank so low that it actually was less than the cost of production. Then, the massive buying added almost 20 cents per bushel. Cutten's associates stated that he was acting entirely alone, going long after studying the market fundamentals. A general suspicion arose that he was acting in concert with the Farm Board, which had large inventory holdings but was committed to modest stabilization operations. Farm Board Chairman James C. Stone acknowledged that the price rise was beneficial to all, but he denied using Cutten to purchase wheat. "The Farm Board has not made any agreements with the private operators," Stone stated emphatically. The marketplace, however, took his comments with a grain of salt.

The Russian affair brought the practice of short selling to a wide audience and proved only the first in a series of revelations about the practice that cast shadows over both the stock and futures markets. The controversy also highlighted the wide differences of opinion that existed between traders and those in government over the state of the economy in late 1930 and early 1931. Stock and commodities exchange officials continued to maintain that the markets and the economy would correct and that the problems were only temporary. Legislators looked past the shortsighted discussions, seeing an economy spinning downward and beginning to suspect even more greatly that short selling was at the heart of the problem. Unfortunately, it seemed that both the exchange officials and the legislators were arguing about arranging deck chairs on the Titanic. Although the real economic issue was much deeper, short selling became the newsworthy topic of the day.

## HOOVERIZING

Whatever the state of the industrial sectors of the economy, the agriculture business was in terrible condition after 1930, and its plight only worsened. By late 1931, the income of the farmer had plunged well below $1,000, while the income of the average industrial worker remained around $2,000. The stock market indices plunged along with commodity prices. Vocal criticism of short selling continued for several years. Herbert Hoover's familiarity with commodities during World War I had always made him skeptical of commodities traders, a mood that spilled over into 1931, when he began his crusade with the support of some corporate leaders whose stocks were plunging on the NYSE. According to Hoover, short selling as a practice had to be stopped in both markets before it destroyed prices and asset values.

Hoover began his campaign by urging the stock and commodities exchanges to put an end to short selling. In summer 1931, he mentioned short sales in wheat for the first time, criticizing the process as ruinous to farmers. Then, in the fall of that year, he directed his criticisms at the CBOT. He requested the exchange's attorney, Silas Strawn, to ask the CBOT for curbs on short selling. The exchange's response was vague, carrying a hint of traders' short-term mentality. Prices were so low already, the CBOT responded that short selling was not feasible. In reality, grain prices were on something of a rebound, with wheat rising to around 55 cents spot. However, the exchange realized that it had better show a united front in the face of the criticism. A few weeks later, Strawn reported to Hoover that the bear raids were finished and that "short selling is not prejudicial." Implicitly, he acknowledged that bear raiding had occurred. But the raiding had now ended and, he vowed, would not resume. Hoover appeared satisfied with the report.

At the same time, NYSE President Richard Whitney reiterated his view that short selling was a natural market technique and that critics, such as Hoover, would be silenced when they fully understood its true function. Whitney, a staunch defender of the status quo at the NYSE, was the most vocal exponent of adopting a hands-off policy toward the markets and considered criticism of the markets to be uninformed. The general Wall Street view was also neutral to moderately supportive of short selling. The *Magazine of Wall Street* acknowledged that there were such forces as "artificial longs and shorts" (meaning corners and bear raids) but suggested that the public report them to the NYSE if it detected irregularities in trading.[8] That would provide little comfort to small investors, who implicitly were at the mercy of the market.

The exhortations against short selling grew and began to assume even greater elements of conspiracy and farce. In winter 1932, Hoover urged the management of the NYSE to limit the amount of stock available for lending so that short sellers would have a limited supply. The NYSE listened but did not act, believing that Hoover did not know what he was talking about. The futures exchanges received the same plea but remained equally silent. Even patriotic overtones had no effect. "Individuals who use the facilities of the Exchange for such purposes are not contributing to the recovery of the United States," Hoover stated assuredly, aiming his remarks at the NYSE. If the stock exchange was not willing to listen, there would be even less incentive for the futures markets, where short selling depended not on the supply of loanable stock but on the intent of floor traders to open a position.

Politicians at the time overlooked the fact that the problem needed a clear origin and bogeyman if it was to be taken seriously. They took for granted that economic conditions spoke for themselves and that the public understood market techniques. However, short selling as a process did not seem to capture the public imagination, nor did the next threat on Hoover's list, although it did elicit more response from the financial markets. Hoover, after making unsuccessful attempts in winter 1932 to stimulate the markets through open-market operations by the Fed, turned his attention to what he thought was an international conspiracy designed to pull the United States off the gold standard. The villains behind this putative conspiracy were familiar.

Machinations in the gold market had a better chance of being taken seriously than short selling. Gold was the standard commodity; it was the metal upon which the dollar was based, and an attack against it was tantamount to an attack on the dollar itself. Since international financial transactions settled in gold, the amount that the country kept in reserve was vital to its economic health. If foreign investors became nervous, they could sell their assets and pull money out the country, draining the gold supply in the process. Clinton Gilbert, a Philadelphia journalist, recounted the episode and added an even more startling connection. He remarked that Hoover "apparently believed a fantastic story. European capitalists had supplied much of the cash needed to engineer the greatest bear raid in history. These proverbially open-handed and trusted gentlemen had accepted the leadership of New York's adroit Democratic financier: Mr. Bernard Baruch."[9]

Baruch was not amused by the connection, especially in light of a decade of anti-Semitism and blaming of Wall Street bankers for all sorts of sins. Somewhat blithely he remarked, "Similar attacks were picked up and mounted by the Ku Klux Klan, Father Charles E. Coughlin . . . to say nothing of Joseph Goebbels and Adolf Hitler."[10] Amid such attacks, Hoover apparently was not taken that seriously. The theory was passed to Hoover by agrarian senators who recognized his vulnerability on the issue. On the basis of what he was told, Hoover called for congressional hearings to investigate stock exchange practices. The Senate obliged in February 1932. Senator Peter Norbeck, Republican of South Dakota and an oil driller by occupation, called for hearings shortly thereafter, which began in April. Smith Brookhart hurried the hearings, for he believed that the market was due for the greatest bear raid in history. More evidence presented itself, all of it international rather than domestic.

Part of the evidence of a purported bear raid and attack on the gold standard centered on a Frenchwoman named Marthe Hanau, who produced a Paris-based financial newsletter called

*Forces.* The newsletter provided erroneous information about the U.S. markets to produce panic in foreign investors who would then sell their U.S. stocks and repatriate their funds, thereby forcing the United States off the gold standard. Matters were given credence by the fact that Hanau previously had spent time in prison for operating a bucket shop.

Motivated by the conspiracies and having a desire to see the United States remain on the gold standard, Hoover called in key congressional delegates in winter 1932 and pressed for a bill to shore up the gold position. One of those in sympathy with him was Senator Carter Glass of Virginia, the senior Senate expert on banking and monetary affairs. The result was the passing in 1932 of the first Glass–Steagall Act, which provided gold for business and industry in an attempt to counteract gold hoarding. An act of the same name was passed a year later and was more famous for its banking reforms. However, the measure proved to be only a short-term solution to the problem of gold hoarding and the developing banking crisis.

The conspiracy theories, however misguided, did point to the predominant popular economic theory subscribed to by Republicans at the time: the *percolator theory,* also known as *trickle-down economics.* The theory states that if the stimulus for economic growth is applied at the top, the benefits will then trickle down to all. According to Hoover, to stop a bear raid meant that its leaders had to be found, not their minions. Walter Lippmann succinctly summarized the difference in attitudes even before Franklin D. Roosevelt (FDR) was elected in 1932. The old Progressives were not as interested in top-down theories as they were to those theories that applied to a wider spectrum. Lippmann wrote, "It was to this progressive feeling that Governor Roosevelt was appealing when he said . . . that the Hoover Administration 'can think in terms only of the top of the social and economic structure' and that it had forgotten or did not wish to remember 'the infantry of our economic army.' "[11] Unfortunately, the farmers were considered only the supply masters of the army rather than its frontline soldiers.

Brookhart continued to believe that a massive bear raid on the stock exchange was imminent and therefore called for congressional hearings to commence quickly. A rumor appeared in the Paris newspaper *L'Ordre* that the National City Bank of New York had suspended operations. Although false, the rumor unsettled overseas markets, and the newspaper subsequently printed a retraction. On the first day of the hearings, a reporter found Brookhart in Washington and asked him what had prompted him to call for the hearings so quickly. "Read the papers," Brookhart snapped at the reporter. "Do you mean under a New York or a Paris dateline?" the reporter pressed. "Read both," Brookhart responded.[12] As it turned out, Brookhart had good reason to hurry the proceedings. He lost the Senate primary in Iowa in 1932 and did not return to Washington.

Ironically, temporary good fortune struck the futures exchanges when the congressional investigation devoted its attention to the stock market and the causes of the 1929 crash. There was plenty of economic damage to be assessed and blame was apportioned accordingly. The stock market crash investigation—known popularly as the Pecora hearings, after Ferdinand Pecora, the Senate committee's chief counsel—involved the interviewing of dozens of bankers and stock traders ranging from J. P. Morgan to Michael Meehan. Revelations from these interviews included income tax evasion, treating of preferred customers to preferential stock issues, and lack of what would later be called due diligence on new issues. The revelations captivated the committee and the country for months. The income tax issue was particularly thorny, because even when executives paid their taxes, the amounts were so outrageously low that public opinion was incensed. Silas Strawn, attorney for the CBOT and member of the United States Chamber of Commerce, was one who reported income and assets requiring only a tax of $120 for 1932. Albert Wiggin, the president of Chase Manhattan Bank, revealed that he sold his own bank's stock short after the crash, netting a handsome profit while hiding the proceeds of the trade in a Canadian account. The committee had more information on the activities of bankers and traders than it had ever imagined. Fortunately for the futures markets, no hearings were held about short selling or cornering during the early 1930s. It was the declining equities market that held center stage.

The gold problem continued despite the first Glass–Steagall Act in 1932, and by the time FDR took office in March 1933, the dollar's link with gold required attention. There was widespread belief that it was contributing to the export problem and the farmers' plight. Most of the Republican old guard favored the link between the dollar and gold, although FDR recognized that access to the metal would need to be restricted because of the country's rapidly falling level of gold reserves. Hoarding of gold and money occurred during the 1932–33 winter, and banks continued to fail. The well-publicized failure of the Bank of United States, a New York–based commercial bank, in fall 1930 destroyed the faith of many depositors in the banking system. As a result, FDR planned to act on the banking and gold problem promptly after taking office.

Within days of his inauguration, FDR was granted the power to restrict the ability of individuals to hold gold and to prohibit the export or hoarding of both gold and silver by the Emergency Banking Act of 1933. Subsequent legislation gave him the power to reduce the gold content of the dollar in an effort to stop the deflationary trend. He issued an order requiring all individuals holding gold to surrender it to the Fed in return for paper currency or a bank account. Shortly thereafter, he cut the weight of gold in the dollar and refused to honor U.S. contracts that provided for official payments to be made in the metal instead of in cash. Most politicians, econo-mists, and civil servants were dismayed by the action, which Director of the Budget Lewis Douglas characterized as the "end of Western Civilization."[13]

Uncertainty came to an end in the gold market when in January 1934 its price was fixed at $35 per ounce. The price remained at the same level until August 1971, when President Nixon unilaterally severed the dollar's convertibility, effectively devaluing the currency again. While the traditional link be-tween gold and commodities prices underwent a radical reex-amination, the most important legislation to affect the markets came in May 1933, when Congress passed the Agricultural Adjustment Act (AAA). The New Deal did not believe the futures markets' claim that they were an efficient mechanism for pricing and marketing commodities. Time had run out for the laissez-faire philosophy that had characterized the markets for the past 80 years.

When in 1933 Congress passed the AAA, farmers had been in a desperate plight. Depressed prices were exacerbated by one of the worst droughts ever experienced. From 1931 to 1935, the drought was so severe that croplands throughout the Great Plains and the Midwest turned to dust as the topsoil blew away, sometimes getting caught in the jet stream to be carried east to such faraway cities as New York. The air would at times become so dusty that cities often had to use streetlights in the middle of the day. The desperate price decreases of 1931 forced many farmers into bankruptcy, and many more eked out only a mar-ginal existence. From 1930 to 1935, almost 750,000 farmers lost their farms through bankruptcy and foreclosure. Most affected were the tenant farmers, who had to leave their land because of a lack of work and migrate to the cities or to California, the promised land for many. The problem became so acute that farmers around the country began organizing penny auctions. When a foreclosed farm was put up for auction, the only bidders attending were other farmers who bid just a few cents for the property. By rigging the auctions, the foreclosed farmers were able to buy back their farms for a few dollars. Outside bidders were actively discouraged from the bidding.

The AAA mandated governmental intrusion into what had been considered a traditional American vocation for generations. Clearly, it sought to fill a void that the futures markets had been unable to fill themselves. The act authorized the government to begin making payments to farmers to take some of their acreage out of production, encouraged farmers to begin storing crops on their farms rather than sending them to the market, and authorized payments to be made to farmers in advance of these actions to help their cash flows. In one stroke of the pen, the New Deal sought to rectify the chronic oversupply problem caused by increased farm efficiency.

Within months, almost everyone was accused of taking advantage of the program for personal use. Harold Ickes, a member of FDR's inner cabinet, recalled a newspaper editor telling him that a rumor was circulating that FDR himself had received an AAA check for crops grown on his property in Georgia. When Ickes mentioned the rumor to the president at lunch one day, FDR "told me that he had denied the superintendent of his Georgia farm permission to grow cotton because that would have entitled him to AAA benefits."[14] Because the AAA program applied to farms of all sizes, almost anyone owning a farm as a full- or part-time business now had to assess whether to accept payments from the government.

Farmers eagerly joined the plan, and over the next two years the government paid out $1 billion in farm subsidies. The continuing drought in the Midwest in 1934 also helped reduce crops, more so than the program itself.[15] In January 1936, the Supreme Court declared the AAA unconstitutional, throwing the program into confusion. Part of the 1933 act relied on payments made to farmers based upon processing taxes, and the

Supreme Court found these taxes objectionable. After short-term patchwork legislation was passed to keep the subsidy programs running, Congress passed the second AAA in 1938, which relied upon appropriations by Congress from the Treasury to make the payments, thereby eliminating the Court's objection. The subsidy program survived and exists to the present day as a cornerstone of agricultural policy.

Farm-price supports were not universally popular by any means. Hoover, the sharpest critic of the New Deal, unequivocally stated that "the whole thesis behind this program is the very theory that man is but the pawn of the state. It is usurpation of the primary liberties of men by government."[16] The population divided along party lines in its support of the program. Public opinion polling was a relatively new art in the country, and when in January 1936 the Gallup organization began asking the public for its opinion about the AAA, it discovered the opinion to be split about evenly. Of polled Democrats, 70 percent supported the act; of Republicans, only 8 percent. The public was, however, fairly perceptive when it came to food prices. Secretary of Agriculture Henry Wallace kept a schedule of what he considered fair prices for basic food and other staple products. When asked what it thought constituted fair prices for wheat and corn, the polled sample responded with $1.00 per bushel for wheat and 75 cents per bushel for corn.[17] Those prices were nearly the retail average for 1937, although they took a sharp dive during the following year.

The AAA was a declaration that the laissez-faire agricultural policies of the past had ended. The role of the futures markets in helping determine prices and marketing was shown to be weak. Most politicians and commentators outside the financial markets in general were tired of bear raids and corners that were making fortunes for their principals while the farmers' plight worsened year to year. The inability of the exchanges to end pit traders' activities culminated with legislation for the futures markets similar to that passed for the securities markets. Despite bad public relations for the markets, however, they continued to flourish, although the old charge that they were no more than gambling dens was beginning to surface once again. In reality, the characterization had never really disappeared. Corners and bear raids were still considered valid floor trading strategies, although traders were more muted in the 1930s than they were in the nineteenth century about their pit prowess.

## BACK IN THE PITS

Arthur Cutten was not the only prominent operator working in the markets during the late 1920s and early 1930s. Thomas M. Howell was the legendary lone wolf of the CBOT. His trading company was a sole proprietorship; he had no partners or employees working for him. Born in 1882 in Nebraska, Howell worked on a small local newspaper before buying a small brokerage operation from the newspaper's owner, who needed cash after the financial crisis in 1907. Finding himself in the brokerage business, he decided that he needed to discover what he had bought, so he set about learning all he could about commodities prices. The firm operated outside the CBOT, along the lines of New York's curb market for stocks. It was a beginning but certainly not his goal, for soon he was on the floor of the CBOT trading for himself in the pits with a taciturn demeanor that made Arthur Cutten seem almost talkative.

Howell's great coup in the pits came in the corn pit beginning in late 1930. Although he was well-known since the mid-1920s as an uncanny trader, his reputation soared when he assumed a massive long position in corn futures. Ironically, this came at the same time that the government, through the Farm Board, reputedly was selling corn futures short. The only tangible explanation for the government action was that it wanted the price stable. Howell accumulated futures, however, and then watched the market slowly awaken to the realization that it was short of the physical corn needed to satisfy delivery, which Howell demanded. The coup became the talk of the Chicago pits. Besides Howell's newfound reputation, the most controversial part of the operation had to do with the short sale by the Farm Board at a time when President Hoover and others were loudly bemoaning the evils of short selling.

Howell abandoned his usual laconic demeanor when the Agricultural Advisory Council accused him of being a short. "Here is an outrageous example of the evils of short selling," the group said. "It helps to depress prices and is absolutely of no benefit to the corn producer." Howell demanded, and received, a retraction of the statement, but not before it was broadcast nationwide by some news services. Indignation was rising quickly in the corn-producing states. Telegrams poured into Washington asking Hoover whether the government had sold corn short. Howell went on the record deploring the government's two-faced attitude toward the markets, then scored points for traders when he used the intervention to the advantage of the exchanges. When asked about the possibility of economic recovery, Howell stated pessimistically, "No, I cannot see any signs of an upturn. But the surest road back to confidence in the markets would be the removal of government influence."[18]

Subsequent information revealed that Howell was both long and short during the operation, revealing his uncanny ability to manipulate the markets. By selling short, he forced many other floor traders hoping for the same price drop to do the same. However, he accumulated physical corn at the same time. When he delivered his own longs against his shorts, he locked in the difference in the two prices. Other traders on the short side were forced to deliver, though, which raised the spot price on corn. In addition, he had a net long position, meaning that he benefited from the price rise. He caught the market in both directions, profiting from the price rise and the price fall. When the transaction was revealed, regulators bristled, given the economic conditions on the farms and in the country as a whole. Regulators claimed that Howell made $1 million on the short sale, to which he countered that he was actually long 8 million bushels. Both claims were correct.

The FDR administration pursued Arthur Cutten and, in 1934, finally decided to ban him from futures trading. Henry Wallace, no friend of futures speculators, charged Cutten formally with failing to disclose his positions in 1930 and 1931 and sought to have him banned from all futures exchanges in the country. As he announced the charges, Wallace jokingly referred to Cutten as "one of our greatest supporters of the law of supply and demand and laissez faire"—an oblique reference to a battle waged in the press between Cutten and the Reverend Clarence Huff. As president of the Farmers National Grain Corp., Huff had recently stated that the grain pits were unnecessary and that the CBOT should be closed. Cynics naturally asked whether the corporation learned about the pits the hard way in 1931 at the time of the Howell controversy. The normally reticent Cutten was beginning to feel the pinch created by the many detractors of the grain pits and lashed back by saying that the statement was "entitled to the booby prize for ignorance . . . when Huff gets rough the title of Reverend becomes nothing less than sacrilegious, losing entirely its caste and significance." He continued by stating, "Economists have held that the elimination of future delivery trading for any commodity of yearly production creates a monopoly. . . . Can it be that the Reverend Huff has dropped his mantle of charity or brotherhood of love. Or has abandoned the Golden Rule itself, with monopoly as his ultimate goal?"[19] Many defenses had been mounted over the years in defense of the markets, but none ever claimed that their elimination would cause a monopoly. The remarks survived for years, much to Cutten's dismay.

According to Wallace's charges, Cutten repeatedly failed to report his true positions in 1930 and 1931. An examination of his books revealed a wide discrepancy between the numbers he did report, beginning in 1931, and the numbers that the government contended were his actual long and short positions. More important, however, was that the Department of Agriculture wanted to pursue him because he would maintain short positions while the price of wheat would decline sharply. The futures price dropped from $1.34 to 56 cents per bushel between the beginning of 1930 and the end of 1931, a decline that everyone except futures traders considered immoral and unpatriotic. Cutten appealed his ban, and politics finally entered the argument when the FDR administration began discussing a new commodities law to strengthen the Grain Futures Act.

When the Grain Futures Commission met shortly after Wallace's charge, Cutten was barred from trading on all futures exchanges for two years. He called the action "outrageous" and vowed to continue the fight in the appeals courts. His defense claimed that he was being singled out because of his prominence. Wallace called him the "greatest speculator this country ever had" when he announced the commission's decision. The commission also pointed out that his response to Hyde in 1930 about short selling was less than appropriate. Almost everyone expected him to pursue the appeal to the end. The burglary incident that he had pursued for years attested to his dogged determination. However, the charges proved that the FDR administration, following Hoover's lead, was determined to clean the markets of what it considered excessive and harmful speculation.

A similar fate soon fell on Howell, whom Wallace charged with violations of the Grain Futures Act shortly after he had made the Cutten charges. As with Cutten, Howell's charges, too, centered on actions he committed in 1930 and 1931. At issue was the corner on corn. Not only was Howell charged but also several members of his family, including his wife and daughter. Wallace claimed that Howell used his family to cover his large positions to avoid being seen violating the act and the CBOT rules. The suit claimed that Howell and associates held 32 percent of all open contracts on July 1931 corn in May of that year but by July 30 held 85 percent of the contracts. The resulting squeeze added 14 cents per bushel, and the visible supply of wheat in the country declined as the short sellers scrambled to cover themselves.[20] The operation was accomplished through dummy accounts, designed with the Grain Futures Act disclosure requirements in mind.

Angered by the charges, Howell filed suit in federal court to test the constitutionality of the Grain Futures Act. His lawyer claimed that the act gave the Grain Futures Commission "quasi-constitutional powers," although he noted that the commission was not a real court. Howell decided to go cruising on his yacht in Florida while the suit was filed and characteristically had little comment. At the Grain Futures Administration's hearing that followed, his attorney turned the tables by calling his client a "public benefactor" who had actually lost over a million dollars on the long position while the market was in decline. He refused to state whether the short side made or lost any money although the defense was clear. Howell maintained that for him to be guilty of the charges, the regulators would have had to catch him in the act—something that they did not do at the time. Because the charges were brought after the fact, Howell felt they essentially were pointless.

Howell's cavalier attitude was not without foundation in the law, as his appeal later showed. Moreover, the sight of a wealthy commodities trader on a cruise off the Florida coast while hundreds of thousands of tenant farmers were being displaced from their homes and meager livelihoods was becoming common in 1930s Americal. J. P. Morgan Jr. liked to sail his yacht, the *Corsair*, in the Hudson River, not far from many of the temporary shantytowns, or Hoovervilles, that were hastily set up along the riverfront to shelter the homeless. America was becoming a nation of stark contrasts and none was more pronounced than the wide chasm between commodity futures traders and farmers. In the mid-1930s, the average income of tenant farmers was about $400 per year, assuming that they even had jobs. That figure represented about one hour's income to a successful trader like Cutten or Howell.

The futures markets began to feel the effects of the changing tide. The price of a CBOT seat fell to $6,000 in 1933 before rising again the following year. The CBOT then suspended Jesse Livermore, the infamous New York stock trader who had been using the exchange as another outlet for speculating in both stocks and commodities. In 1935, one of its largest trading firms, the Rosenbaum Grain Corp., filed for bankruptcy and sought reorganization. Each year, traders large and small were expelled from the pits, either for flagrant rules violations or the occasional bucket shop dealing. Until Cutten ran afoul of the Grain Futures law, however, no substantial trader had been sanctioned for violations of the $500,000 contract limit.

The tide definitely turned in favor of regulation by the mid-1930s. Free markets appeared to not be able to right the economy and occasional government intervention did not seem successful either. Prices of commodities rose from their 1931 lows but were still extremely volatile and the grain pits attracted more press coverage than did the mass exodus of farmers from their homes in the Great Plains and Midwest. The FDR administration indicated that the futures exchanges needed regulation in much the same way that the stock markets had after the passing of the Securities Act of 1933 and the Securities Exchange Act of 1934. Futures traders could not escape the same fate that befell others. The time was at hand for legislation to help clear up the markets and it was Wallace who spearheaded the administration's campaign.

A new law designed to encompass all of the futures markets, just as the Securities Exchange Act was designed to include all of the stock exchanges, was needed to prevent traders from distorting the price of essential commodities. Such a law was passed in 1936. Known as the Commodity Exchange Act, it was intended to apply to all the futures exchanges by replacing the piecemeal laws already in existence. The cotton exchanges fought hard to be excluded from the bill, claiming that the Cotton Futures Act of 1915 was sufficient regulation. Their drive was spearheaded by Senator "Cotton Ed" Smith of South Carolina, who lobbied effectively for the exclusion of the cotton exchanges. Finally, he succumbed at the request of the administration, and the law included all of the exchanges. A similar exclusion was unsuccessfully sought for butter and eggs by the CME. In many respects, the new legislation was similar to the Securities Exchange Act but lacked the muscle of the securities laws.

The law created a Commodities Exchange Commission, which included three cabinet members—the secretary of agriculture, the attorney general, and the secretary of commerce. The three cabinet members had ultimate jurisdiction over the exchanges. They required brokers to be registered with the body. They could also limit the amount of trading in any one day on a given exchange and require brokers to segregate customers' margin funds from brokerage house funds so that no confusion would occur concerning whose funds were placed by brokers in the market. The avowed purpose of the commission was to reduce the kind of rampant speculation in the markets that had been experienced since late 1929.

Most important, the Commodity Exchange Act banned options from being traded on agricultural commodity futures.[21] The options market that shadowed the boards of trade since the nineteenth century was finally prohibited. The commission reserved the right to review all requests for new options trading, although the issue would not rise again for over 30 years.

Traders naturally disliked the new law. Many predicted that the futures markets would die a quick death because of what they saw as government interference. The CBOT's management claimed that the current rules were sufficient and saw no need for the new law. About 70 of its floor brokers took the idea a step further by refusing to register with the new commission, preferring to do business as usual. The CME's management disliked having butter and eggs included in the final version, claiming that the Commodity Exchange Act was essentially a grain bill and should be kept that way. Their protests, however, came after the fact. Reality finally arrived at the futures exchanges. After the new law's passage in 1936, they would have to suffer the indignation of what they saw as unwarranted government regulation in their affairs. However, the law also had weaknesses that many recognized.

Unlike the securities acts of 1933 and 1934, futures exchanges did not have a full-time regulator to keep tabs on them. The 1934 Securities Exchange Act created the Securities and Exchange Commission (SEC), a panel of five commissioners whose full-time job was to monitor the activities of the primary and secondary equities markets. The SEC was designed with the original Federal Reserve in mind. Since its inception, the Fed had been manned by bankers whose full-time obligations laid elsewhere, especially at the district bank level. The New York members of the local Federal Reserve Bank were all bankers involved heavily in the stock market both before and after the 1929 crash. However, the commodities law was not designed in the same fashion. The regulatory and monitoring powers were given to political appointees who had many other obligations and duties as well.

## LAST HEE-HAW

The appeals of the agrarian Progressives cut across social and party lines during the 1930s as the Depression continued. Agrarians proved useful to the New Deal, since they were allied with many of FDR's policies. However, it is doubtful that the president and his cabinet otherwise had much use for them as a group. The simple ideology of putting farmers first and blaming Wall Street bankers for most of the country's social and economic ills also allied them to other firebrands, including Father Charles Coughlin—the "Radio Priest"—and Huey Long. The rhetoric found a willing audience in the 1930s, although on occasion it sounded much like the inflammatory prose of the newspaper *Dearborn Independent* from years before.

The last gasp of the agrarians came in early 1936. Senator Gerald P. Nye of North Dakota called hearings to investigate bankers and financiers one last time. The topic was sure to titillate a public already accustomed to sensational hearings such as the Pecora proceedings of several years before. It appeared, however, that the committee was grasping at straws. Their topic did not inspire the imagination. It was already far-removed from the public's mind. Did bankers lead the United States into World War I simply to make excessive profits selling war materials and commodities to its European allies? The source upon which they based their allegations clearly claimed that they did.

The basis for the hearings was a book published in 1935 by Walter Millis, a reporter for the New York *Herald Tribune*, entitled *The Road to War*. According to Millis' book, the United States was dragged into the conflict by bankers who desired to

128

profit from war financing. It was well-known that J. P. Morgan & Co. made more than $30 million as both purchasing agent and supply master for U.S. and British war efforts. As the 1930s progressed, the resentment against bankers rose to the surface. The strictures of the Glass–Steagall Act of 1933 did not quench the desire for what appeared to be revenge against bankers. Added to that was the introspective nature of American society in the 1930s. The United States appeared to be adopting a neutral stance as European politics again became highly volatile. The country's domestic problems were too great to allow for concern about European developments.

The irony was that the thesis of the book was the same as the position held by the grand old Progressive of the Republican Party, Senator George Norris of Nebraska, made in 1917. At the time, Norris was the sole voice raised against the influence of bankers on Woodrow Wilson. As *Time* magazine noted, "In 1917, Senator Norris was almost alone in his interpretation of why the U.S. went to war. By 1936, a vast army of people and politicians, still sick and sore with the memory of what their country had gone through, were ready to agree with him."[22] Norris was instrumental in helping establish the Tennessee Valley Authority (TVA) in 1933. One of the dams built by the TVA was even named after him. The new allegations proved that there was still some mileage to be made at financiers' expense.

Almost 20 years later, the criticism arose again and had many more supporters. The 1936 Senate committee, hearing testimony from mostly bankers, including J. P. Morgan & Co., was headed by Senator Nye of North Dakota, one of the last members of the 1930s Progressives left in Congress. A former small-town newspaper editor, Nye originally came to the Senate in 1925 by filling the vacancy of a recently departed Republican. Prior to that, the highest-ranking public job he had ever held was as a member of his local school board. After a slow start in the Senate, he won reelection on his own merits and became known as one of the Sons of the Wild Jackass, although most of his speeches and demeanor were models of restraint and reason. Representing North Dakota was a difficult job; most politicos in Washington looked with disdain at the state, especially because it was known for its own brand of prairie socialism. The state was a major wheat producer and claimed to have suffered mightily at the hands of the pit traders in Chicago. Someone had gotten rich during World War I, and although during the war bankers procured record amounts of commodities for the Allies, farmers had never gotten wealthy from the purchasing program. The best they had was several years of decent prices and demand before the recession of 1920.

The proceedings were known as the Nye Committee hearings and were conducted primarily by Nye and General Counsel Stephen Raushenbush, who interrogated some of the bankers at great length. Many of the bankers' private correspondence during the war years were perused with great interest by committee members, but when questions arose, they were met with the response that J. P. Morgan & Co. could not remember what had taken place almost 20 years before. This was especially true of commodities sales, for which the bankers were accused of arranging loans to the British so that commodities, along with rifles and other materials, could be purchased. That the bankers lined their pockets—from both the banking fees for war bond issues and Morgan's procurement fees—was at the heart of the accusation. The hearings, however, never floated a balloon with any air. The bankers forgot their past dealings, so the proceedings ended on a tame note. Without hard evidence or an outright admission of collusion, the committee was nothing more than a tame cross-examination of bankers with bad memories.

Even the New York *Daily News*, a strong supporter of the

New Deal programs and severe critic of bankers, concluded that Nye proved nothing at all. "What does Senator Nye think he has proved by digging up these old facts once more and parading them across the witness stand?" asked the *Daily News.* "Let's give the devil his due. Morgan and the rest of the bankers did not get us into that war. And Nye's intimation that they did so is unfair, unhistorical, and untrue."[23] Given the political climate, the conspiracy theories that had plagued the 1920s and 1930s were still in vogue. Before the 1930s were almost over, a major law affecting public utilities was passed and a study of monopoly formation in American business would begin. Only World War II would eventually relieve the pressure on business, Wall Street, and LaSalle Street.

## VINDICATION

After years of appeals, Cutten's case finally was heard by the Supreme Court in 1936. The outcome did not please the administration or foes of the markets, for the court dismissed the charge. The court blamed the language of the Grain Futures Act, which the court said called for preventative measures against excessively large trading, not punishment for prior actions. "The language of section 6 (b) [of the Grain Futures Act] is clear," wrote Justice Brandeis. "Its language is plain and unambiguous. What the government asks is not a construction of a statute but, in effect, an enlargement of it by the court, so what was omitted, presumably (possibly) by inadvertence, may be included within its scope."[24] So the charges were thrown out and Cutten was free to trade again without the inconvenience of having to go through other brokers, something that the CBOT had previously allowed both him and Howell while they were on suspension. Persistence paid off once again.

A month later, Howell was also clear of his charges. A U.S. Circuit Court of Appeals set aside the ban ordered by the

Grain Futures Commission on the same basis that the Supreme Court had ruled for Cutten. But by mid-1936, the actions were rapidly becoming dated. Cutten's exoneration by the Supreme Court helped provide impetus for the Commodity Exchange Act, although it had been well on its way toward being passed by the time the verdict was reached. The appeal demonstrated that the language of the Grain Futures Act was too vague to deal with trading infractions. Most in Congress were aware of the problem and proposed the new law as a result, the Cutten case only having helped amplify the need. The major unanswered question was whether the Commodity Exchange Act had the necessary means to prevent the problem's reoccurrence. It was clearly a step in the direction toward greater regulation, but was it strong enough?

The bear hunt officially finished when the Commodity Exchange Act was passed. Short selling was the catalyst that finally brought about the legislation, although it was only serendipity that allowed futures markets to escape meaningful regulation for as long as they did. Taking a backseat to the stock exchanges in the late 1920s certainly had its advantages for the pits. The revelations of the Pecora hearings, as well as the travails of Richard Whitney at the NYSE—who was sent to prison on charges of fraud and embezzlement—and the wrenching changes to Wall Street caused by the Securities Act, the Securities Exchange Act, and the Glass–Steagall Act all combined to deflect unwanted attention from the pit traders. And the reluctance of Congress to create an SEC-style agency to regulate the future markets on a full-time basis certainly led to future battles between Washington and the markets, although the latter were again able to escape the full wrath of lawmakers.

During the later years of the Depression, the CME also felt the pinch of the lack of business. Unlike the CBOT, the much smaller produce exchange never participated in the bear raids of the early 1930s, nor did attract big-time speculators to its floor. In fact, it attracted very few speculators. As a result, the exchange began a public relations campaign wherein it asked other brokers and stock traders to become members. The price of a seat was only a few hundred dollars, and the CME hoped to attract the speculators and scalpers necessary to generate revenue. The campaign worked successfully. By 1939, a significant proportion of butter and egg contracts were held by traders outside of the butter-and-eggs business—meaning speculators, not hedgers.[25] World War II would, however, put its products on hold again as shortages became common after 1941.

Commodities prices slumped again in the late 1930s. Wheat and corn retreated to prices recorded in 1931 and 1932. Despite the attempts of the AAA to limit production, agricultural production always ran slightly ahead of demand, having a depressing effect on prices. The war in Europe also dampened demand for imports, interrupting farm exports. The federal government found itself propping up prices as best it could because of overproduction and slack demand, but the depressed prices would rally quickly once the war intensified. Behind the price rises was a factor that had not been seen in decades—a war economy, characterized by intense demand for commodities of all sorts, from silk for parachutes to cocoa for soldiers' rations of chocolate.

After years of pursuit, Washington finally imposed regulations on the securities and commodity futures industries. Of the two, the futures legislation in 1936 has been less well-known than the Wall Street regulations, especially the Glass–Steagall Act and the SEA. Although certainly rivaling Wall Street in speculation and scandal, traditionally the futures business always was associated with LaSalle Street, even though New York did a thriving futures business in the nineteenth and early twentieth centuries. Only after World War II did the futures industry become more closely associated with Wall Street. Prior to the war, it was erroneously associated exclusively with the Midwest and farmbelt legislators whose political voices were outside the mainstream. The period from the late 1920s to mid-1930s was one in which these loud voices, criticizing the effects of gambling and speculation, were heard clearly. After the bear hunt was over, however, other topics vied for national attention.

## HALF MAST

By 1940, the depressed prices and the more stringent regulatory climate had taken a toll on the pits. The price of a CBOT seat had declined to $750, the lowest since the 1890s. Within a year, the price would drop below $200. Business was so slow in 1940 that the exchange shifted to half-session days in December to offset the lack of business. Many wealthy investors, such as the Annenberg publishing family, gave up their seats as a lost cause and cashed out for relative pocket change. The message seemed to be clear. Without wild prices, bear raids, and corners, the pits were worth neither the time nor effort of many speculators. Hedging by itself was not a worthy—or profitable—exercise.

Commodities prices rebounded in the early to mid-1940s as World War II intensified. Both wheat and corn recorded price increases of 70 percent between 1939 and 1941 yet the increases did not spell success for futures traders. Two government agencies stepped into the market to ensure that price gouging and rampant speculation did not drive the commodities prices even higher. Normally, this would have given cause for pit traders to complain about government interference in their business. However, in 1940 nobody complained, at least publicly.

During the early years of the war, the Commodity Credit Corporation became even more prominent than it had been during the 1930s. Originally begun in 1933 as a lending agency by executive order, it received funds from the Reconstruction Finance Corp (RFC). After 1939, it was transferred to the Department of Agriculture. During the 1930s, it made billions of dollars in loans to farmers to support cotton, corn, wheat, and other commodities. The idea behind the lending was to allow farmers to store their harvested crops rather than dump them on the market immediately, thereby helping to stabilize prices—an activity that from a pit trader's perspective would hinder the ability to make assumptions about supply in the market. Jesse Jones, a Texas businessman who became head of the RFC in 1933, described how the program got started. "One afternoon in 1933," he recalled, "President Roosevelt called me to the White House and, as soon as I entered his office, said 'Jess, I want you to lend at 10 cents a pound on cotton.' "[26] Jones recalled having difficulties with the request, for cotton was only selling at 9 cents per pound at the time. The implications were clear, however. Lending at more than the actual price of the commodity would help raise its price and, if interest charges were sufficiently low, would enable the farmer to harvest and store the crop rather than be forced to sell it immediately to raise cash at distressed prices.

Even before Pearl Harbor in December 1941, the commodities exchanges were coming under fire for excessive speculation. J. M. Mehl, chairman of the Commodity Exchange Commission, warned 18 futures markets against excessive speculation in May 1941. If speculation continued, he said, the markets risked being closed. Two exchanges in particular—the New York Produce Exchange and the New Orleans Cotton Exchange—were singled out for allowing excessive speculation in their products. He wrote to them, stating, "The exchanges cannot afford to treat lightly the responsibility of seeing that this [a potential closing of the markets] does not occur."[27] Although the warning against speculation was aimed at the major exchanges, some of the smaller exchanges traded commodities considered vital to the war and were therefore felt to be vulnerable to speculation. John Kenneth Galbraith, working for the Office of Price Administration (OPA), was dispatched to hold consultations with several of the exchanges. As part of internal changes to ensure against speculation, the exchanges were asked to raise their margin requirements above the minimums that normally prevailed.

The OPA became the true problem for futures traders. It was a wartime agency established to monitor and impose maximum price ceilings for most commodities—using the prices recorded in March 1942 as its base—and had the authority to ration scarce consumer goods, including tires, automobiles, gasoline, coffee, meats, and processed foods. It took a couple of years for the OPA to bring prices under control. The implications for futures traders were clear. Vacillating prices, especially those that increased rapidly, were not going to be tolerated during the war. Prices were, in fact, not officially released from their 1942 levels until mid-1947.

Stable prices and rationing also had their effect upon the national psyche. Years of depression had taken their toll. After years of slow economic activity, the public mood toward speculation and gambling turned distinctly conservative. No state lotteries were in existence after 1930, and many state constitutions had amendments added to outlaw them. A Gallup poll in 1941 revealed that only about half of those surveyed favored a national lottery to help pay for war expenses. Even more revealing was another poll, taken during the same year, in which only 24 percent of those questioned admitted to buying a ticket in a church raffle or lottery and only 14 percent claimed to have ever made money on a game of chance.[28] Pit traders were not necessarily constrained by public opinion, but the times were not conducive for the usual bear raids and corners. The public would not tolerate market manipulation during the war. Normal supply-and-demand factors were in disarray, and only the bravest bull would attempt a corner under such conditions. Short sellers for the most part recognized that market conditions were too stable for profitable selling and the OPA guidelines only complicated matters.

The labor shortage during the war finally persuaded the exchanges to open their doors to women, but only in support capacities. The CBOT lifted its ban on female employees in 1941, although those who worked on the exchange floor had to wear suitable uniforms. Pit trading, however, was still off-limits to women, who were relegated to backroom jobs and positions such as telegraph and phone operators. The stock markets, most for the first time in their histories, also liberalized their rules to allow women to work on the exchanges.

Throughout the war years, the grain exchanges managed to remain open for trading, although limits were imposed from the outside. Some of the more specialized exchanges were shuttered and did not resume until the war ended. Trading in silk futures halted in 1940; in copper and coffee, 1941; in rubber and sugar, early 1942; and in hides and skins, late 1942. Many agricultural commodities, among them cottonseed oil and black pepper, felt the pinch in 1943, and butter trading stopped entirely, going from a staple item to something of a rare delicacy for the balance of the war. Meat became scarce as well and remained so until 1946. Despite the many inconveniences, not much dissent was heard from traders, who understood that the normal factors affecting the markets were seriously out of kilter.

Although the grain exchanges escaped closing during the war, some did close after the war ended. The major grain exchanges suspended operations in June 1946 because of the temporary price controls. Within a month, however, the exchanges were again open and reported record one-day price increases on almost all commodities. Grain prices rose in some cases by 40 cents per bushel as OPA controls were discontinued and prices were free again. Within hours of the OPA demise, many exchanges relaxed their OPA margin requirements so that speculation could resume to prewar levels.

The exchanges opened with great fanfare, especially for trading the lesser-known commodities that were vital to the war effort. The Commodity Exchange (COMEX) in New York resumed trading in hides in November 1946, four-and-a-half years after trading was halted. Curiously, it was the hide market that first attracted the young Jay Gould a century before, giving him his first taste of futures trading. Although only a handful of contracts were traded, the opening price was almost twice that of the previous close in 1942. The exchange, which traded mostly metals at the time, watched the price of a seat increase almost fivefold since the trading halt, at which time it traded at $600. By 1946, a seat sold for $3,000.

Almost as soon as the exchanges were operating again, pit traders reverted to their old tactics, attempting corners either for themselves or for others. In 1947, the Great Western Food Distributors attempted a corner on the CME's December egg futures contracts. The company's long position exceeded the total stock of available eggs in Chicago during December. It was not the first time that a company attempted a corner rather than a pit trader. The CBOT suspended the Cargill Grain Co. during the 1930s for similar antics, although it reinstated the company shortly thereafter. The CBOT suspended Great Western in 1940 for attempting to corner butter futures and again in 1949 for attempting to corner eggs. The CME became so alarmed at the last corner that it suspended the October contract in eggs, and outstanding contracts had to be delivered or negotiated at a specific price.[29]

Old tactics were adopted in the pits after the war, in the late 1940s, because of rapid increases in consumer and wholesale prices. Volatility returned to the commodities markets, attracting speculators to the pits again after years of limited trading. Most other financial markets did not react well to price volatility but the futures markets demonstrated that they thrived on it; without it, their functions could not be fulfilled. Hedgers would have little reason to hedge and speculators would disappear without the prospect of being able to scalp. The post–World War II period was not the first time this old principle had been demonstrated, although it did underline the fact that the futures markets marched to their own tune and would continue to do so during this period.

The presence of federal agencies during the 1930s and the war years was not an indictment of the futures markets. Even if the markets had been able to achieve some price stability for farmers, other agricultural problems were outside their scope of influence. Increasing production, cyclical swings in supply, and changes in consumer tastes all affected the markets and were factors well outside the markets' influence. As an intermediary in the process of production, the markets' main job was to provide prices for future delivery that benefited farmers and processors. How well they provided the services depended upon the intent of the users and conditions in the cash, or physicals, markets. However, there was still a general discontent on how the markets provided their basic services. The assumption was that futures prices were wagging the dog by abnormally affecting the cash prices rather than the other way around.

Normally, futures prices were expected to be a reflection of not only the current cash price for a commodity but also other factors, such as the cost of storage and expectations over the short term. When short sellers or corners focused on specific future delivery months and began their operations, however, the cash market often swung wildly in price as other traders tried to determine what effect such operations would have on them. Short sellers often were forced to start buying in the cash market to cover themselves or the longs might start selling. In the prewar years, almost since the time that the CBOT and other exchanges began trading, the link between the futures and cash markets was more than theoretical; it was distinct, causing the farmers woe at many times, especially when least expected. A question of primary importance was whether this link would continue or whether the futures markets would develop into more sophisticated hedging and speculative markets during the postwar years. Only time would tell.

## NOTES

1. *New York Times,* September 21, 1930.
2. Ibid.
3. Ibid.
4. Ibid., September 23, 1930.
5. *Magazine of Wall Street,* November 29, 1930.
6. Ibid., September 27, 1930.
7. Reported in the *New York Times,* January 13, 1935.
8. *Magazine of Wall Street,* November 29, 1930.
9. [Clinton Gilbert], *The Mirrors of Wall Street* (New York: Putnam, 1933), p. 255. The book was published anonymously.
10. Bernard Baruch, *My Own Story* (New York: Holt, Rinehart & Winston, 1957), p. 51.
11. Walter Lippmann, *Interpretations, 1931–1932* (New York: Macmillan, 1932), p. 325.
12. Charles R. Geisst, *Wall Street: A History* (New York: Oxford University Press, 1997), p. 210 ff.
13. Peter Bernstein, *The Power of Gold: The History of An Obsession* (New York: John Wiley & Sons, 2000), p. 321.
14. Harold L. Ickes, *The Secret Diary of Harold L. Ickes: The First Thousand Days* (New York: Simon & Schuster, 1953), p. 566.
15. Willard W. Cochrane, *The Development of American Agriculture* (Minneapolis: University of Minnesota Press, 1979), p. 141.
16. Herbert Hoover, *The Challenge to Liberty* (New York: Charles Scribner's Sons, 1934), p. 88.

17. Gallup polls of January 5, 1936, and December 19, 1937. See George H. Gallup, *The Gallup Poll: Public Opinion 1935–1971* (New York: Random House, 1972), pp. 9, 79.

18. *New York Times*, September 13, 1931.

19. *New York Times*, August 24, 1932.

20. Ibid., November 17, 1934.

21. Commodity Exchange Act, US Code, Title 7, Section 6.

22. *Time*, January 20, 1936.

23. *Daily News*, January 13, 1936.

24. *Wallace v. Cutten*, 298 US 229 (1936).

25. Bob Tamarkin, *The MERC: The Emergence of a Global Financial Powerhouse* (New York: HarperBusiness, 1993), p. 62.

26. Jesse H. Jones, *Fifty Billion Dollars: My Thirteen Years with the RFC* (New York: Macmillan, 1951), p. 88.

27. *New York Times*, May 14, 1941.

28. Gallup polls of February 19 and October 4, 1941. The February poll, concerning a national lottery, was most strongly supported in the Northeast, with 60 percent favoring it. It was least popular in the Midwest, where only 39 percent favored it. See Gallup, *Gallup Poll*, pp. 264, 300.

29. Tamarkin, *The MERC*, p. 85.

# CHAPTER 4

# EXPANDING THE MENU

ESPITE YEARS OF BAD PUBLICITY AND ATTACKS BY critics, the futures markets survived the World War II years remarkably free of regulation. The Commodity Exchange Act of 1936 put a regulator in place, but its effectiveness was questionable. Policy makers paid attention to the markets only when complaints mounted and could no longer be ignored. If a national crisis developed, as it did during both world wars, the government could always effectively shutter the markets or regulate prices. Over the years, the futures markets were just lucky. Stocks were more popular and attracted the most public attention. Despite their importance in ensuring the stable flow of commodities at firm prices, the futures markets were still considered somewhat marginal to an industrialized nation moving further away from agriculture.

The financial markets only became free of regulatory influences after the Korean War. Price controls were halted, causing commodity prices to rise, and the Federal Reserve relaxed its control of interest rates, marking the end of extraordinary measures that had kept the markets restrained since the begin-

PENNSYLVANIA BEEF CONTRACTOR. "Want Beefsteak? Good Gracious, what is the World coming to? Why, my Good Fellow, if you get Beefsteak, how on earth are Contractors to live? Tell me that."

Thomas Nast in *Harper's Weekly*, August 17, 1861.

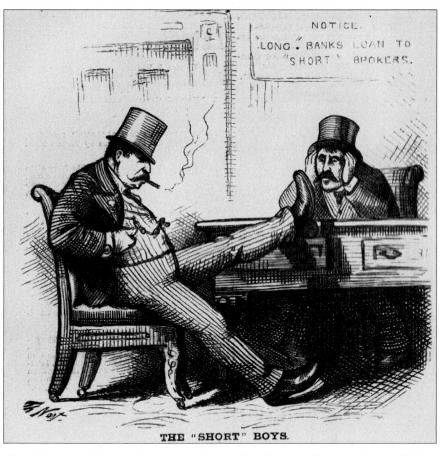

THE "SHORT" BOYS.

The "short boys" lamenting their bad luck. By Thomas Nast in *Harper's Weekly*, October 18, 1873.

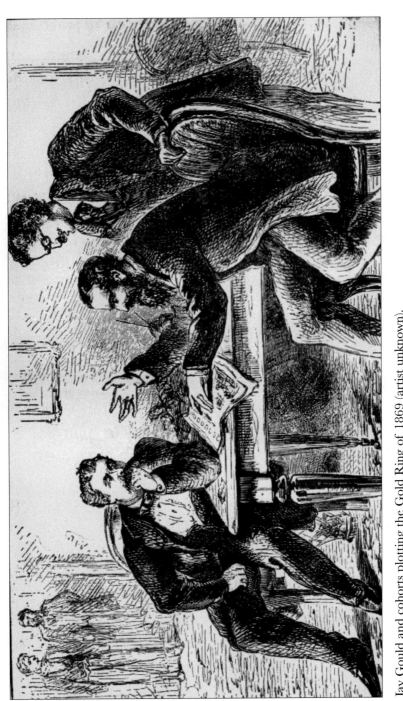

Jay Gould and cohorts plotting the Gold Ring of 1869 (artist unknown).

The Liverpool Cotton Exchange, 1881. Courtesy of Liverpool Cotton Association.

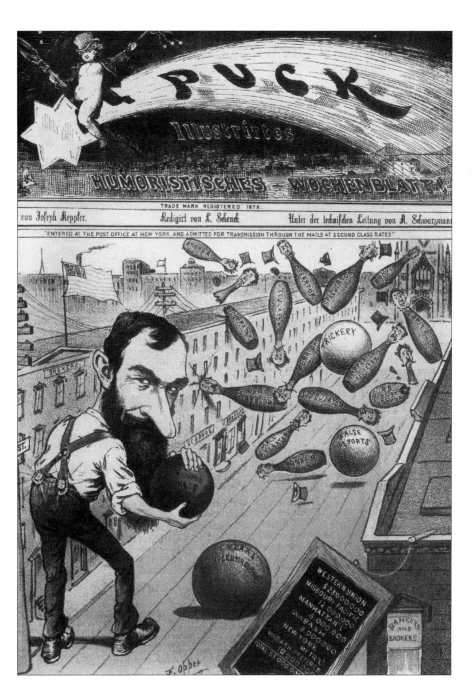

Jay Gould using Wall Street as a bowling alley. By F. Opper in the German edition of *Puck*, March 29, 1882.

An artist's sketch of Benjamin P. Hutchinson.

EXCHANGE HALL OF THE CHICAGO BOARD OF TRADE.

CBOT Exchange Hall, 1895. Courtesy of the CBOT.

A CBOT runner, circa 1895. Courtesy of the CBOT.

A CBOT chalkboard, circa 1895. Courtesy of the CBOT.

The wheat pit at the CBOT, circa 1900.

Hennessy LeRoyle as the wheat king in "Other People's Money." Courtesy of the Library of Congress.

A bucket shop, circa 1900.

The wheat pit at the CBOT, 1925.

The New York Corn Exchange, circa 1890.

The New York Coffee Exchange, circa 1890.

Arthur Cutten, by Seymour Marcus.

A contemporary CBOT trading floor. Courtesy of the CBOT.

ning of World War II. After the Korean War, the stock markets began their first prolonged rally since the 1920s and the economic picture was brighter than at any time in 20 years. Despite the prosperity, the futures markets still managed to stumble politically. Antifutures forces gained their first significant victory over the markets since the Hatch bill was passed 60 years before. On this occasion, the victory was a real one.

At the beginning of the 1950s, Wall Street scored a major victory in the courts when a judge threw out an antitrust case filed by the Justice Department against 17 investment banks, alleging violations of the antitrust laws. The case was reminiscent of the Nye hearings, charging collusion among investment bankers since World War I. It was, however, dismissed for lack of conclusive evidence. As a result, Wall Street's star began rising both socially and politically. Being a stockbroker was no longer a matter of opprobrium, as it had been in the 1930s, but was now a profession admired by the public. Washington and Wall Street began to forge ties not seen since the 1920s. Business conditions were better than any in recent memory, and growth became an acceptable market term again, not just a synonym for a market bubble.

On LaSalle Street and in the New York commodity markets, conditions also were improving. Commodities prices began to rise, and domestic consumption again fueled demand for agricultural products. However, futures brokers were far behind their Wall Street counterparts. Marketing to the small investor was not yet a well-established art. In the 1950s, the large wire-house brokers such as Merrill Lynch, E. F. Hutton, Bache, and Dean Witter rapidly expanded their operations nationwide to cater to the retail investor, a growing source of investment funds. The commodities brokers remained specialized, however. Their business increased during the 1950s and 1960s, but those were nevertheless to be the decades of Wall Street, not LaSalle Street.

The long-standing differences between Wall Street and LaSalle Street persisted through the 1950s and 1960s. The securities business was still a gentleman's preserve, with good connections and education important for success. LaSalle Street, on the other hand, was a rough-and-tumble place where education did not spell success by any means. Only pit instincts ensured survival. Former runners, truck drivers, physicians, and college instructors occupied the same trading pits as MBAs and professional traders. Floor trading on Wall Street was hardly polite but it still was less frantic than the open-outcry pit trading of LaSalle Street. The occasional fistfight still occurred in the pits when trading became heated. The commodity futures markets had no other polite side to their business. Trading was all that existed; there was no investment banking or corporate finance side to the futures markets, only the pits.

The rough-and-tumble side of the markets did not help when times got tough. Futures traders traditionally had little political influence and almost no powerful connections in Washington. When Congress applied pressure in the past, traders always managed to escape through a combination of good luck and serendipity. When the Pecora committee pursued Wall Street bankers in the early 1930s, the futures markets remarkably kept away from (but not above) the fray. Even the Commodity Exchange Act of 1936 was less stringent than its securities counterpart and had less bite to it. At the heart of the problem was the futures markets' relative importance to the economy as a whole, especially when compared to Wall Street. After 100 years of development, they were well established and considered necessary for the development of commodity prices, but beyond that, they were not considered legitimate financial markets. Being purely secondary (trading) markets, they did not raise capital for investment, nor was their influence felt far from the agricultural heartland. When compared with Wall Street, LaSalle Street's importance was still regional at best.

146

# EXPANDING THE MENU

Marketing futures trading to the wider investing public was not an easy job. Although not difficult to understand, the large contract amounts in which the futures markets traded could be daunting to the small investor. Even though margin requirements were low, most knowledgeable retail traders realized that they would have to be quick when trading their accounts, acting more like a scalper in the pits than a long-term investor. As a result, futures contracts were not easily marketable unless the risks and rewards associated with trading were understood. The days of the bucket shop were long gone and investors now had to be informed of the pitfalls involved in trading.

Nevertheless, futures market operations made strides. Many of the large stockbrokers acquired futures brokers or trading firms, incorporating them into their overall operations. In 1941, Merrill Lynch acquired Fenner & Beane, a commodities broker, and merged the operations into its own. The new firm was then called Merrill Lynch Pierce Fenner & Beane. As a result of the acquisition, Merrill Lynch gained access to the smaller firm's seats on the commodities exchanges. Although Merrill Lynch offered commodity brokerage to its clients, part of its strategy also was to employ the futures markets for the firm's own proprietary trading, by which it traded for its own account rather than for customers. As Don Regan, president of Merrill Lynch noted, the income from commodities trading often complemented commission revenues from brokerage operations. Selling the public on futures trading would not generate much commission revenue by itself for commissions on futures trading were often quite small when compared with stock trading, where costs could be scaled up as the value of the trade increased for retail investors. Large futures traders demanded—and received—flat commission rates that declined in percentage terms as the number of contracts increased. Only the most active traders proved profitable for brokers, a structural anomaly that became a sore point for the markets during the early 1960s, leading to the largest financial swindle yet recorded.

Despite the miscues and their growth, the futures markets began to take on a more serious aura in the post–World War II years. Futures prices began to be studied by academic and professional economists and many of the old shibboleths about the markets began to be challenged. Did cash (spot) and futures prices have any correlation as the Farm Bloc maintained or were they separate as the futures markets had asserted over the years? The markets began to attract as much study as stock price behavior and the scrutiny would do much to help the markets develop some integrity, which was greatly needed. However, trading scandals were always on the horizon, as they had been for decades, and showed no sign of abating.

## *ONION SOUP*

Over the years, new futures contracts constantly were being introduced to the mix traded on the exchanges. Some contracts succeeded while others failed. The only way to test the viability of a contract was to open it for trading and see whether traders would adopt it. Ordinarily, trading in a contract reflected the importance of the commodity itself and the way the contract was structured by the exchanges. In 1942, one of the more elusive contracts was introduced by the CME when it began onion futures trading.

The onion contract was an attempt by the CME to reinvigorate itself during wartime. Its two traditional mainstays—eggs and butter—suffered when the butter contract ceased trading for the duration of the war. Butter trading never revived and some contracts subsequently introduced failed to generate much enthusiasm. As a result, onions began to be traded quite actively, perhaps more than that suggested by their economic role on the farm. While commonplace in the kitchen, onions were not considered agricultural staples. They became one of the most volatile contracts in the entire futures market, experiencing wild price swings that often crashed outside the daily limit movements. While pit traders loved them, frequently harsh criticism arose among onion growers who claimed that the trading was hurting them economically by its deleterious effect on cash prices.

Originally, onion futures did not fall under the aegis of the Commodity Exchange Act. New contracts were slow to be included under the act, and the trading patterns reflected this. Onion prices were volatile, whereas price controls were still in effect in the early 1950s. The CEC issued notice that it was beginning to monitor the price of onions in 1952 after they had risen almost $1.00 per sack. Yellow onions had to be shipped from Texas or California, where most were grown, and then forwarded to Chicago for delivery. Because of where they were grown, yellow onions had a rarity value despite being a common household item. Traders naturally thought that they could predict the supply and they speculated accordingly. Three onion growers from California soon discovered that trading onions was far more profitable than growing them. They traveled to Chicago from California in late winter 1953 to buy onions because their own crop was late. Only a few months before, onions were so plentiful that supermarkets were giving away free bags of them with other purchases just to reduce their inventories. The growers intended to buy up to $1 million worth on the CME and proceeded to spend about half that amount, buying March futures between $2.80 and $3.00 per sack. They happened to make their trip at a time when the CME was doing record business. Overly wet weather threatened the supply of onions and prices quickly advanced. The price of their contracts soon increased to $4.30 per sack, netting them a profit of $180,000 in 10 days. The price would be a record.

Heavy trading in all commodities helped increase the price of seats on the exchanges. In 1952, the price of a CBOT seat was $4,000, but within a year it doubled. Similarly, the price of a CME seat jumped to $4,500 in 1954. Both were the highest prices recorded since the Depression. Moreover, the mercantile exchanges also began to offer trading in foods, a new departure from the traditional wholesale agricultural commodities. The New York Merc introduced broiler chicken contracts and frozen poultry contracts in 1954 and other exchanges quickly followed suit. Futures trading had not been so active since the 1930s.

Within a year of the run-up in onion prices, the Senate approved a bill to put onion futures under the aegis of the Commodity Exchange Authority (CEA). The price volatility caused Congress to put onions under the same guidelines as other commodities so that the CEA could look into the markets' and traders' activities if necessary. Coffee also came under the same scrutiny. Senator Guy Gillette, a Democrat from Iowa, tacked coffee onto the onion bill in Congress, causing both commodities to be regulated. Coffee also had been rising in price, and Gillette claimed that each 5 cent rise in its price cost consumers $1 billion in additional expenses. When retail coffee prices hit $1.00 per pound, there was a loud cry from homemakers and consumer groups over the cost. Food contracts were beginning to draw attention. A New York City coffee roaster was convicted of fraud and sentenced to prison for adulterating coffee with cereal to take advantage of higher prices.

One young runner employed on the CME at the time that onion trading was heating up was Leo Melamed, who took the job to help put himself through law school at night. After working his way through the ranks, Melamed became president of the CME and one of the futures markets' more popular figures. Like more senior officials on the CME, all he could do was watch in amazement as Congress debated a ban on onion futures. The straw that broke the camel's back was the speculation in the onion contract that attracted the California farmers. That long-dated contract traded as high as $2.50 per bag in 1955 then plunged to a low of 15 cents near its expiration date. Onions had fallen into a Depression-like trap where it was no longer economical to harvest them. Years of speculation, accompanied by loud criticisms from consumers and farmers alike finally prodded Congress to act. In the House vote on a possible ban, a Republican congressman from Maine, Clifford McIntire, tried to jump on the bandwagon and get Irish potatoes—which he also claimed had become extremely volatile— attached to the bill, but he was ruled out of order.[1]

The CME adopted the position that activities on the floor were beyond its control, with traders simply reacting to supply and demand as they perceived them. To a House subcommittee investigating onion futures, CME President Everette B. Harris said, "The futures market does not in any way set prices. We merely furnish the hall for trading and what we hope are fair and equitable prices . . . we are like a thermometer, which registers temperatures. You would not want to pass a law against thermometers just because we had a short spell of zero weather or break a barometer because the air pressure fell."[2] Unfortunately, the argument was an old one that had never fully convinced critics. But never did anyone imagine the result of this latest bout of antifutures fervor, especially after 100 years of market history.

Finally, the unthinkable occurred in May 1958 when Congress banned onion futures trading. The onion debate enlisted some later familiar names on both sides on the aisle. Senator Paul Douglas, Democrat of Illinois and an economist, argued in favor of futures trading generally and did not favor curtailing trading in any commodity. Michigan farmers seeking an end to speculation enlisted the help of Representative Gerald

Ford, a Republican, in their quest to have trading banned, along with Senator Hubert Humphrey, Democrat of Minnesota. Both were convinced by the National Onion Growers Association that speculation was rife and that prices were being destroyed by the old bête noire of farmers, short selling. The law left the CME and the New York Merc, which also traded onions, startled. In the turbulent history of the futures markets, this was the first time that trading in a specific commodity was banned. Onions hardly seemed that significant. An appeals court upheld the ban in 1959.

The CME sought outside help and hired Archibald Cox as its adviser and counsel. Cox would later gain fame as the Watergate counsel fired by President Richard Nixon. After studying the CME's problem, he advised that the exchange not appeal the ban. He advised that an appeal might bring more unwanted attention and possibly even lead to more troubles for the exchange. The CME was not politically influential, and the other exchanges had done nothing to fight the ban in principle other than offer their moral support.[3] As a group, the exchanges did not have a powerful industry association or lobby group to argue their cause in Washington. For all practical purposes, the CME reverted to being a one-commodity exchange: eggs were its only successful contract. If the exchange wanted to survive, it would need to acquire new contracts quickly. Its membership therefore set about studying new products in the late 1950s.

Fast-moving developments in the markets finally led the CBOT to elect a full-time paid president in 1956. It selected 33-year-old Robert Liebenow, a lawyer and previously board secretary, to be its CEO. Liebenow was the first nonmember elected to the job and his salary was not disclosed. The choice demonstrated the success of the CBOT during the 1950s as economic conditions improved substantially. In 1955, the CBOT transacted over $32 billion worth of business, representing more than 400 million bushels of cash grain and 13 million bushels of grain futures. Its membership was actually lower than at the beginning of the century, with around 1,450 members comprising producers, wholesalers, traders, and warehousemen from around the globe. It also employed over 200 support staff.[4] Although other exchanges were gaining quickly, the CBOT remained the major commodity futures market of the period.

By the late 1950s, futures exchanges were doing active business although their customers were the usual array of hedgers and speculators. Small investors also played the markets but their numbers did not approach the increasing numbers attracted to stock investments. Retail futures speculators were a fairly specialized group, usually understanding the risks and rewards of speculation. Margin requirements differed for the different types of activity. Hedgers had lower margin requirements than speculators, who had to put up more cash because of the intrinsic riskiness of their activities. Straddlers had lower requirements than both hedgers and speculators, since they were long and short at the same time and the combination of the two positions reduced their trading risk.[5] For the most part, however, margins were generally low to begin with and the differences in requirements for the various classes of activity were mostly nominal, in keeping with regulations imposed by the CEA.

As the economy progressed, it became evident that the markets' success depended largely upon the comfort of hedgers who used the futures exchanges to ensure a steady supply of raw commodities at a price known at the present. One large firm, Corn Products Refining Co., with extensive dealings in futures markets hedged its operations in the 1930s and 1940s to protect against the Depression-era price swings that had caused so much trouble for traders and farmers. The company was one of the largest manufacturers of products made from corn, including starch, syrup, sugars, and animal feeds.

The wildly fluctuating price of corn in the mid-1930s caused the company to start purchasing corn futures contracts to ensure itself a steady supply in the years ahead. If the company subsequently found that it had too many contracts, it would simply sell the excess and keep the balance of the long positions for delivery. The method was standard among processors of agricultural products and from the late 1930s to the early 1940s the company used about 65 million bushels a year. Later, the company claimed that the profits and losses from these positions involved capital assets, not short-term trading profits or losses. By making this claim, it sought favorable tax treatment. However, the lower courts disagreed with the claim and the case found itself before the Supreme Court. In the past, the high court did much to help define the role of futures markets and this case was no exception.

The court ruled that the company's transactions produced only ordinary profits or losses. In doing so, it helped establish several terms that would be used in later years to describe the role of futures markets. Justice Tom Clark wrote that "it appears that the transactions were vitally important to the company's business as a form of insurance against increases in the price of raw corn . . . it is difficult to imagine a program more closely geared to a company's manufacturing enterprise or more important to its successful operation."[6] Simply put, buying for future delivery was a normal part of the company's operations and could not be segregated for any special tax treatment.

This case became a milestone in the evolution of the futures markets. It demonstrated how the idea of buying and selling for future delivery had become so clearly established in the markets that it was now considered part of the ordinary process of doing business. The company's claim was actually something of an anachronism, for the hedging process had already become thoroughly ingrained in the agribusiness over the years. In the 50 years since the *Christie* decision, the language of the court amply illustrated the progress that the futures markets had made in becoming an integral part of the manufacturing and processing processes.

In the late 1950s, the bull market on Wall Street presented an opportunity for the New York Merc. The exchange introduced a plan to open a subsidiary stock exchange in 1959. The National Stock Exchange was established and planned to trade smaller stocks than those traded on the NYSE, intending to become a competitor with the American Stock Exchange. It was not the first time the name was used. The first National Stock Exchange was a short-lived attempt by Daniel Drew and Cornelius Vanderbilt after the Civil War to establish an exchange to vie with the NYSE. The pedigree of the proposed exchange was better, however. Its counsel was James M. Landis, former chairman of the SEC, whose support would give the exchange validity. He claimed that the new exchange would be preferable to having stocks trade over-the-counter (OTC), as many small issues did, because the new exchange would have to list them and presumably give the SEC a greater measure of control.[7] Landis' reputation as no friend of the NYSE in the mid-1930s gave the application serious credence. He was known for years as favoring strict control of stock trading. The argument was successful but the new market never developed into a first-class arena for stock trading and remained a small exchange for second-rate issues.

The price of a New York Merc seat at the time was only about $4,300. An NYSE seat sold for $135,000, so traders had little to lose by buying a seat as a speculative investment. The Merc recognized this and made one of its commodity seats a prerequisite for a stock exchange seat. The price then increased accordingly. However, the exchange was fighting an uphill battle for the NYSE and the American Stock Exchange were now well-established and recognizable names in the markets. Then, with a dreadful sense of timing, a new scandal arose to cast a cloud over all the markets.

## INSALATA VERDE

The post–World War II years were a crucial time for the futures markets. After the onion ban, the markets appeared to be chastened and developments suggested that they were moving into the mainline of financial markets more so than at any time in the twentieth century. The activities of pit traders were not, as would soon be discovered, the only concern for the markets. The activities of a former meat packer from Bayonne, New Jersey, would give the markets their largest collective black eye ever and taint their reputation for almost a generation.

Anthony "Tino" De Angelis was born in the Bronx in 1915, the son of an immigrant family of modest means. Demonstrating little talent at school, he dropped out at age 16 to become a meat packer. He made his reputation by his adroit efficiency with a meat cleaver. Able to dismember hogs on a moving production line while jogging alongside, De Angelis quickly found his forte in the meat-processing business. After opening his own processing company during the Depression with borrowed money, he became quite successful providing provisions for the government during World War II. After the war ended, he moved his company operations from New York to New Jersey and began selling meat to foreign governments. Almost from the beginning, its operations were plagued with legal troubles. Complaints abounded regarding delivery problems and the inferior quality of his meats.

Lacking education and not being well spoken, the portly 5-foot-5-inch, 250-pound De Angelis did not pay particular care to the fine points of his business, even at an early stage. Frequently, he was sued by his foreign clients for delivering substandard meat. His litigation and tax problems soon forced him into bankruptcy court in the early 1950s. Then in the mid-1950s, he recognized an opportunity created by the overproduction of agricultural commodities, a problem that usually plagued others in the commodity business. At the time, the United States was producing a surplus of vegetable oil derivatives which were heavily in demand in other countries. These oil derivatives, including soybean and cottonseed oils, became known simply as salad oils although they were used in a variety of foods as additives. Once De Angelis recognized their potential, the basis was laid for the largest financial fraud in American history.

After organizing the Allied Crude Vegetable Oil Refining Corp., De Angelis began his fraud in the port section of Bayonne, New Jersey. Beginning with a small amount of capital, he acquired large petroleum storage tanks and had them cleaned, refurbished, and converted into storage tanks for vegetable oil. From this port location, he was able to ship vegetable oil to his foreign buyers. Almost immediately, the company's sales began to skyrocket. De Angelis was highly successful, selling oils abroad at prices that his competitors thought were ruinous. The mechanics of the selling operation operated under the general auspices of the federal government which was supporting an export program called Food for Peace. This program was used to sell American agricultural surplus to foreign countries through a labyrinthine operation designed to off-load the surplus. However, the former meat packer understood its intricacies well. By most estimates, De Angelis was selling more than 75 percent of exported vegetable oils.

Allied itself did not crush the beans needed for the oils but instead bought the oils from traditional Midwest manufacturers who had been in business for years. To get the oils expeditiously, De Angelis would pay slightly above market prices. "He paid quote 'fantastic prices' for vegetable oil," one executive said. "He would pay ¼ of a cent per pound for soybean salad oil over the rest of the trade."[8] De Angelis apparently was buying high and selling low, a formula that should have led to ruin. By all accounts, however, his company was highly successful, and the rotund, giggling De Angelis appeared to be rolling in disposable cash. While not the most appealing businessman, he seemed to have the producers and buyers of vegetable oils convinced that he indeed was the "salad oil king."

By the late 1950s, the commodities had a new king but not of the wheat pits. De Angelis remained a supplier rather than a pit trader although he did buy a CBOT seat. His enormous buying power held the attention if not the respect of the commodities business. He could not, however, escape his past. The SEC and the Internal Revenue Service pursued him periodically for his activities in the meat-packing business. He also kept himself surrounded with some unsavory characters who were on the payroll as aids or administrative assistants. Occasionally, a foreign buyer would complain that the salad oil bought from Allied was of poor or inedible quality. Despite his past foibles, De Angelis was acknowledged as the most successful supplier of salad oils and was courted by food processors and bankers alike. Clearly, his operation was unorthodox, but nobody seemed to care as long as he continued to buy huge amounts of oils from the Midwest processors.

De Angelis was able to accomplish the seemingly impossible by defrauding the well-established American Express Co. out of millions of dollars. One of the company's subsidiaries was involved in inventory financings. In the commodities business, the financing took the form of issuing warehouse receipts. Based upon an inventory of commodities on hand—in this case, salad oil in the Bayonne, New Jersey, tanks—a trading firm would issue a receipt using the commodity as collateral. The receipt could then be used as collateral itself if the firm needed a loan. If the firm faltered, the inventory could be liquidated to repay the loan. Many banks turned down requests from De Angelis for guarantees in the 1950s but American Express embraced it and began issuing receipts based upon the amount of oil that Allied claimed it had in the tanks.

The problem was that De Angelis overstated that amount by vast quantities. On the odd occasion when an inspector was sent by a creditor to Bayonne to check on the operation, De Angelis would have dummy amounts of oil put in special compartments in tanks otherwise filled with water. When the inspectors inserted a dipstick into the tanks full of water they would register oil instead. Incredibly, most of Allied's lenders never diligently checked the tanks beyond these spot checks conducted infrequently to see whether the oils were actually stored in Bayonne as De Angelis claimed. Allied was a legitimate exporter of salad oils but the scale of its operation was not. It was difficult to determine whether the company was corrupt from its very beginning or became corrupt only after the business had started to succeed but such a distinction made little difference. De Angelis' cunning, as well as some major oversights by his lenders, allowed the business to prosper. By 1961, American Express issued receipts for over 170 million pounds of oil when Allied had only 60 million pounds in its tanks. Nevertheless, the 110-million-pound difference was pledged against loans, amounting to millions of dollars. Allied's bank account was over $165 million at the time, the entire amount of which was in the form of cash advances against the receipts.[9] Basically, Allied was printing money using American Express' guarantee.

The fraud was maintained throughout the later 1950s and continued into the 1960s. De Angelis was successful at selling salad oil abroad although he apparently believed that organized groups were out to get him. He had a particular distrust of the Catholic organization Opus Dei, which had substantial influence in Spain, especially during the Franco dictatorship. He consistently believed that social and political forces conspired against him and were becoming even more successful. That paranoia eventually led to events that caused his downfall.

Like many commodities dealers, De Angelis became involved with the futures markets in the early 1960s and quickly became hooked on trading. He began trading on the New York Produce Exchange and on the CBOT, the two homes of salad oil futures. He was able to do so without much fear of the CEA, although that agency was the watchdog of the markets. The agency was poorly staffed in the early 1960s; it had less than 120 employees altogether, of which only 25 were investigators and auditors needed to patrol the futures markets.[10] As it turned out, doubling the number of investigators would not have prevented De Angelis from dominating the markets. All sorts of theories abounded regarding the nature of his trading. Because he was in the salad oil business, many assumed that he was a hedger. However, his background and track record up to that time suggested something different.

While the fraud concerning warehouse receipts was in full swing, De Angelis began speculating in salad oils on the New York Produce Exchange and the CBOT. He sold a large amount of oil to the Spanish government and needed to cover his supply because his tanks were short of the required amount. The Spaniards reneged on the offer. De Angelis claimed that Opus Dei was actively working against him since the conservative organization did not fully recognize his genius. He was now long in the futures markets, however, and selling his contracts would have created a loss. So, he employed what he considered the next best strategy. He continued to buy.

Allied's machinations in the futures markets originally were confined to smaller Chicago futures brokers but they soon spilled over to Wall Street. One firm approached by De Angelis was Ira Haupt & Co., a brokerage house better known for its stock market presence than its commodities brokerage. The firm was a partnership, as were most Wall Street brokerage houses of the day. In fact, the firm knew so little about futures trading that some of its senior executives admitted to never having visited their own commodities department as well as not understanding that side of the brokerage business. They could appreciate the fact that De Angelis was already a large trader in futures and that the commission business he could bring to them would certainly help their bottom line. The only way that futures commissions proved successful was by high-volume trading and De Angelis certainly filled the bill.

Trading on the CBOT was substantial and Allied had open positions of more than 3,000 contracts. That represented about 200 million pounds of oil, of which De Angelis had no intention of taking delivery. To forestall delivery problems, he rolled over contracts (swapped close delivery months for those further out in time) at small losses and found money to buy even more by forging warehouse receipts drawn on American Express. Eventually, he persuaded Ira Haupt & Co. to accept the warehouse receipts as margin against his account so that he would not have to pay any cash up front for his speculations. Basically, he was using worthless receipts to buy on margin. Some of the better-known brokers, including Merrill Lynch and Shearson, declined his proposition for similar financing so it fell to the smaller firms to pick up the slack. The end was in sight for Ira Haupt & Co. when the firm accepted the receipts.

By spring 1963, De Angelis' trading was attracting unwanted attention. He was suspended from trading on the CBOT. Then, several months later, he was expelled from his personal seat on the CBOT for unauthorized trading. The CBOT was quick to point out that Allied was not a member of the exchange; only De Angelis was. That action came after the CEA detected that he was using dummy accounts to mask his activities. However, the CBOT action was the only one taken. The CEA failed to act immediately against Allied and would be sorry for its oversight. In the interim, the massive speculation was hurting De Angelis' business by forcing up the cash price for oils and beans. With high prices, foreign buyers were less inclined to purchase from him so he was doing himself double damage.

His brokers' activities in the pits suggested that a massive corner was underway. De Angelis would order his brokers to place large buy orders at the end of each trading day, presumably to force the price higher at the close. Doing so ensured that no margin notices would be sent out on his accounts since the price finished each day strong rather than weak. Danger signs were developing that could not be ignored, however. In August 1963, De Angelis held 79 percent of cottonseed oil futures on the New York Produce Exchange and 40 percent of soybean oil contracts on the CBOT.[11] He mounted a classic corner in the tradition of Hutchinson and Cutten. The classic pit traders, however, always had a plan when they entered the pits to begin cornering. De Angelis never had a plan; he simply hoped for a lucky break to bail him out.

De Angelis practiced the traditional tricks of the corner, which suggests that he might have had some professional but unnamed assistance in his operations. A rumor began to circulate in the pits that perhaps the high prices were justified after all because the Soviets planned to buy a massive amount of oil from Allied. As it turned out De Angelis himself began these rumors. The attempted corner in soybeans and cottonseed oil also underlined the weaknesses of the CEA. Striking a chord that would have sounded familiar at the time of Arthur Cutten, the CEA claimed that its hands were tied until De Angelis actually violated the law. They saw no immediate evidence of a corner or manipulation. Mounting a large position was, in their opinion, not a violation of any rules, although the dummy trading accounts probably would have proved a corner conclusively. Of course, the size of the positions should have been sufficient evidence. By fall 1963, De Angelis held 22,600 contracts worth $160 million. The precarious nature of the positions was clear to all. A 1-cent drop in the market price of the positions would have cost him over $13 million in margin calls at the end of any trading day. It is not surprising that he did his buying toward the close of a business day. Allied's trading accounted for 90 percent of the contracts outstanding on the New York Produce Exchange. Ira Haupt & Co. alone purchased over 70 percent of the cottonseed contracts for him.[12] The CEA reported the numbers to the exchanges. Apparently, the transparency created by the CEA did serve some useful purpose after all.

De Angelis finally ran out of both time and money. An investigator from the CEA informed him that the agency finally was beginning an investigation into his trading activities. By then, he had been involved in what was the last stage of his market deception but he was unable to finish the operation because of the investigation and, as a result, ran out of time and money. Quickly, he attempted to declare Allied bankrupt so that he could stave off his creditors. His timing was poor, however. Word had reached the trading pits of his troubles and salad oil prices began to fall precipitously. The losses triggered margin calls, which De Angelis was unable to meet.

The immediate problem reached Ira Haupt & Co. very quickly. The firm soon fell below its capital requirements mandated by the SEC for brokerage firms and it became insolvent. The rudest shock came when the firm discovered that all the warehouse receipts it held as collateral were worthless. The firm was a partnership and its capital (partners' funds) was not adequate to meet its obligations. After much debate, the NYSE forced the firm to liquidate. It joined a very small list of firms that had met a similar fate over the years. The NYSE acted to demonstrate that it was in control of the situation and that it wanted to assure Haupt's customers and others that business could continue as usual despite the liquidation. Although it clearly was too little too late, the NYSE's actions were exemplary when compared with those of the futures exchanges involved.

The revelations came at a critical moment in American history. While the De Angelis affair was making headlines, President Kennedy was assassinated on November 22, 1963, sparking a national crisis. Since the news of De Angelis' plight first hit the futures exchanges, short selling became heavy in salad oil and in other commodities. The New York Produce Exchange had closed temporarily before Kennedy's assassination to assess its problems. Activity on the CBOT was heavy, with prices continuing to fall as the positions were unwound by forced margin selling by De Angelis' brokers to close his longs. The commodities exchanges said little to assuage public fears. The futures exchanges were, after all, traders' exchanges, so as soon as the traders' positions were squared there was little more to be heard from them.

Robert Liebenow stated that the CBOT's activities could not be construed as a cause of the scandal. "The losses suffered by people who dealt with the bankrupt Allied Crude Vegetable Oil Refining Co. of Bayonne, N.J. are in no way connected with commodity exchanges," he stated emphatically in December 1963, well after the damage had been done.[13] Nevertheless, the CBOT passed some new regulations in the wake of the scandal but they did not seem reassuring. The most obvious of them was imposed on warehouse receipts, which now could not be used as collateral for margin lending unless the warehouse itself could be inspected easily. American Express had that opportunity with Allied but never pursued its doubts about De Angelis, even though the Bayonne tanks were only a short commute from its New York City headquarters. Another regulation placed limits on the number of outstanding contracts that a trader could hold on salad oils but the matter of dummy accounts was not addressed. The largest commodity trading swindle to date produced no realistic regulations on the futures exchanges or in the CEA itself. The CEA was still shorthanded and answered to the Department of Agriculture, which was always concerned about the effects that regulatory actions might have on the agricultural industry in general.

When the smoke cleared on De Angelis' operations, there were losses aplenty. When Allied went bankrupt, American Express was owed almost $144 million; Continental Illinois Bank, $34 million; Chase Manhattan, $25 million; Ira Haupt & Co., nearly $32 million; and the NYSE, nearly $10 million. Grain companies, food processors, and storage companies, as well as other bank creditors, were owed around $200 million altogether. Over 50 banks were involved in some manner. The actual net losses were estimated to be around $200 million, with American Express the largest loser by far.

In the aftermath of the affair, De Angelis became something of a working-class folk hero. Even as he was awaiting sentencing in 1964, he still traded salad oil on a small scale through some of his other related companies. Although the damage was extensive, he simply was considered the most recent example of white-collar crime and the product of a lax banking system and commodities trading market. The judge who eventually sentenced him in 1965 to 10 years in prison seemed highly sympathetic in his presentencing comments although he finally threw the book (somewhat abridged) at the salad oil king. The maximum prison time for De Angelis' collective offenses was 185 years. The several sentences ran concurrently, however. As the case wound its way through the courts, it became obvious that De Angelis was not necessarily the mastermind of the operation. The operation was too complex, for it required an extensive knowledge of the futures markets that he did not possess. One commentator remarked after the trial and sentencing that De Angelis "looked more like a front or stooge than the mastermind."[14] De Angelis, however, remained resilient. After serving his time in a Pennsylvania prison, he moved to Newark, New Jersey and in 1990 was contemplating writing his memoirs. Fortunately for his former bankers the book never materialized.

Regardless of his role in the affair, Allied's trading in the markets helped underscore some serious structural weaknesses that the futures markets needed to fix in the years ahead. De Angelis easily had come to corner cottonseed oil on the New York Produce Exchange and his positions on the CBOT, although smaller as a percentage of outstanding open interest, were still substantial. The exchanges stood by and watched the corners mount without actively intervening, hoping that all of the activity would help their businesses. After decades of bad public relations and the demise of the onion futures contract, the exchanges were still gambling dens of sorts, with Allied being the largest gambler to date. The rest of the financial markets could only hold their collective breath and hope that this latest round of traders behaving badly would not infect all of the markets' reputation for integrity. Unfortunately, it did.

The affair had a devastating effect on the New York Produce Exchange. Once known as the Grand Lady of Bowling Green, this exchange located on lower Broadway suffered badly after the Allied positions were unwound. It had discussed a merger with the New York Cotton Exchange but that idea fell through in fall 1963 after the De Angelis scandal erupted. Never large by futures exchange standards, the market had a paid staff of 50 and traded soybean oil and black pepper in addition to cottonseed oil. Its mix, however, was too narrow and its reputation too tarnished after De Angelis cornered such a large percentage of the salad oil contracts. By 1965, the exchange was on its knees and its trading pits deserted. Sitting on a lucrative lease for its premises, it hoped for—indeed, its survival depended on—a merger with a larger exchange.

Two years later, the Produce Exchange came up with a

166

solution to its problems by borrowing a page from the New York Merc's book. It proposed that it begin trading stocks and filed with the SEC for permission to begin trading a handful of common stocks. The Merc's own experiment with common stocks was still active although the exchange traded only 20 issues, with names such as Whale Electronics and Yoo-Hoo Chocolate Beverages dominating trading. Wall Street was not intrigued by the proposal, with one broker commenting, "I don't think the Fed will allow this proposal to go through since it's a beautiful way of getting around the margin requirements."[15] At the time, the margin requirement on common stocks was 70 percent, raised by the central bank to curtail speculation on the stock exchanges, which had increased considerably since the 1950s. Allowing a commodities market to trade stocks would have taken the margin requirements out of the regulators' hands. The SEC—which administered the margin percentages laid down by the Fed—had no control over futures exchanges.

The aftermath of the salad oil swindle reverberated for years, extending well beyond the fascinating but hubristic story of De Angelis himself. A well-known, if not major, Wall Street broker had collapsed and the mastermind of the scandal spent only a short time in jail, considering the extent of his swindle. Brokers from Wall Street to LaSalle Street became acutely aware of the slogan "know thy customer" as a result of the affair. Don Regan of Merrill Lynch noted that the swindle served as a precedent, as Wall Street firms and the NYSE established a reserve fund to help bail out members in financial trouble so that public confidence in the stock market could be maintained. "Acting in concert through the Exchange [NYSE] its members agreed to a levy based upon their gross revenues to indemnify the customers of firms that had failed," Regan later noted.[16] Ironically, that reserve fund would prove useful in the late 1960s when Wall Street underwent one of its most serious crises. The De Angelis scandal provoked a loss of confidence in brokers that continued well into the next decade and the damage it caused extended far beyond the futures exchanges.

## EGGS . . . AND BACON

History began to move quickly for the futures exchanges in the wake of the salad oil affair. The stock market and the foreign exchange markets were growing in importance, as indicated by their increasing trading volume, and the financial world in general was becoming more sophisticated as time went on. The futures markets, however, were still relatively thin. They traded only basic agricultural commodities and foods. Even within that narrow realm, there was a genuine need for new futures contracts. Without them, some of the smaller exchanges faced extinction.

Such was the case on the CME. In the absence of onions, the exchange was left only with its egg contract. Without something new to trade, its lifespan would certainly be limited. All futures contracts require two elements for success. First, the commodity that they trade must be central to the economy so that sellers, or producers, will recognize the necessity of protecting their price by selling forward. Second, users, or processors, must recognize that a purchase can protect against an unforeseen price rise in the future that could otherwise damage their economic interests. Another important element, however, is that the environment must be volatile enough to create enough uncertainty so that both sellers and users become convinced of the virtues of the markets.

By the 1960s, agricultural production was so efficient that its success almost victimized the futures markets. With many commodities in abundant supply, only unforeseen events were likely to upset supply-and-demand schedules, reducing the need for trading in the process. Ironically, this was the problem in which the CME found itself with its egg contracts. As an important staple, eggs were being produced in record amounts, and without a threat to their potential supply or the intrusion of external forces unforeseen at the time, they risked being taken for granted with the futures market becoming less necessary. The cash market had more than enough eggs to supply ordinary demand, so without a new product to trade, the CME's existence looked tenuous at best.

The new futures contract launched on the CME was for pork bellies. The contract, announced in spring 1961, caused some early confusion. Pork bellies refer to the part of a hog used for bacon. Initially, nobody understood and cared much for the new contract and it languished for well over a year before trading began to increase. The CME also discussed other contracts in such foodstuffs as orange juice futures and frozen broilers but these suggestions were eventually rejected. Soon, the pork belly contract began to attract attention and began trading in reasonable amounts, helping to revive the exchange's prospects for the future. As with all other futures contracts, the contract called for physical delivery if the buyer or seller needed to take or make delivery of the commodity. Encouraged by its modest success, the CME and the CBOT introduced another contract, adding a new twist to the standard futures game.

Beginning in 1964, the CME introduced a contract on live cattle—the on-the-hoof variety. The exchange assumed that the cattle industry needed a contract of this sort to revive its own prospects because of currently low beef prices. The contract was risky for the exchange for no one was certain whether the cattle industry understood the futures market or actually wanted it intruding in their business. The president of the Chicago Livestock Exchange noted that "farmers were leery about futures because they don't know the ins and outs of the market. We have not found a great deal of interest among our customers. Maybe it's because of a lack of education in futures trading."[17] That was a century-old lament still ringing true even in the mid-1960s.

In 1965, the CBOT took the opposite tactic and introduced a contract on beef carcasses, but the contract soon died for lack of interest. However, the live cattle future began to attract interest on the CME among hedgers and speculators, and before long, it became quite active. Market wags could not refrain from drawing parallels with the infamous Daniel Drew of NYSE fame, who was New York's best known speculator before the Civil War. Before moving to New York City from upstate, Drew had developed a reputation for selling watered cattle to farmers. He would put thin cattle on a train headed for New York State farms, give them water, and hope that the cows would not develop cystitis before reaching their destinations. Once delivery of the new contract had been ironed out, it became one of the CME's most popular contracts, and the CBOT soon followed suit by introducing its own contract on live cattle. The CME added live hogs in 1966; that same year, the New York Merc added some more exotica by introducing futures on mercury. The CBOT also continued to add new contracts, with iced broilers in 1968 and plywood and silver in 1969. The silver contract, the exchange's first in precious metals would be the focus of much unwanted attention within a decade.

Delivery of a live commodity proved a radical departure for the markets, for the traditional commodity had been perishable, depending upon the quality of the technology that preserved it. Despite their differences, however, all commodities could be delivered against a contract if desired, dead or alive. The new contracts were still based upon tangible products grown or raised on farms. The success brightened the exchanges' prospects considerably. The price of exchange seats began to reflect the new activity. By 1967, CME seats were selling for $23,000 while those on the New York Merc were selling $18,000. Two years later, both doubled as the prospects of even more new products loomed on the horizon. A whole new generation of futures contracts and other derivatives developed in the late 1960s that would depart from the time-proven formula for agriculturals and break new ground. The futures markets were about to enter a new era of innovation on a scale never before imagined.

Since the nineteenth century, futures exchanges—especially wheat exchanges and mercantile exchanges—have in many cases traded similar contracts. However, the different contracts could never be switched from one exchange to another. Arbitrage between the exchanges was not possible. For instance, a trader could not sell wheat in Chicago and cover it in Minneapolis. Despite the exchanges having become larger and more sophisticated over the years, they were still regional in that respect. Standardized contracts were something of a misnomer. Contracts were standard on the exchange on which they traded, not on a nationwide basis.

The gender barrier finally fell in 1965, when the New York Merc admitted its first woman as a floor trader. Muriel Edelstein became the first woman to trade on the floor of a commodity futures exchange after clerking for her husband, a pit trader, for several years. A grandmother by the time she entered the pits, she specialized in Maine potato trading. When asked how it felt to be trading in the fast-moving pits, she replied, "Oh, it's far more exciting than the P.T.A. meetings I attended when we lived in Westchester." Most of the other Merc traders readily accepted her, and no one seemed to be bothered by her gender. One trader admitted that women were not in danger in the pits, because "we don't have the fist fights like in the old days"—the reason for which was perhaps that "modern women tend to inhibit masculine activity," as another trader put it.[18] The CBOT admitted its first two women members in 1969.

As the markets expanded, old debates again surfaced. The most notable debate to resurface in the 1960s was whether futures markets actually affected cash market prices or were simply arenas where those who wanted to establish a price either for hedging or delivery could be accommodated. The discussion began to attract a number of academic commentators as well as market participants who strived to show that the markets did have legitimate economic value, especially in the embarrassing wake of the onion contract. Fundamental analyses were made of the relationship between cash and futures prices and the role of storage costs in determining futures prices. Technical analysis also made strides as traders and analysts studied charts, hoping to detect trading patterns that could possibly be repeated.

The back-office, or backroom, crisis on Wall Street in the late 1960s was a direct result of the De Angelis scandal and threatened the integrity of the marketplace. As a result of the failure of Ira Haupt & Co., the NYSE had a reserve set aside to help its members who were falling into financial distress. The bull market of the late 1960s provided the stimulus. Volume on the stock exchanges became so heavy that many of the backroom operations began to fall woefully behind trading volume. Most of the securities dealers had poorly run settlement departments which could not cope with the increased activity. As a result, in 1969 the NYSE actually called for a trading holiday to occur during the business week so that it could catch up. Doing so did not help the situation, however. Investigations showed that theft was rampant at some securities dealers with stocks and bonds disappearing without a trace.

As a result of the increased volume and the frauds, Wall Street slipped into its worst crisis in decades. The $25 million reserve fund established at the time of the Ira Haupt & Co. liquidation was tested on several other occasions as major securities houses required bailouts. Goodbody & Co. and Hayden

Stone & Co. both required assistance from the fund, and F. I. DuPont & Co. and Bache & Co. both fell upon hard times as well. The larger, more healthy brokers, led by Merrill Lynch, stepped into the breach and provided assistance but usually at a price. Goodbody & Co. was shut down and Merrill Lynch assumed its accounts so that the NYSE would not be faced with the bleak prospect of providing assistance by itself. As a result of the affair, Congress provided assistance by creating the Securities Investor Protection Corporation in 1971, which provided insurance for securities held in brokerage accounts.

The NYSE implemented other corrective measures before the integrity of the market was damaged beyond repair. In addition to forming a group of strong brokers to help bail out the weaker, other more mundane but necessary reforms were instituted. To weed out potential criminals before they began working in the industry, all securities and commodities brokers began the practice of fingerprinting their employees. Even before the crisis erupted, the CBOT in 1966 introduced the first licensing examination for commodity brokers to put them on par with securities brokers who already had licensing exams of their own. The exams were not industrywide but only a CBOT requirement. True to form, Wall Street and LaSalle Street would respond to crises only after their onset but certainly before Congress would respond to do it for them.

## INTO THE MIX

The true value of the futures markets was tested in times of turbulence. When prices became volatile, hedgers needed to establish futures prices that would remove uncertainty from their core businesses. Even though buyers hoped against cash-price rises in the future and sellers hoped against cash-price drops, prudent hedgers established a price, either long or short, at which they could take potential delivery regardless of where the markets turned. In the late 1960s, the markets began to witness the sort of volatility that pit traders dreamed about and hedgers detested although the source was foreign to most traders.

The stock and commodities markets became very volatile in the 1960s. Most of the explanations cite familiar causes of that time. The Vietnam War helped create inflation, and antiwar dissent created uncertainty in politics and in the markets. New technologies were appearing in the marketplace for defense-related industries, and large communications companies and the conglomerates were on a buying spree that made many smaller companies potential takeover candidates. Price-earnings ratios were historically high but volatile. Commodity prices were increasing with inflation, and the nation was in the midst of a residential building boom, as the CBOT plywood contract attested. However, racial problems persisted despite the Civil Rights Act of 1964, and political assassination cast a long shadow over the political process.

In the face of all these issues, nobody was interested in the problems surrounding the commodities markets' favorite old link—gold. Since the New Deal, Americans were not permitted to own gold bullion for investment purposes, so the commodity developed its investment identity overseas, becoming the favorite bellwether investment during times of economic and political uncertainty. The dollar was pegged to gold at $35 per ounce although it did fluctuate during times of currency market unrest. The metal was of vital importance to international monetary authorities and central bankers since it was still the lynchpin of the currency system. In the United States, however, gold was not a particularly newsworthy item in a world that had become much more complex since the days when Benjamin Hutchinson considered it the force that moved the wheat market.

That state of affairs was about to change in the late 1960s, as turmoil began to rock the foreign exchange markets. Several currencies, including sterling and the dollar, were considered major reserve currencies, meaning that central banks held them as assets. Reserve currencies reflected the strength of a country's economy and its prestige in international trading terms. If a country did substantial business with the United States, then its central bank would normally keep a percentage of that business in reserve in the form of dollars to cover its import costs. If a currency fell out of favor, however, it could fall dramatically on the markets, signifying a potential demotion of the country in international trade.

Beginning in 1964, economic problems began to plague Britain and sterling suffered as a result. The British government was forced to devalue or support sterling several times—in 1964, 1965, and 1967. The 1967 devaluation trimmed sterling by 14 percent, from $2.80 to $2.40 per pound. Over the years, the pound's value had fallen nearly 50 percent. In 1929, at the time of the stock market crash, it stood at $4.80. The latest crisis demonstrated how far the currency had slipped in purchasing power terms, not to mention the loss of international prestige.

During the last sterling devaluation in 1967, a new term, the "gnomes of Zurich," began to circulate in the currency markets. A British civil servant had coined this term, referring to the foreign exchange (forex) traders of Switzerland whose speculation had driven down the value of the pound. The term quickly caught on in Britain and then in forex markets around the world. Faceless little moneychangers were victimizing the pound, bent on driving down its value. Following their speculations, gold began to gyrate on the markets as well and before long, the dollar was under pressure as well.

Although the dollar was the major international trading currency, it was not immune to fluctuations in value, even under the fixed-parity exchange rate system established at Bretton Woods, New Hampshire, at the close of World War II. In

175

1967, it came under pressure as gold became increasingly popular as a result of political and economic turmoil in Europe. The fear among American monetary officials was that if gold appreciated substantially in value, foreign governments would demand conversion of their dollars into gold. If that occurred, the dollar eventually would have its link with gold cut, undermining the entire international monetary system established since the 1940s. Even if that did not occur the system had limitations that encouraged arbitrageurs to insist on buying gold at the fixed price of $35 per ounce and then selling it in the market at the higher price.[19] The international gold market closed for several months in 1968 as a result and the metal stabilized. However, continued American trade problems put further pressure on the dollar leading to more serious problems in the early 1970s.

During the period of gold and currency turmoil, the normally esoteric forex market came to the forefront of the news more than at any other time since the 1930s. Unlike the futures markets, the forex market was huge but invisible. Operating on an OTC basis, the market has no central location. Instead, it is conducted among international banks via telephone. Those banks choosing to make prices are called market makers. Corporate and government customers traded currencies on either a spot or forward basis. Most large money-center banks traded in the market, dealing in those currencies that they knew best. In many respects, the forex market was very similar to the old to-arrive market in futures conducted on the original boards of trade during the Civil War.

Unlike the futures markets, the forex market never developed legendary traders. The market primarily was conducted between banks and their established clients and although it was called a market, it was—and remains—a bank service provided to customers only. Like some futures markets, both spot and forward markets are conducted in the same location—at the

176

banks. The rates quoted are market rates, determined by the market makers trading with each other over the telephone. In this corporate environment, well-known traders are few and deals are not publicized or published in newspapers. Only large government-inspired forex deals ever reach the press, usually when a central bank intervenes on behalf of its own currency.

The most important difference between forward markets and futures markets was the nature of the obligation buyers and sellers contracted. Spot deals were for immediate settlement in forex and these are the prices reported on a daily basis. Prices for future delivery, known as forwards, are struck for delivery up to 360 days. However, the counting always starts from the day the deal is struck. A 90-day forward means that it delivers 90 days from today, not on a standard delivery day in that month. No secondary market exists in forwards; once a deal is struck, it must be delivered on that same day. It cannot be sold to a third party and remains irrevocable between bank and customer.

When speculators wanted to buy or sell in the market, they traded an irrevocable contract. Since it could not be sold, the only way to offset its effect was to enter another contract. This caused a great deal of trading in the market. When the market became volatile, trading would increase considerably, for new trades were often made to offset older positions. This nonnegotiability of forward contracts was the major difference between forward and futures markets. In the nineteenth century, futures markets began trading contracts that originally were never intended to be passed to a third party. That intent, however, was soon overridden by the need for flexibility and the desire of traders to buy and sell established contracts frequently.

The problem for users with forward contracts was that they were for relatively large, standard amounts, usually $1 million lots or the foreign currency equivalents. Because small contracts did not exist, small businesses usually could not access the forward market although they could have used the protection it provided just like multinational corporations. A market for smaller contracts would not compete with forwards but only complement them by allowing smaller hedgers and speculators into the market. Futures traders recognized this as a window of opportunity in their quest for new products to complement their existing products.

When in the late 1960s the dollar became volatile, the need for smaller contracts with more flexibility than forwards became obvious to the futures exchanges. After the pound was devalued, the dollar came under pressure. President Johnson failed to balance the budget in 1968, a serious issue at the time, and the United States was running balance-of-payments deficits. A flight from dollars weakened the currency and the country found itself in the odd position of requiring devaluation. Under fixed-parity system of the International Monetary Fund (IMF), devaluations or revaluations needed to be orchestrated in consultation with the fund and other major trading nations. The raison d'être of the IMF was to avoid the kind of unilateral devaluations that had occurred in the 1930s causing serious trade distortions and international animosity. The futures markets remembered that period well because it was a time of a serious drop in grain exports.

The volatility resulting from the 1960s and 1970s uncertainty gave new life to the futures markets. The benefits were not seen immediately, however. Because volatility motivated hedgers and inspired speculators, the markets thrived on it. But this period of international uncertainty was not agricultural or domestic. Currency volatility, inspired by inflation, was a new phenomenon for most commodities traders, although they quickly saw opportunity in turmoil. The futures markets continued to detect opportunity in uncertainty when the securities markets were in a funk over declining prices.

Inflation became the major problem confronting the Nixon

178

administration. As inflation rose, workers began demanding higher wages to compensate. Workers at General Motors negotiated a 20 percent increase in their pay package at the same time that investors drove Treasury bond yields to an historic 8 percent yield. As a result, in August 1971 Nixon and his advisers proposed a package of anti-inflation measures which included a 90-day wage and price freeze and special excise taxes. During the previous spring, the administration had steadfastly maintained that devaluing the dollar was not a viable option and that gold would remain at its official price of $35 per ounce.

In an August 1971 nationally televised address, Nixon discussed his administration's gold policy toward the end of his address. Almost as if it were afterthought, he dropped the bombshell that would reverberate in the financial markets for years, saying, "In the past seven years, there's been an average of one international monetary crisis every four years. Now who gains from these crises? Not the workingman, not the investor, not the real producers of wealth. The gainers are the international money speculators: because they thrive on crisis, they help to create them."[20] The gnomes scurried for temporary cover. Not since Harold Wilson's devaluation had such a direct reference been made to speculators and their "malevolent" effects on currencies. Futures traders could appreciate the reference for they had heard it many times in the past.

Crucial for the forex markets was the last part of Nixon's address in which he severed the link between gold and the dollar. The dollar effectively was devalued at the Smithsonian in December 1971 when an agreement among the major trading nations revalued gold to $38 per once. The dollar declined across the board by an average of about 10 percent. The IMF fixed-parity system died with the severance. The major currencies began floating against each other within 18 months of Nixon's unilateral August announcement. Inflation was the culprit, causing the international financial system to shake on its foundations. Moreover, domestic financial matters did not help the situation. Wall Street was embroiled in its own crisis of confidence and the stock market was low as a result. The conglomerate craze of the 1960s was coming to an end and many of the decade's growth stocks were falling in value. Fraud was rife. In addition to backroom scandal, the stock market was dealt another severe blow when one of its former favorites—the Equity Funding Corporation—was exposed as a fraud, sending the market and other insurance stocks into a tailspin. The Dow Jones fell below 1,000 points and equity investors were beginning to abandon the market.

At what appeared to be an inauspicious moment, the CBOT wanted to reenter the stock trading arena during the bull market of the 1960s. Between 1928 and 1953, it had traded some stocks listed by the Chicago Stock Exchange but never became a major force in equities. Then in 1969, it announced that it wanted to reenter the equities arena by trading put and call options on common stocks. CBOT President Henry Wilson announced that the exchange was considering the move, which would require substantial regulatory approval. Stocks were regulated by the SEC and the agency had no control over the futures exchanges. In the wake of the Wall Street scandal, it was unlikely that the agency would permit the CBOT such latitude although no one argued that a form of stock hedging would prove beneficial. Before anyone could entertain the notion the CBOT needed to demonstrate how its proposed options differed from the privilege trading of the past.

The state of the financial markets made new-product development difficult if not impossible. Put and call options had been traded in Europe for years and Wall Street firms also offered them to large clients on an OTC basis. However, the market was far from developed. Options remained illegal in many states and the Commodity Exchange Act also effectively banned them on the boards of trade. Any new developments needed to be carefully monitored. Besides the legal obstacles, the major problem confronting the CBOT was education. Options were somewhat esoteric and would require a thorough grounding before traders and investors could feel comfortable with them.

## BAND OF GOLD

When President Nixon severed the link between the dollar and gold, he also severed the official price of $35 that had stood for decades. The old gold standard was something of a myth although the dollar–gold link provided the international financial system with its foundation. Once that foundation crumbled, the world moved toward a dollar standard. When this was fully recognized, the whole financial landscape changed. Volatility became the norm in the stock and currency markets, and phlegmatic interest rates became a thing of the past.

Almost from the beginning, futures traders recognized the opportunities and began to explore new contracts in financial futures, a new class of instruments designed to cope with the new environment. However, traditional futures practices needed to be revised if expansion was to succeed. For over a century, futures and the commodities upon which they were based traded in the same markets. Cash and futures markets were not physically removed from each other. Chicago was still the center of the agricultural universe and New York the center of the financial. If Chicago attempted to trade crossover products, such as stock options or financial futures, the adjustments would have to be made in the traditional way in which actual commodities were provided for physical delivery.

Futures traders had two choices. If they traded a financial instrument rather than an agricultural commodity, they would have to ensure as smooth and problem-free a delivery as possible. In short, they needed to prove they were as adept with the Japanese yen as they were with soybeans. Some traders entertained notions of trading contracts which technically could not be delivered. This was true of financial futures, such as index futures, based upon a stock market index or an inflation-linked index. Because these contracts were mathematically constructed indicators, they could settle only by way of cash, not by way of actual delivery. If this could be accomplished, the markets' potential for expansion would be unlimited.

In the late 1960s, the CBOT was leaning toward equity options while the CME contemplated trading futures on foreign currencies. While the CBOT had some limited experience with stocks in the past, currencies were a radical departure for the CME. The exchange did have substantial support from such powerful economists as Milton Friedman at the University of Chicago who recognized the virtues of currency trading during the turmoil of the 1960s. Increased opportunities for small traders carried a bevy of financial benefits that the forward market did not provide. The real question facing the CME was whether traders accustomed to agricultural futures could make the transition to currencies successfully. Contracts that died on the exchanges for lack of interest or adequate public education rarely got a second chance.

The CME made great strides in catching the CBOT in the 1960s and by the end of the decade, it rivaled the CBOT in terms of contracts traded and dollar volume. Leo Melamed assumed the presidency in 1969 when the exchange had attained unprecedented prosperity. Pushing the CME to strive for innovative contracts became a distinct goal. In December 1971, at the height of the currency crisis, Milton Friedman presented the exchange with a research paper entitled *The Need for*

*Futures Markets in Currencies* which had been commissioned by the exchange in the aftermath of Nixon's August 1971 announcement. In the paper Friedman wrote, "It is highly desirable that this demand [for foreign exchange hedging facilities] be met by as broad, as deep, as resilient a futures market in foreign currencies as possible . . . such a wider market is almost certain to develop in response to the demand. The major question is where. The U.S. is a natural place and it is very much in the interests of the U.S. that it should develop here."[21]

Encouraged by Friedman's support and having gained the tacit approval of Washington, the CME's newest creation—the International Monetary Market (IMM)—began to develop slowly. It initially traded futures in the most popular currencies against the dollar, in modest contracts of around $50,000 equivalents. Begun in 1971, the new exchange was trading a few thousand contracts per day within a year as traditional agricultural commodities traders tried their hands at the intricacies of currency trading. It was treated as a separate operation from the CME itself, however. Seats were separate, as were the trading facilities.

The new contracts also added to the century-old debate about the effects of futures trading on the cash markets. These markets—notably the CBOT and later the CME—consistently argued that futures markets were places where traders could find a price for delivery. The only contribution they made to physical commodities was providing a place where the contracts could be traded easily. In other words, they had no effect on the cash price. Over the years, critics of the markets begged to differ. Populists, Progressives, and Farm Bloc Republicans all maintained that these markets did indeed affect prices, often negatively, by short selling. After years of corners and bear raids, protests by the exchanges that futures markets were only trading places rang hollow. The volatile prices experienced during the 1920s and 1930s seemed to confirm the critics' opinions.

The new contracts could make the exchanges' claim legitimate. When financial futures began trading, there was no debate over the effect that futures would have on the currencies themselves. A relatively small futures exchange could not affect the spot rate or futures rate on a currency, regardless of heavy volume. It was believed that the real effect of futures on the currencies might develop into arbitrage with the forward market, but that, too, was a very large order to fill. For the first time, futures market were what they claimed—trading places only.

Not to be outdone by its rival, the CBOT pursued new products and planned to open a new options market for common stocks. The two exchanges began development on products that would revolutionize both LaSalle Street and Wall Street by proving that derivative instruments did have a contribution to make to the securities and foreign exchange markets. Agriculture remained important but trading agricultural commodities remained limited and seemed less important than it had been 50 years before. The new experiment would test Wall Street's tolerance for competition and new hedging instruments while ushering LaSalle Street into a more sophisticated financial world.

Necessity became the mother of invention on all the financial markets by the late 1960s. The volatility caused by inflation and uncertainty made investors nervous and less likely to hold securities for the long term. As in the past, such conditions spawned new products and increased trading for short-term profit. They also awakened a speculative fever that would increase gambling on a scale not seen since the Civil War. The brave new world of the late 1960s and early 1970s had volatility lurking in the background and experience proved that it would remain on the financial scene for decades to come.

## *NOTES*

1. Irish potatoes grown in the United States, known by their Latin name *Solanum tuberosum,* in the Commodity Exchange Act.
2. Bob Tamarkin, *The MERC: The Emergence of a Global Financial Powerhouse* (New York: HarperBusiness, 1993), p. 103.
3. Ibid., p. 114.
4. *New York Times,* December 5, 1955.
5. A *straddler* is a trader who is long and short at the same price and is able to take advantage of an upward or a downward price movement although the position is more expensive to maintain than an outright long or short.
6. *Corn Products Co. v. Commissioner,* 350 US 46 (1955).
7. *New York Times,* September 17, 1959.
8. Norman C. Miller, *The Great Salad Oil Swindle* (Baltimore: Penguin Books, 1965), p. 21.
9. Ibid., pp. 94, 96.
10. Ibid., pp. 67–68.
11. Ibid., p. 133.
12. Ibid., pp. 147–148.
13. *New York Times,* December 21, 1963.
14. Leslie Gould, *The Manipulators* (New York: David McKay Co., 1966), p. 111.
15. *New York Times,* December 29, 1967.
16. Donald T. Regan, *A View from the Street* (New York: New American Library, 1972), p. 113.
17. Tamarkin, *The MERC,* p. 135.
18. *New York Times,* February 17, 1965.
19. Robert Solomon, *The International Monetary System, 1945–1976* (New York: Harper & Row, 1977), p. 115.
20. Quoted in the *New York Times,* August 16, 1971.
21. Tamarkin, *The MERC,* p. 185.

# CHAPTER 5

# METALS AND MONEY

**A** S THE 1970s APPROACHED, TWO CONVULSIVE EVENTS rocking the markets would leave their mark permanently on the financial landscape—the backroom crisis on Wall Street and the shocks to the international financial system. Both helped create financial markets that would emerge from the period with a different complexion and structure from preceding decades. The post–Bretton Woods environment brought with it new challenges that would seriously question the futures pits' ability to fashion themselves into acceptable financial markets. If they were not met, their future would be in serious doubt.

For the first time since World War II, the markets were thrown into an instability that had effects extending beyond New York and Chicago. The weakness of the dollar, as well as inflation and foreign competition in manufacturing, all began to spread doubts about American economic supremacy. Making matters worse, speculation increased with inflation. In an attempt to find ways to beat inflation, many investment schemes appeared, promising high returns in short periods of time. Naturally, many were related to the commodities markets.

Financial magazines and newspapers were cluttered with anti-inflation schemes involving traditional commodities and precious metals. Metals especially became alluring because of their long-standing restriction in the United States. Speculating in them was seen as a way to keep abreast of foreigners who seemed to have the Americans at their mercy.

While stocks and bond prices declined, commodities came to the forefront. Commodity prices were expected to increase along with inflation, so investors believed—rightly or wrongly—that futures prices would always be higher. Clearly, the idea overlooked the fundamentals of many individual commodities, but American investors believed that precious metals in particular filled the bill. What could be so difficult to understand about gold or silver? The suppliers were well-known and somewhat limited, and stockpiles were well documented, so their values would only increase as they attracted more and more devotees. Obviously, their prices had nowhere to go but up.

In the wake of the collapse of the Bretton Woods agreement, the major event of the 1970s causing much uncertainty was the rapid increase in the price of oil. As if on cue, the Organization of Petroleum Exporting Countries (OPEC) raised the price of oil shortly after the August 1971 dollar announcement. In December 1973, the price was officially doubled to $11 per barrel. Since the United States was a net importer of oil, the price increase had an invidious effect on prices and inflation. The increase caused long lines at filling stations around the country within a short time. The dollar was hit hard on the currency markets. Within the six months following the price rise, it fell against all its major trading partners' currencies. The new oil volatility also gave rise to discussion about oil (petroleum) futures of different types, although it was not until the late 1970s, when oil approached $30 per barrel, that futures markets began developing new contracts to trade it.

Americans could not own gold but they could buy gold futures. That simple fact would make gold futures a favorite speculative tool since the vast majority of speculators could not take delivery. Silver was a different matter. A futures market for it did exist and the average citizen could actually own the physical commodity. Unlike gold, silver was a precious metal that could be cornered easily. Physical silver was available in sufficient quantities and was popular in some parts of the world, rivaling gold. However, its popularity was not universal, and it was considered a second-rate investment.

Fighting inflation became an American industry in the 1970s. The financial world was structured much as it had been since World War II. Events began to change quickly, however. When interest rates began to rise after the collapse of the Bretton Woods system, investors and savers were no longer content to leave their money in banks, where interest rate ceilings were still controlled by the Federal Reserve. Wall Street developed a new mutual fund, called a money market mutual fund (MMMF), that was sold to investors seeking higher interest. The funds paid the money market rate, approaching 9 percent, while banks continued to pay about 3 percentage points lower. The results astonished everyone. Money poured out of banks and into the funds. By the end of the 1970s, over $100 billion had been redirected to the money market and many banks and savings and loans associations were feeling the pinch. The average investor demonstrated that increased yield did mean something in inflationary times. No one was willing to tolerate static interest rates anymore.

Reviewing 1973, the *New York Times* identified inflation as the problem of the year. The paper also offered its readers an "Econ Game" that they could play, charting their knowledge of ways to keep abreast of inflation. Keeping abreast, however, was not the same as getting ahead. The more adventurous investor had many more schemes available to beat inflation.

190

Most such schemes involved commodities in one form or other. There appeared scores of books advertised in leading business publications, that advised readers on how to beat inflation. Many advertised exponential gains on an annual basis, climbing into the ether. Closer examination of the ads revealed that a one-time gain in the commodities market of 20 percent, recorded in a month, could be hypothetically converted to 240 percent annual rate if the fine print was not misleading. The exotic world of spreads, straddles, and rollovers now became widely advertised for as little as a few thousand dollars down. The investment world changed dramatically because of the fear of further inflation.

Even the sometimes dubious integrity record of the commodities markets was being overlooked in the speculative atmosphere. In this respect, all the markets had some serious help from academic quarters, where new investment theories emphasized intrinsic quality and potential performance over history. Stock markets were now being described as "efficient," meaning that past history played no role in determining securities prices. All investors were theoretically on a level playing field, with no investor having access to information that would give undue advantage over other investors. The theory applied only to stock markets and spilled over to all markets by implication. In the futures markets, history played a much larger role than anyone wanted to admit. Events in the 1970s would only underline its importance once again.

All financial markets suffered scandals over the years. The stock markets had seen their share of frauds but managed to survive. The backroom crisis and Equity Funding scandal were just two recent examples in the 1970s. Of course, futures exchanges were always equated with fraud and self-serving behavior, more so than the stock markets would ever endure. No matter what the exchanges did to spruce up their image, the public seemed not to care. Retail investors did not play the futures markets in large numbers and despite the exchanges having a major presence in New York, most people outside the Midwest never even heard of them. Although the markets were determined to develop new, meaningful products, they were still susceptible to trading scandals that would only tarnish their already tatty reputation. The 1970s would prove to be no exception.

After a century of success and scandal, the futures markets were poised to enter the brave new world of the 1970s with an expanded menu of products and concepts. For the first time, futures contracts included nonagricultural commodities and would move even further away from farmers and processors as time passed. While markets for agricultural commodities would always exist, an advanced industrial society needed to begin acknowledging that basic commodities also included such things as Treasury bills, foreign exchange, and long-term Treasury bonds—in addition to wheat, cotton, and soybeans. In the nineteenth century, Benjamin Hutchinson recognized the fundamental link between wheat and gold. In the twentieth, the link was between interest rates and the markets. The fundamental commodity in society was no longer measured in bushels but rather in basis points.

None of this was new in the 1970s. However, by adopting contracts on currencies, interest rates, and stock market indices, futures markets were tacitly admitting that volatility had crept into what previously had been sleepy quarters of the markets. Futures markets need volatility to thrive and found plenty of it in interest rates and interest rate–related instruments. For most of the 1940s and 1950s, interest rate volatility was an oxymoron. Bill and bond yields were relatively stable, and bank deposit rates were protected by Federal Reserve regulations that limited the amount of interest paid to depositors. Currencies were pegged to gold and the dollar, and although the financial world was not totally peaceful at that time, it would begin to look positively idyllic when compared to the 1970s.

If the introduction of new futures contracts did not excite investors, there was always the other new product of the decade—options. Since the nineteenth century, options on common stocks had traded quietly OTC style in New York. Options on commodity futures contracts, the more noxious of the two, remained outlawed since the Commodity Exchange Act was passed in 1936. Stock market volatility, however, demanded that both come out of the closet and prove their worth to those investors who began abandoning the stock market in droves by the late 1970s. Futures traders loved volatility while producers and processors sought refuge from it. A bear market in stocks was another matter entirely. Volatile stock markets chased away investors, hurting both the primary and secondary markets. Without investors to purchase new issues, the capital-raising process was in serious trouble and company balance sheets would become skewed in favor of debt rather than equity. Any instrument that could help abate this process would find an immediate reception. The question was whether options were up to the task.

With much immediacy and fanfare, the futures and options markets began their brash experiment in the early 1970s. Terms such as rollovers, puts, calls, and straddles became popular and were no longer confined to professional traders. Investors were faced with a bevy of new instruments with their own exotic terminology. Yet many stockbrokers were unable to grasp the new concepts quickly and failed the initial options licensing exams put in place by the new and expanded derivatives exchanges. More than one cynic felt that the whole trend was ephemeral and would dissipate quickly. The agricultural futures markets were no longer the only game in town and the generic term "derivatives" came into vogue.

New York and Chicago began to do battle for the right to be called the home of options. Futures were never in doubt and remained the offspring of the Chicago markets although some interesting contracts sprang up in other, more unlikely places. Amidst the squabbling and boasts about territorial rights, it did seem that the good old days in the futures markets had finally disappeared. In the brave new world, scandal seemed to have receded from view. The new markets employed higher math to work out complex trading and arbitrage models. When Henry Wallace made his reputation as a forecaster of the 1920 recession, he employed a hog-to-hog ratio to explain his prediction. Fifty years later, traders began employing regression analyses and other statistical tools to predict future price trends. Two economists would win a Nobel Prize for their model explaining options pricing. Clearly, it seemed these were not the type of markets that could be manipulated.

Over the years, futures markets proved that a little scandal could always be expected and the 1970s proved no different. Quick to disavow Tino De Angelis in the 1960s, the markets had another major scandal to contend with in the 1970s. The perpetrators this time were hardly working-class unknowns from Bayonne, New Jersey. They came from one of the country's richest families, with ties to international oil money. Despite the background, the scandal was a classic nineteenth-century-style corner. New products were springing up rapidly but old habits died hard.

Recognizing that futures markets needed better monitoring, Congress acted again in the 1970s to put more teeth into regulation. The stock market had been relatively free of scandal until the 1970s. Although regulatory agencies could never prevent scandal and fraud, they were able to deal with it once it occurred. In futures markets, there was widespread suspicion that the CEA was only partially effective at best, especially with a small staff and budget. But once the plethora of new derivatives products arrived regulatory issues became paramount. Who was responsible for the new products? What classification did they fall under? Regulatory squabbling began in the 1970s and continued on and off for years. No one wanted to be blamed after the fact for not recognizing problems as they developed. Nevertheless, in several cases, problems were recognized at their onset but still turned out to be major fiascoes.

## CALLS AND PUTS

The CBOT pressed ahead with its plan to offer options on common stocks after its initial announcement in 1969. The idea ran into regulatory difficulties immediately. Although clearly not futures options, as privileges were years before, eyebrows were still raised at the prospect. Which regulatory body would have jurisdiction over the new exchange-traded options? The existing market as such was known simply as OTC options. Although it existed in New York among certain securities dealers, it remained a market for professionals and individual large-scale traders.

The advantage that the new options would have over their predecessors was that the new class of puts and calls would be marketable—that is, they could be bought and sold prior to expiration. Existing OTC options, like their European counterparts, were either bought or sold by investors and held until expiration. They could only be exercised on the expiration date; otherwise, they expired worthless, in which case the seller would keep the proceeds. The new planned market would be a continuous market where options could be easily bought and sold until their expiration date.

Since one option contract—either put or call—represented 100 shares of its underlying stock, it did not seem appropriate for the CEA to have jurisdiction, since the market was an adjunct of the stock market. However, the SEC assumed jurisdiction, arguing that the market bought and sold derivatives of equities that could easily be converted into stocks if investors chose to do so. In May 1972, the SEC received a formal application from a group headed by J. W. Sullivan to establish the Chicago Board Options Exchange (CBOE), a new options exchange separate from the CBOT. The agency had previously dithered since 1969, when the CBOT first announced its intentions. As a result the options markets became the first and only derivatives market to fall under the SEC's aegis. The SEC approved the application and the market opened in April 1973.

Listing new options was a slow process and the SEC allowed the listing of calls only in the beginning for fear of the potential manipulative effects of put trading. The original 16 options represented the most widely held stocks. Trading scandals in the past made the SEC proceed with great caution to allow the new market to develop slowly but with integrity. However, the market itself reacted more strongly. Over 15,000 calls per day were initially traded and the volume rose quickly to over 20,000 calls per day even before the exchange expanded its trading to 32 listed companies.

Within a year and a half, a seat on the CBOE was trading as high as $35,000. By late 1974, the CBOE was trading the equivalent of more than 4 million shares per day (40,000 calls) and, because it was running out of trading floor space, began searching for larger quarters. All of this was occurring while the stock market was declining in the wake of not only the Wall Street backroom fiasco but also a recession. The market, though, touched a responsive chord in small investors. The *Wall Street Journal* praised the CBOE as a "glittering success, attracting flocks of individual investors." It was not long before other exchanges saw the possibilities in options despite the dreadful stock market. They were not futures exchanges but instead smaller stock exchanges. In January 1975, the American Stock Exchange announced that it was opening trading, followed by the Philadelphia and Pacific exchanges. The stock exchanges created separate facilities for options trading as the

CBOT had in 1972. Technically, options had to be listed on the exchanges, designating them as "new" options as opposed to the older OTC types.

The CBOE's popularity was due almost entirely to individual retail investors. Options took away some of the risk of investing. For a fraction of a stock's price, an investor could purchase a call and potentially reap the rewards if the stock price rose. If the stock did not perform, the risk would be limited to the amount that the investor paid for the call. That one simple mechanic spelled the major structural difference between options and futures contracts. When investors purchased (or sold) a futures contract, they were exposed to the entire value of the contract itself, which could amount to hundreds of thousands of dollars. Options were structured differently. Investors bought or sold calls based upon the option's strike price—the price at which they could take (or make) delivery of the stock if they chose. The price buyers paid for the option, known as a "premium," was at risk, nothing more. Options could expire worthless, but futures contracts could not. Futures positions that were not closed had to be delivered. The risk was in the structure of the contracts themselves.

The options market quickly became a miniature stock market. There was little doubt that this new trading was having a negative effect on the stock markets. After all, 40,000 calls per day represented 4 million shares of stock—a significant number of actual shares, considering that the average volume on the NYSE was only about 50 million shares per day. Despite poor economic conditions, the NYSE looked at the CBOE as a potential rival that had already caused it some harm. From 1973 to 1974, volume on the Big Board declined, the value of stocks traded declined, and the price of a seat declined substantially, from a high of $190,000 to around $65,000.[1] From nearly total obscurity, the CBOE had progressed so rapidly that by late 1974 a CBOE seat cost half the price of an NYSE seat.

Wall Street felt the pinch. Options seemed natural Wall Street products yet these remarkably successful instruments were being traded in Chicago. The price of a CBOE seat naturally increased when many Wall Street traders recognized the arbitrage possibilities between the CBOE and the stock exchanges and hurried to buy. However, there were complaints about options that extended beyond simple envy. It appeared that options investors were interested only in buying and selling quickly, not in investing for the long term. The argument was first made in the early 1970s and reverberated for years to come. Although trading calls was one way in which to accomplish long-term investing, doing so was siphoning funds away from the stock exchanges at a critical time. The reasoning was sound but not obvious to the small investor. Investors ignored new issues of stock by trading options and when many companies came to market to raise fresh cash, they did not meet with great success. Equity price volatility appealed to traders. However, traders did not find the actual stocks as appealing when they could trade options instead. It seemed that the stepchild was upstaging the parent and the NYSE and the other stock exchanges did not like it. The other exchanges were quick to open their own options floors to take advantage. The NYSE did not, for the CBOE already had stolen its thunder.

In the mid-1970s, the Big Board traded around 75 to 80 percent of all stocks traded on the exchanges. Making matters worse, the old OTC market in stocks was now organized under the National Association of Securities Dealers Automated Quotation (NASDAQ) system and the country's oldest exchange found itself in competition from two sides. The NYSE responded by publishing a study predicting an equity capital shortage that would fail to adequately produce enough fresh equity for American companies over the next decade. Of the $250 billion it anticipated the economy would need to raise from 1975 to 1985, a net shortfall of $71 billion was predicted.[2]

Obviously, to make up the shortfall, the amount would have to be raised by either issuing bonds or not raising the funds at all, causing a slackening of capital investment that could potentially damage long-term prospects for the economy.

The argument was a bit disingenuous, however. The role of the stock exchanges was to trade existing issues of stock, not raise new issues for companies. That function was performed OTC style by the primary market among the investment banks. The NYSE was clearly trying to make a sophisticated case against the new options markets without actually naming them. It was playing to the fears of regulators and critics of options who felt that the markets were nothing more than gambling instruments depriving the market of badly needed equity. The CBOT had heard arguments like that for years but never in such a slick form. In the nineteenth century, gambling was claimed to erode the morals of the public in much the same way that Prohibitionists in the post–World War I years claimed alcohol drained the moral fiber. This new type of gambling, it was felt, eroded the capital base of American corporations, thereby causing potential harm to capital investment and competitiveness.

Early in the life of options markets, a major contribution to their effectiveness was made by three young academics studying the factors that priced individual options. What became universally known as the Black–Scholes model was developed in 1970 and 1971 by Fischer Black and Myron Scholes, in collaboration with Robert C. Merton. The model was not published until 1973 because of a less-than-enthusiastic reception from some academic journals. The complicated model illustrated how greater volatility in stock price leads to greater volatility in options prices, presenting the option holder with potential benefits for profit with limited downside risk.

The model relied on an underlying arbitrage argument. In theory, since a stock and a bond can be combined to replicate the payouts of an option, the price of the option must be the same as the price of the securities otherwise there would be an arbitrage opportunity that investors could exploit. The model was based upon what are known as European options, which do not have a secondary market like the one instituted by the CBOE. The Black–Scholes model calculation worked so well that it became the standard by which options of all sorts were priced. It became the best known model used in finance and won Scholes and Merton the Nobel Prize in economics in 1997. Black died two years before.

All of these factors helped the options markets for calls make an auspicious debut. Introducing puts was a much slower matter. Several years after the launch of the CBOE, put trading was still on hold. In March 1976, I. W. "Tubby" Burnham, president of the Securities Industry Association (SIA), held a news conference in which he urged the options markets to go slowly when introducing puts, claiming that the industry was not ready for trading. The CBOE, however, was pressing the SEC for permission to begin as soon as possible. The astonishing success of calls only wetted the exchange's appetite for more success. However, selling the SEC on puts would not be easy. A year passed before the SEC would give the green light.

The mechanics of puts made them very appealing for two reasons. A speculator who decided to sell a stock short would sell it in a margin account. Doing so meant that the trader would deposit the margin—usually 50 percent of the stock's price—and hope that its price would diminish so it could be bought back cheaper. If puts existed, the trader could buy a put for a fraction of the stock's price. If the stock declined, the put would appreciate in price and could be sold for a profit. In the case of options (both puts and calls), margins did not apply. Options required cash only but the put strategy was still cheaper than selling a stock short and did not carry the same risks. If the strategy did not work, the investor could lose no more than the price paid for the put. After a century of complaints about the effects of short selling, introducing put trading could not be expected to occur quickly.

Unlike futures contracts, dual listing of share options became a major source of contention among the options exchanges. The popularity of options led the exchanges to begin listing similar options, and an ensuing options war rattled the industry. SIA President Edward O'Brien called on the options exchanges to "carefully reappraise what they are doing," claiming that the unprecedented garb for options business was doing more harm than good to the industry.[3] The battle began when the Amex announced that it would begin trading calls in National Semiconducter Corp., one of the CBOE's favorite options. The CBOE immediately retaliated by listing some Amex options. At the time, the CBOE traded about 60 percent of the market, with the Amex in second place with 25 percent and regional stock exchanges accounting for the remainder.

The SEC helped settle the matter, taking it out of the hands of the exchanges. The commission was already annoyed at floor traders on both the large exchanges who reported fictitious trades, so when the prospect of a trading war between the two exchanges broke out, it stepped in, calling for an inquiry into the markets. This inquiry had the immediate effect of freezing new options listings. Only those options already traded before July 15, 1977, were allowed to continue until the SEC was satisfied. Put options were at the heart of the matter. The SEC had just sanctioned put trading a month before so the freeze hurt them most. It had taken the SEC almost five years to approve the creation of these options.

## RUSSIANS AND GNOMES

Although years passed since their wheat had crossed paths, in the early 1970s Soviets and Americans became involved in con-

201

troversy again. This time, the deal was more straightforward than it had been in the 1930s when it was cloaked in relative secrecy. In 1972, the deal was public and seemed to be completely above board. But when the wheat pits became involved nothing was as simple as it seemed.

The Soviets had a terrible wheat harvest in 1972, with production down 50 percent from the previous year. As a result, the Soviet government approached the United States about buying a large quantity of grain to tide it over. On July 8, President Nixon announced a three-year plan to sell at least $750 million of wheat, corn, and other grains to the Soviets, the largest deal ever between the two countries. The grain was to be purchased from private American grain dealers and the United States limited the Soviets to no more than $500 million of export credits. The Americans were not alone in supplying wheat abroad nor were the Soviets the only buyers. India, China, and Pakistan also placed orders for grain in other major wheat-producing countries such as Canada and Argentina. The policy dovetailed perfectly with Nixon's foreign policy of trying to reach a more friendly accommodation with both China and the Soviet Union. What could not be foreseen at the time was that the Russians appeared to be up to their old tricks. Unlike the 1930s wheat scandal, this one had a champion. The Nixon administration was not aware that the deal would prove a public relations nightmare.

A year later, in 1973, Secretary of the Treasury George Shultz acknowledged that the United States had been "burned" in the deal for the Soviets had sold the newly purchased wheat to the Italians at substantially higher prices. Senator Walter Huddleston, Democrat of Kentucky, waved a copy of the Italian newspaper *Il Tempo* containing details of the deal on the floor of the Senate to embarrass the administration. The terms of the deal were printed in the newspaper. The deal was not popular with the American public either. While farmers were counting their cash, demonstrators gathered in New York protesting deals with the Soviets, who allegedly were persecuting Jews at the time.

Huddleston followed in the shoes of other notable antifutures legislators. Better known as "Dee," he was born in Kentucky in 1926 and graduated from the University of Kentucky. After serving in the Army, he worked at several radio stations before being elected to the Kentucky State Senate in 1965. He was elected to the U.S. Senate in 1972. Considered a moderate Democrat, he opposed many of Nixon's domestic policies and also had harsh words for the futures markets on more than one occasion. His effectiveness, however, was limited when in 1984 his reelection bid failed.

Old fears began to surface after the wheat scandal. Traders on the CBOT feared that Congress would finally take action to control trading. CBOT President Frederick G. Uhlmann noted that the goodwill and political clout that the exchange had built up over the years was in danger of being overlooked as the public ranted against food prices and dealings with the Soviets. Reiterating a century-old lament when he testified before the House Small Business Subcommittee in 1973, he complained that traders and speculators in agricultural commodities were being made "whipping boys" for soaring food prices.[4] Denying that traders were responsible for high food prices, he blamed high interest rates and inflation instead. He also deplored the activities of brokers unconnected to the exchanges who were selling unlisted commodity options to the public. His argument harked back to the days of the anti–bucket shop campaign. After years of development and increasing public acceptance, the markets again found themselves in a bitter dispute that recycled many old arguments in contemporary form.

Fortunately for the futures markets, the flap ended quickly. The new financial products gave them something positive to demonstrate. Currency futures proved very successful for the new IMM and also wetted the exchanges' appetite for more financial futures. The logic behind new product development was very simple: trade anything with underlying volatility. By the early 1970s, it became apparent that volatility was a permanent feature of the securities markets and that it was now possible to treat financial instruments as if they were commodities. Once that realization set in, the door opened for futures exchanges to establish themselves even further. Not to be outdone, the New York Merc announced that it was introducing currency futures in August 1974.

There was also a nationalistic element in currency trading that was especially strong since the general dollar float. The gnomes had traveled west to Chicago. Rightly so, said IMM chairman Leo Melamed. "Predictably, our market has already experienced a number of significant changes," he stated, "subject to modifications brought about by our own daily dealings with this new vehicle of finance, previously the sole possession of the gnomes of Zurich, London, and Frankfurt. Why we asked, should this be so? By what right should European centuries-old markets be the sole determinants of the value of the dollar?"[5] None, as far as anyone in Chicago could see. However, the shift was overstated. The futures market for currencies, as useful as it was, did not develop as a substitute for the foreign exchange market, only as an adjunct of it.

To date, volatility had been witnessed in both the currency markets and the stock markets. In the financial world, though, it was understood that currency rates and stock prices were a function of interest rates. That was probably more easily understood in the forex markets than in the stock markets. Currency spot and forward rates were tied directly to interest rates, and once a country changed its official interest rates, it could expect a change in its currency value. Traditional economics textbooks taught that increases in the money supply—later understood to be an integral part of inflation—were good for stocks because they made more money available for investment. What was not clear was the link between inflation and stock speculation. If inflation rose and interest rates were adjusted upward as a result then margin rates would also increase. The cost of carrying stocks on margin would increase which would dissuade many speculators from the market. The link between interest rates and other financial instruments became more clear as a result of the turmoil but it was an expensive education.

While the futures pits were becoming transformed in the 1970s, the settlement process was being changed as well. In 1970, the CBOT moved its reporting- and data-processing systems 15 miles from the exchange, placing them under the management of a company that specialized in data processing. The move was the first for an exchange and marked the inroads that computers had made in reporting and processing transactions. The move was necessary for volume was increasing dramatically.

Financial futures held center stage during the early 1970s but did not entirely dominate the markets. The humble soybean became a cause célèbre in 1973 in the anti-inflation war being fought by the Nixon administration. The beans actually became the country's top cash crop in 1973, outselling wheat and corn. The importance of soybeans was that they were an integral additive to many foods as well as a major export item. Soybean prices doubled in the year prior to the action and the effect on inflation proved worrisome. Soybeans had become the favorite food of the day. In 1973, the first soyburger was introduced in New York, albeit to somewhat less-than-enthusiastic reviews from meat lovers. A soybean shortage developed in the summer of that year causing the administration to halt the export of soybeans (along with cottonseed) and their derivatives for a week. The action was taken primarily to prevent a shortage of food for cattle and hogs so that core food prices could be kept stable. After the initial ban, the administration intended to reassess the strategy and provide a planned system of export controls. Needless to say, futures prices skyrocketed on the news. Suddenly, soybeans were on everyone's lips if not in their stomachs.

President Nixon left most of the battle to his cabinet. He then unfortunately confided in an interview that although he thought the price rise was a problem, he had no idea what a soybean looked like. Upon hearing his remarks, Representative J. Litton of Missouri—a major soybean-growing state—sent Nixon five sacks of the ubiquitous bean so that he would no longer claim to be unfamiliar with it.

The futures markets reacted immediately. The CBOT suspended soybean trading for a few days until the situation could be resolved. In New York, the COMEX also suspended silver futures as well, allowing trading only for those traders liquidating positions. Silver also had been subjected to wild price swings. The silver problem was temporarily overshadowed by soybeans but would emerge as the major financial market scandal of the 1970s. In one rare case in which the SEC intervened in a commodities-related problem, the agency filed suit in Las Vegas, charging Western Pacific Gold and Silver Exchange Corp. with selling investment contracts on the metals without the necessary futures contracts to back them up. The company operated a Ponzi-style scheme by paying off old investors with the funds of new ones. The company promised to purchase gold and silver coins from customers but had little or no cash in a rising market and little intent to do legitimate business. The company's president, a former candidate for governor of Nevada, ran afoul of the SEC by financing his fraudulent campaign with a bank loan, collateralized with the company's stock. The CEA was powerless in this case for silver was not an agricultural commodity and did not fall under the aegis of the 1936 Commodity Exchange Act.

## ENTER THE CFTC

The fast-moving futures world finally evoked a response from Congress. Since the salad oil scandal of 10 years before, a great amount of criticism had been leveled at the CEA for not having a clear mandate or the labor resources to deal with the quickly expanding futures markets. The SEC did not have jurisdiction in the field. Therefore, a new body was needed to regulate the markets. In 1974, Congress passed the Commodity Futures Trading Commission (CFTC) Act, which was designed to give futures markets a badly needed SEC-style regulator for the first time in their history. The CFTC became the watchdog of futures markets, including those in agriculturals and financials.

Although the CEA had existed since 1936, it was not felt to be effective and it accomplished little. If the opposite had been true, there would have been no need for a new regulator. Similar to the SEC, the CFTC was a five-member body that had broad regulatory power over the 16 futures markets. Section 201 of the CFTC gave the commission exclusive jurisdiction over the markets. Its powers included increasing the personnel of the new agency to 500, requiring registration of commodity futures brokers, segregating the margin funds of customers from those of brokers, and potentially banning options trading on futures contracts. Although options on futures were already banned, trading did occur in some metal futures contracts because the CEA had no authority over nonagricultural contracts. Unlike some other federal agencies, the CFTC was formed with a "sunset clause" attached, meaning that it would require renewal periodically in the future. That clause kept pressure on the commission during its early days. Its first renewal was required in 1978.

Many in the futures industry were opposed to the commission. The reasons for opposing it were traditional and had been heard many times before. The body would stifle the markets' spirit and be unduly costly and an unnecessary layer of federal bureaucracy. However, senior management at the exchanges recognized the handwriting on the wall and decided to accept the CFTC rather than oppose it. Other markets were already regulated. Leo Melamed described the new arrangement as "something akin to a shotgun wedding. Thus I felt that if a federal regulatory agency was unavoidable, it would be best for our industry to accept its fate and partake in its creation."[6] Traders complained but the exchanges' management realized that the new regulator was destined for permanence. Within a short time, the CFTC developed its own guidelines against market manipulation.

There was more discussion over the composition of the new body since traders knew that the personalities of the commissioners would dictate much of the CFTC's activities. William T. Bagley, a former Republican California State Senator, was named by President Ford to be the first chairperson of the commission. *Business Week* characterized him as "an inexperienced amateur," but his lack of experience did not prevent him from predicting that "we will be a bright star in the regulatory heaven." A graduate of the University of California at Berkeley and its law school, Bagley had never bought or sold a commodity before assuming the chair and it was widely assumed that his role would be mostly passive. The 47-year-old chairperson was well aware of the futures industry's hope that his lack of experience would result in a hands-off policy but he was determined to show some toughness. Surveillance was foremost on his agenda and he proclaimed that the CFTC would not simply rubber-stamp policies made by the former CEA. Within a couple of months, applications for new products to be listed on the exchanges began to reach Bagley's office.

One of the first applications was for mortgage futures. By its very nature, the new contract was too sophisticated to have originated in the pits. It was designed by Richard Sandor, a finance professor at Berkeley. Having the distinction of being the first interest rate future, it was introduced in 1975 when the CBOT launched a contract on the Government National Mortgage Association (GNMA) mortgage-backed certificate. The GNMA, more popularly known as Ginnie Mae, actually was a 30-year bond having a yield only slightly lower than the mortgage rate itself. The agency sold its bonds to investors and used the money to buy guaranteed mortgages from banks, which made them to homeowners under the agency's guidelines. In short, the agency was supporting urban mortgages made under guidelines established by the Department of Housing and Urban Development (HUD). If long-term interest rates rose, mortgage rates would rise with them, making home loans more expensive. If the Ginnie Mae bond could be hedged, then the new futures contract would help stabilize the mortgage market. Investors would have less reason to sell mortgage bonds and mortgage rates would be more stable.

Ginnie Mae and HUD were both products of civil rights legislation that had been passed during the 1960s. Part of their mission was to provide affordable urban housing in the wake of the race riots that rocked many cities during the mid- to late 1960s. The bonds issued by the agency became popular very quickly. Salomon Brothers developed a market for them and quickly began trading heavy volume. The CBOT saw an opportunity both to make money and do something futures exchanges seldom could claim; provide a distinct benefit to mortgage investors and urban homeowners alike. Although traders and mortgage investors, such as banks, greeted the futures contract enthusiastically, it was never as successful as originally anticipated and was eventually suspended from trading in the 1980s.[7] Nevertheless, its introduction spawned more futures that would survive the rough-and-tumble world of the pits.

Not to be outdone by its rival, the CME applied for permission to trade futures on U.S. Treasury bills at the same time. While the Ginnie Mae contract represented $100,000 face amount of bonds, the bill contract was for $1 million. Both were considered round lots for their respective instruments. While the contracts represented the short and long ends of the yield curve, they were only the tip of the iceberg. New contracts were beginning to be introduced frequently. In addition to those made for financials, there were applications for cotton-seed, crude oil, and coal futures, as well as for contracts on ocean-freight rates. *Financial World* remarked that it hoped the CFTC would "bring more credibility to the futures industry," although, it said, "Wall Street feared the effects of over-regulation."[8] However, that would be the price of admission given the futures markets' reputation for fast trades and lax self-regulation. The SEC opposed allowing Ginnie Mae futures to be regulated by the CFTC. As far as it was concerned, mortgage bond futures were securities, and therefore it—not the commodities regulator—should regulate the contracts.

The CFTC faced a rocky road almost from its inception. Bagley took off the gloves in 1977 when he filed suit against Texas oil tycoon Nelson Bunker Hunt. Hunt and his family had exceeded the limits on trading in soybean contracts and caused serious price distortions in the market. The CFTC sought to block them from further trading after the fact that their efforts had made them more than $50 million had been widely publicized. The episode vividly illustrated the trials and tribulations of the markets in the 1970s.

The soybean corner began when Nelson Bunker Hunt, son of the legendary Texas oil tycoon H. L. Hunt, set out to corner the soybean market with the assistance of several family members, including his brother W. Herbert Hunt. Position limits on the number of futures contracts any trader could accumulate was equal to 3 million bushels, or 5 percent of the market. The Hunts' position was much larger, topping out at almost 24 million bushels, or 40 percent of the market. If Nelson Hunt had acted alone, he would have been comfortably within the limits. However, in the classic tradition of a corner, he had employed family members to help violate them. Having joined Nelson Hunt in the corner, they duplicated many of his positions to avoid the position limits.

When the CFTC sued to prevent further trading, it cited the price rise in soybeans, which had increased from $5.15 to $10.30 in a year. The heavy volume in soybeans and its derivatives accounted for almost half the volume on the CBOT at the peak of trading. Named in the action were Hunt, his brother W. Herbert Hunt, and five of the brothers' children, most of whom were college students. The dummy accounts created by the Hunt family did not fool the CFTC nor were the accounts particularly well disguised since they all used the same mailing address. One of the CFTC commissioners remarked that the only member of the family who did not have a trading account was the family dog.[9]

Everyone, though, enjoyed the results. The profits from the rise in soybean prices were estimated to be around $100 million. Bagley contended that the single mailing address was proof of a corner. Nelson Hunt's reply was that Bagley was "full of baloney." He claimed that each family member traded individually but with similar patterns because of their access to similar research reports on soybeans. They also had a substantial short position independent of the longs. In an original twist, Nelson Hunt accused the CFTC of "trying to manipulate the market by forcing people to sell. I call that attempted blackmail." For his part, Bagley contended that the CBOT should have done more to prevent such large positions but questions remained about under whose jurisdiction the Hunts fell. Unlike

Tino DeAngelis, the Hunts did not own a seat on any of the exchanges; they remained simply "outside investors." Bagley, however, remained resolute. "I am not playing God nor economist," he explained, "but enforcing a congressional mandate."[10]

The case appeared to be a certain victory for the CFTC but in the world of futures regulation it could not be considered fait accompli. The suit went to court in April 1977 and the CFTC asked the court to force the Hunts to liquidate their excessive positions to protect the public. The CFTC also claimed that the Hunts continued to trade "even in the face of repeated admonitions from the Commission and its staff that [the] violations were serious and a threat to the market." The CFTC also made their positions public, infuriating the Hunts in the process.

The disposition of the case surprised many and cast a long shadow over the effectiveness of the CFTC. In September 1977 the court ruled that the Hunts had indeed violated the regulations but it refused to impose any penalties. In short, it was the business of the CFTC to impose penalties, not the court. Members of the CFTC admitted later that they needed proof that the Hunts intended to manipulate the market, a contention for which they did not have good evidence to support.[11] As a result, the case was a victory for the speculators and a black eye for the CFTC. The battle, however, was not quite over.

Conscious that its good name was at stake, the CFTC instituted an administrative hearing a few months later. An appeal court finally reviewed the case and overturned the lower court's ruling. It ordered the excessive trading in the Hunt accounts beyond the limits to cease and the illegal profits to be returned. It appeared that the CFTC had won its victory after all. The Hunts settled the case with the commission in 1981 for a nominal sum so that both sides could claim victory. The settlement, like the case itself, was surrounded by statements from the Hunts about the intrusions of government in the private sector and their innocent intentions. The fact remained that the soybean affair was only one of two in which the Hunts were involved. The second would make them infamous.

Concerns about the CFTC's effectiveness surfaced quickly. One of the agency's former policy-level staff members commented in October 1977, after the Hunt case, that "the place is a Titanic; it's a disaster." Senator Huddleston was also making similar comments. The laundry list of complaints against the young agency already was long. Besides the Hunt soybean case, it included illegal tax rollovers, commodity options problems, a Maine potato fiasco, and alleged price manipulation in the coffee futures market. Critics were vociferous because of a review underway by the General Accounting Office (GAO) into the agency's operations due to be released to Congress in February 1978. Supporters also offered reassurance that the agency was new and needed time to work out its operations smoothly. Size was a crucial factor. The agency had a staff of 500 and an annual budget of $13 million and it was expected to supervise over a dozen independent markets that were constantly introducing new products. By contrast, the SEC had a staff of over 1,900 and an annual budget of $49 million to supervise fewer markets with less dollar turnover.[12]

But the older regulatory agency did not want to make any concessions to its younger counterpart. In early 1978, the SEC sent a 10-page memorandum to the GAO as part of the same review. To Washington's surprise, the securities regulator proposed that it, not the CFTC, regulate the financial futures markets. Since financial futures were introduced in 1972, the SEC continually expressed doubts about any regulatory body for the nascent market except itself, and the founding of the CFTC never changed its mind. When the contents of the memorandum were made public, both Wall Street and LaSalle Street were surprised and dismayed. A CBOT official remarked that the memo had "some people up in arms but the rest of us can't believe that we'll have to fight this battle again." The president of the CBOT, Robert Wilmouth, stated that "I don't like it. Only one agency should regulate the commodity industry and if it's the CFTC, so be it."[13] Critics heard that remark and noted that the CBOT would naturally prefer the weaker of the two regulators. The memorandum set up another jurisdictional battle that the CBOT would win.

The full board of the CBOT interpreted the problems at the CFTC somewhat differently. Despite Wilmouth's previous comments, the CBOT board failed to give the agency an endorsement when its reauthorization was due in 1978. Wilmouth was directed to support any proposed legislation that would change the CFTC back to a division of the Department of Agriculture—in short, to return to the status quo of the old CEA. A similar proposal at the CME was dismissed. As Leo Melamed put it, it would be a "step backward." The CBOT's action was hardly a reassuring vote of confidence in the new regulatory body. If any fragmentation of regulators passed the reauthorization hearings, the futures industry would have been in a quandary. Even in the face of the CFTC's checkered but short history, it seemed that the CBOT was adopting a divide-and-conquer strategy.

Making matters worse for the CFTC, the GAO recommended to Congress that some of the agency's authority be transferred to the SEC. It wanted Congress to give the SEC authority over any financial future that represented such securities as stocks, corporate bonds, and government securities. Stock index futures were also included, although they were not yet trading. The Kansas City Board of Trade applied to the CFTC for permission to trade futures on a stock index and was waiting approval. The Philadelphia Stock Exchange did the same but submitted its application to the SEC instead.

Despite all of the posturing, the CFTC was renewed and kept its powers over the futures exchanges. The futures markets had only one regulator while equity options markets had the SEC. Within a year, the CFTC was authorizing the expansion of financial futures. In 1979, the American Stock Exchange's commodities division and the COMEX both received authorization to trade Treasury bill futures. The CBOT and the CME were given authorization to trade medium-term Treasury notes. The NYSE soon entered the fray by applying for its own financial futures exchange, the New York Futures Exchange (NYFE). Expansion was on the agenda for all the futures exchanges. A year earlier, the once-proud New York Merc had announced plans to trade petroleum futures and currency futures. Petroleum futures were currently traded at Rotterdam, the Netherlands, and the exchange saw an opportunity to have similar contracts traded in the United States in smaller-contract amounts. It regretted its lack of initiative in currency futures which it originally launched in 1974 only to watch the CME dominate the market. In a succinct explanation of why the New York Merc decided to reenter the market, a spokesperson declared that the new volatility in the currency markets gave it a new opportunity, adding that "we believe that we will generate additional business in New York rather than siphoning business away from Chicago." The lesser exchanges did not want to pose a direct challenge to the market leaders for fear of retaliation, which would only stymie their development even more.

## GNOMES IN CHICAGO

Currency futures on the IMM were born out of crisis and naturally it was fitting that a crisis tested the IMM's resolve. On September 1, 1976 Mexico officially devalued its currency by almost 40 percent in the greatest peso crisis of the post–World War II era. As one of the largest trading partners of the United States, Mexico had pegged the peso to the dollar since 1954. However, trade problems loomed for the peso was universally acknowledged to be overvalued and Mexican trade was suffering as a result. Because of the peso's popularity, the IMM introduced peso–dollar futures contracts and successfully traded them for several years. When the devaluation came, the peso volume on the IMM increased exponentially. The exchange traded almost $100 million in contracts before the confusion subsided. The stability provided by the IMM prompted Leo Melamed to note, "A hundred million dollars changed hands and we were safe and secure. And the world took notice that the Chicago IMM stayed in business and continued to trade Mexican pesos."[14]

The popularity of currency futures led to problems. In 1976, an investigation began into what were known as tax rollovers on the CBOT, the CME, and the IMM. The Justice Department and the Internal Revenue Service subpoenaed trading documents from the exchanges to determine whether traders had been rolling futures profits and losses further out by switching soon-to-be-due contracts into those with longer life-spans. The Internal Revenue Service estimated that over $100 million in tax revenues had been lost between 1972 and 1976 and concluded that currency futures trading had been employed in the process along with agriculturals. The exchanges sought to quash the subpoena but it was carried out after a federal district judge denied the exchanges' request and ordered them to produce the requested documents.

Precious metals always attracted attention during inflationary times. Futures on gold were finally introduced in 1974 and began trading on the CBOT, the IMM, and the COMEX. Silver was already trading and the markets now had basic contracts for almost every financial contingency. While the role of gold in the international monetary system clearly was on everyone's mind, its old compatriot, silver, became the metal that made the most headlines during the mid-1970s. The scandal that developed around the almost-forgotten metal was so reminiscent of Jay Gould's gold corner in 1869 that it seemed as if someone had rewritten the story, only changing names and dates in the process.

Both options and futures were growing by leaps and bounds in the 1970s but the CME saw problems with the way the IMM was developing. While the CBOT and the CBOE were operating separately and developing a professional animosity for each other, the CME realized that it was in its own best interests to bring the IMM back to the fold. A merger was proposed whereby the two would again share seats and physical facilities. However, a proposed union would not be sold easily to the membership. The IMM members felt they did not need the CME and its traditional commodities while the older exchange looked at the financial futures traders as upstarts. The CME wanted to expand the number of seats available for sale and realized that including the IMM would enhance its prospects considerably. After much debate and some very hard selling, a merger was approved in October 1975. The boards of the two exchanges approved the merger with little dissent and their members followed suit. Members of the CME voted 343 to 23 for the merger; members of the IMM, 396 to 57. At the same time, a nonlivestock division eventually called the Associate Mercantile Market Division, was created, which traded eggs, lumber, butter, and frozen turkeys.[15] Although traditional agricultural commodities were not dead, they had certainly taken a backseat to the new financial futures.

Despite scandal and controversy over the effectiveness of the CFTC, product development showed no signs of abating. What would prove to be the most popular financial future of all was introduced in 1977, when the CBOT listed contracts on the long-term Treasury bond. Designed by Richard Sandor, these contracts allowed traders to speculate or hedge both the long and short end of the yield curve and they were quickly adopted by mortgage bankers and professional traders exposed to long-term interest rates. Originally, the future represented 20-year Treasury bonds, but during the same year, the Treasury announced that it would begin issuing 30-year Treasury bonds. As a result, delivery became much more complicated and it took a couple of years to sort out the problems. However, within a few years long bond futures became the most popular type of futures contract. Although other bond and short-term interest rate futures would later be introduced, it was obvious that interest rates, as with other financial instruments, were now being treated as commodities.

The proliferation of new products found a warm reception among wholesale and retail speculators. By early 1977, the NYSE approved options trading in principle although it did not establish facilities for trading. The CBOE was trading almost 90 listed options, all on blue-chip issues. The *New York Times* cited the IMM as a leading monetary market for forex futures, based on its success in handling the peso crisis of several months before. However, describing the market in such terms was somewhat misleading because the true market for currencies was still conducted among banks.

True to the history of futures markets, one progressive step forward was followed by one step back. In 1976, a major scandal erupted when traders on the New York Merc defaulted on delivery of 50 million pounds of Maine potatoes, as specified by their contracts. Normally, the New York Merc imposed limits of 150 contracts on speculators but when the May 1976 future expired, an extraordinary number of contracts were left outstanding. Usually, the delivery average of outstanding contracts was about 3 percent, but when the May contract expired, over 1,900 contracts were left undelivered. Suspicions were immediately aroused, for the U.S. potato crop was very strong while a potato shortage existed in Britain and the rest of

Europe. An agriculture department spokesperson described the situation as eerily familiar. "It sure reminded us of 1973 and their grain deal with the Russians," he commented.

Investigation showed that two competing groups had taken opposite positions—one long and the other short—in the futures market. One of the groups, representing potato farmers from the Pacific Northwest, sold 15,000 tons to a European importer. When the news agencies reported the deal, however, a typographical error appeared; instead of 15,000 tons, the amount was reported as 150,000 tons—all on the buy side. The market price rose immediately even though the seller maintained to the CFTC that it was an honest mistake. Richard Levine, president of the New York Merc, took the matter very seriously. He realized that the integrity of his market was at stake. "The situation is unprecedented," he stated. "Even one default is a grave matter. Those responsible will face extreme penalties."[16] Apparently, the shorts refused to cover at the higher prices and simply decided to let the situation work itself out.

A year later, the CFTC investigated reports that manipulation was involved with the May 1976 contract and came to the same conclusion as the New York Merc. Levine stated that he thought the problem was due to a simple misunderstanding. The CFTC concurred, saying, "The evidence did not establish that new stories were purposely misleading or that violations of the Commodity Exchange Act occurred with respect to those news stories."[17] The deliveries were covered and the CFTC appeared to try to hide its embarrassment at the whole affair. Its public relations were not helped by the original default or its subsequent conclusion.

## *PRIVILEGED*

By the mid-1970s, equity options were developing quickly but options on futures contracts still languished under the 1936

Commodity Exchange Act. Options on metal futures had developed into a small specialized market simply because metals did not fall under the original act. However, the CFTC had the ability to rule on futures options and was about to make itself unpopular in some quarters for exercising its regulatory muscles.

Futures options were sold by brokers in California, New York, and Massachusetts to relatively unsophisticated investors. For the most part, these options were traded overseas in London, not domestically. They were either puts or calls that called for the delivery of a futures contract—in other words, a derivative based upon a derivative. The brokers realized that the products were beyond the reach of American regulators. With a relatively weak record of pursuing less-than-scrupulous brokers, there was little reason to think that the regulators would take much notice. The options were essentially the product of bucket shops that were capitalizing on both the reputation of commodity volatility and the popularity of equity. The term "bucket shop" was no longer in vogue. Now, the preferred term was "boiler room," after the high-pressure sales tactics used by such a room's brokers to close a sale.

The brokers sold options on futures listed on the London Commodity Exchange. Most of their clients were Americans who thought they were purchasing negotiable options but because these options were actually of the European variety, they could prove very risky to the seller at expiration date, especially if the buyer demanded delivery of the underlying contract. The CFTC knew about the operation but refused to ban options trading. Instead, it planned to have the dealers register so that they would fall under its jurisdiction. The agency preferred to regulate rather than punish during its early years. However, before any useful policies could emerge, scandal struck once again.

In January 1978, the CFTC charged a New York broker

with fraud in the sale of commodity options. The agency claimed that Neuberger & Co. used high-pressure boiler-room tactics to sell unwitting small investors London options, misrepresenting the risks in the process. The firm pleaded no contest, claiming, "We agreed to this action without admitting or denying any of the allegations in order to avoid protracted litigation and bring this matter to an end."[18] Another boiler-room operator did not prove to be so compliant, however. Similar charges were leveled against Lloyd, Carr & Co., a Boston-based futures brokerage firm run by a James A. Carr. When his background was revealed, it was obvious that the markets still had a long distance to go before claiming that they were free of corrupt influences.

When the charges had been made, Carr was already under indictment for fraud by the Massachusetts securities authorities. The firm was served with a cease and desist order but continued to operate. Carr then fled for places unknown, later reputed to be hiding in the Caribbean with approximately $2 million of the firm's funds. An FBI investigation revealed that his name was not Carr but Alan Abrahams and that he had escaped from a New Jersey prison in 1974. He had a 22-year record of criminal activities and was wanted by several law enforcement agencies. Carr was eventually apprehended in Florida and sentenced to two-and-a-half years in prison for violating probation in a 1971 tax case. Consequently, the CFTC began thinking about better registration procedures for brokers. The agency then made an embarrassing revelation. It admitted that it had never examined Carr's books during all of its troubles. The explanation did not satisfy many of its early critics. With all of the litigation pending against the broker, the CFTC claimed that it did not want to add more confusion by insisting on an audit.

The CFTC still managed to establish a reputation for toughness early in its history. In 1976, it told the New York exchanges in no uncertain terms that it wanted them to tighten their operations. The agency wanted the "establishment of new or improved rules and procedures that will protect investors and traders, while governing boards should be more than a token gesture representing the constituency of the exchanges, including the general public."[19] Some of the exchanges complied and asked well-known public figures to sit on their boards. Andrew Brimmer, a former Fed governor, sat on the board of the COMEX, as did William Simon, former treasury secretary. The exchanges were encouraged to consolidate their operations in the new World Trade Center being built at the time. However, the agency did not stop in New York; it gave the Chicago exchanges the same message shortly afterward. Finally, in June 1978, the agency banned the sale of commodities futures options until it was able to resolve the issue.

The CFTC was reacting to the continuing problems with commodity options. In 1977, it issued guidelines for a pilot program that would allow options to be reintroduced into the markets officially after a 40-year absence. The speed of the proposal was greeted skeptically in the markets, however, where most traders thought the CFTC's timetable much too ambitious. It was trying too quickly to stamp out OTC options by replacing them with approved contracts. The proposal was made by CFTC Vice Chair John Rainbolt, who—aware of the industry's history and the CFTC's new role in trying to regulate it—allowed himself to muse publicly by saying, "I wonder if the futures industry ever would have gotten off the ground if the CFTC had been around back then."[20] The markets had been through tough patches with regulators before but it remained to be seen whether good luck or serendipity would again bail them out.

Many of the CFTC's early problems were simply growing pains and resentment from the futures industry which (the CEA notwithstanding) had its own way for over a century.

222

However, even the exclusive jurisdiction found in the 1974 act did not clarify the messy situation that existed from years of overlap by the SEC, by state and federal courts, and, most important, by new product development. Even when the myriad state and federal courts, legislatures, and securities agencies could agree on jurisdiction over the markets, new products stretched the limits of regulation. Although not obvious to the casual observer, research and product development teams were designing products that confused regulators. Who was responsible for them? The original Black–Scholes model gave a hint of the problem. A stock and a bond could be combined to replicate the potential payout on an option, meaning that options should fall within the SEC's ambit. However, what if the derivative instrument was not tied to a security? Suppose the same replication could be achieved by a futures contract? The answer was far from obvious and would not be easily solved.

By the end of the 1970s, the problems were more acute than ever. James M. Stone, an economist and former insurance commissioner of Massachusetts, succeeded Bagley as chair of the CFTC in 1979. When he took office, three other federal agencies were actively plowing ground that was originally designated for the commission—the Federal Reserve and the Treasury, which were studying the effects of Treasury bond futures on the government's debt-management policies, and the SEC, which continued with another of its studies on the stock options market. The CFTC itself was in the process of further study on the feasibility of commodity options after its first blush with them had stalled two years before. The results were more than just academic inquiries. They could be used for official position papers to frame public policy in the future.

The new products allowed brokers to begin marketing to the small investor. New products meant more diversity and brokers began packaging investment vehicles, affordable to small investors, that did not expose them to just one or two commodity futures. For $5,000, investors could buy into a limited partnership, or commodity fund, that allowed a group of investors to take advantage of price swings in the funds' futures contracts. Managed accounts were also added so that the manager, not the investor, would be able to trade them at his or her discretion. Those types of accounts attracted many brokers to the business. *Money* magazine warned its readers that "investors can be wiped out suddenly. And business ethics also may not be scrupulous . . . of the 140 firms trading in deferred delivery contracts on record with the CFTC in 1979, around 30 have folded or are operating under different names."[21]

Commodity funds, or pools, became breeding grounds for fraud. If a fund had fewer than 15 investors, it would not be required to register its activities with the CFTC. Many would charge investors for their services, taking their fee before calculating gains or losses. Others employed traditional bucket shop techniques. They would accept investors' funds, pocket them, and record fictitious trades on paper, showing small losses. Because the losses were too small to panic investors, they would not ask for their money back. If the market was poor, the small losses appeared to be good management on the part of the fund managers. Then, the fund would end its operations or shift to a different locale and begin again. Given the presence of the CFTC in the market, the activities of pool operators began to give commodities investing a bad name. Critics began demanding nonrenewal of the sunset clause, arguing that the CFTC was ineffective or had the wrong set of priorities.

Financial futures and investment vehicles dominated the market in the 1970s, leading many commentators to pronounce the traditional futures market dead and all but buried. The agricultural sector actually was very alive and well but old criticism began to flare up again. When financial futures and options were introduced, many commentators wondered if pit traders could grasp the intricacies of currencies and interest rates. They discovered that it was not difficult. "If it has a bid and offered price," responded one trader, "I can trade it." The whole concept was then turned upside down when farmers and others in the agricultural business realized that their favorite commodities were being given short shrift by traders who preferred financial futures to the less exotic soybeans and pork bellies.

Farmers had always questioned the role of futures exchanges in producing valid prices but in the late 1970s they also began to question the role of the CFTC. No commissioner had an agriculture background and the CFTC seemed content to allow traders with no knowledge of basic agricultural supply-and-demand factors to set prices on commodities.[22] The complaint was a century-old one but this time it carried more urgency for the CFTC was in line for renewal again shortly. Washington, however, had reason to worry about expert agricultural futures experts and traders in the markets because of another corner mounted in 1978 and 1979—this time, by members of the CBOT commission itself.

In winter 1979, another corner was unearthed on the CBOT. The CFTC sent a warning letter to a speculator who accumulated a large position in wheat. That speculator, Alan Freeman, was a partner in Rosenthal & Co. with Leslie Rosenthal, the firm's vice chair and also a director of the CBOT. Rosenthal received a similar warning. More embarrassing for the CBOT, keenly aware of its image in the marketplace, was the fact that Rosenthal was elected vice chair of the exchange in January 1979. The positions were revealed publicly when Freeman and Rosenthal attempted to block the CFTC action in court. Freeman controlled about 2.5 million bushels in futures contracts while his positions combined with Rosenthal's suggested that they held 90 percent of the positions in March wheat and owned about half of the physical supply. The two's combined positions amounted to a classic squeeze on the market because when the shorts were forced to cover, they found physical wheat to be in short supply.

Conflict of interest abounded when it was revealed that Rosenthal was part of the CBOT's internal discussions on how to best respond to the CFTC's concerns. The exchange did not react quickly enough to satisfy the CFTC and the agency ordered a halt in March wheat trading. At the time, the March futures were trading as high as 55 cents more than the next nearest delivery months, May and July. The trading halt was reversed by a Chicago court a day later. The CFTC backed away from pursuing a further ban because it claimed that its action apparently prevented a further jump in the futures price.[23] The affair was another case of all sides claiming victory, although it was clear that the fox was still in the henhouse at the CBOT.

Despite all of the advances made by the exchanges during the 1970s, the decade still witnessed an unusually large number of corners and attempted market manipulations. While the breakdown of the Bretton Woods system led to many new, clever futures products, it also unleashed skepticism about the value and future of the dollar. The attitude led to the largest and best known corner of the decade. The great irony was that it occurred while the markets seemed to be making their greatest strides toward integrity and regulation.

## *HI-HO SILVER*

Economic conditions in the early 1970s caused a great many wealthy investors to turn to speculation as a means of keeping ahead of declining asset values and inflation. Their penchant for trading added to the volatility because the constant buying and selling became something of a self-fulfilling prophecy for securities and derivatives markets. These developments occurred not because the general public took a new interest in the futures markets but because wealthy investors with an excess of time and money decided to play the markets.

In spirit, they were not alone for the public clamored for the return of lotteries, the old favorite for small speculators. After being banned for years, lotteries began to make a slow comeback. As the 1970s began, New Hampshire, New York, and New Jersey all instituted state lotteries and several other states planned to follow suit. Speculators—large and small—now had more opportunity than ever to make a killing. The increased interest in gambling and speculation was the greatest ever since the Civil War changed American attitudes toward easy money. War was the first cause of a major shift in attitudes toward speculation. Inflation was the second.

The scions of a wealthy Texas family entered the fray on a scale not witnessed since the Tino De Angelis affair had rocked the markets a decade before. Nelson Bunker Hunt and his brother W. Herbert Hunt were oil tycoons who made a fortune in the oilfields of the Middle East and North Africa. But after seizure of the Libyan oilfields, Nelson Hunt in particular was at something of a loss for investment opportunities for some of the $4 billion he was reportedly worth.

In many respects, silver was the opposite of gold. It had a limited monetary use, and its significance was diminishing quickly. In 1965, the Coinage Act eliminated its use in dimes and quarters and reduced its content in half-dollars. Two years later, the Treasury ended its managed sales of silver and its price increased about 60 cents to $1.87 per ounce. At the same time, the Treasury announced that it was no longer possible to redeem its silver certificates. The price rose on this news and gave heart to silver aficionados who believed that the metal had been given a new lease on life as a hedge against inflation. Silver futures, unregulated by the CEA, were introduced at about the same time. As a result, silver futures contracts had no position limits imposed on them; traders could buy or sell as many contracts as needed with no regulatory implications. Silver traded primarily at the COMEX and the CBOT.

Even before the soybean affair, the Hunt brothers had been speculating in the silver futures market with great abandon. As early as 1973, Nelson Hunt had been purchasing silver in the Middle East, apparently to accumulate a sizable physical horde of the metal. In December of that year, the Hunts purchased $20 million worth of silver and had contracts for another 35 million ounces at a price of $2.90 per ounce.[24] Holding that much physical silver, in addition to the huge position in futures, suggested that a squeeze was developing. As a result, the price increased dramatically to $6.70 within two months, and as in the past, short sellers were faced with a physical-supply problem so the price began to run up. Without the government's planned sales program of the previous decade, no stabilizing influence existed on the market. Moreover, the price increased without a substantial change in demand factors other than speculation. While the market abounded with rumors, serious demand was no different than that before the squeeze.

A classic squeeze and corner was being mounted and the Hunts apparently had some outside help. Bunker made many trips to the Middle East during the mid-1970s where he enlisted the help of wealthy Saudi investors who did not mind making a few extra dollars. Using his past oil connections to good advantage, he was able to convince several of these investors who had substantial assets to join him in buying silver. Among the investors were three wealthy Saudis: Khalid bin Mahfouz, Prince Abdullah of the Saudi royal family, and Gaith Pharaon. Mahfouz's family ran the National Commercial Bank, Saudi Arabia's largest bank that would later have close ties with the Bank of Credit and Commerce International (BCCI). That bank was accused of international money laundering and was closed by both the Fed and the Bank of England in the early 1990s after a major scandal involving almost $20 billion in lost assets. Introductions to the Hunts were made by John Connally, former governor of Texas and treasury secretary under Richard Nixon at the time of the collapse of the Bretton Woods system. Connally was on Nelson Hunt's payroll at the time.

Many of the Saudi investors, including Prince Abdullah, did not participate directly in the corner but used brokers designated by the Hunts to preserve their anonymity They did, however, provide substantial amounts of money. Additionally, rumors constantly abounded in the market that Saudi investors had taken a special interest in silver and such rumors helped to fuel speculative fires, for the Saudis—because of their vast oil wealth—were the world's nouveau riche. The Saudi Arabian Monetary Agency (SAMA) was also directly connected to the royal family and its immense dollar reserves were the constant subject of discussion and rumor. Although the speculators were individuals, their institutional relationships gave the markets the impression that the speculation was official, only adding to the price appreciation.

Using a related company that would not reveal its identity, the Hunts took delivery of over more than 20 million ounces of silver that added to their already well-established horde, bringing the total to 53 million ounces. The price was around $4.30 at the time, in summer 1976. The CFTC finally became interested in the movements in the silver market now that the market knew of the Hunts' involvement. Their explanation was simple. They told the CFTC that they were using the silver as payment for a trade-related deal in the Philippines for sugar.[25] Commodity-based trade and barter deals were common at the time because of the vacillating currency markets so their explanation was somewhat plausible. Despite the silver squeeze, the soybean corner was still their first serious challenge from the CFTC, which had known about the silver-related shenanigans for several years already.

Throughout the 1970s, the Hunts continued to accumulate silver. The silver markets—notably the COMEX and the CBOT, as well as the European markets—knew full well that the Hunts were on a long buying spree but they and their Middle East cronies were able to accumulate without interruption. Unlike previous corners (with the exception of De Angelis), there appeared to be little the futures exchanges could do since the buying activity originated from outside the exchanges. A corner mounted by a pit trader was easier to detect and ultimately prevent. However, simple customer orders were difficult to deal with, especially those of this magnitude. Moreover, silver did not dominate the news; other political news from the Middle East—including the Iranian hostage crisis of 1979 and the Soviet war in Afghanistan, also beginning in 1979—all competed for the news, along with the continued effects of inflation and the inexorable rise in the price of gold. In 1971, gold increased to $38 per ounce. By the end of the decade, it stood at $500 per ounce, reflecting international political turmoil and unrest.

In the wake of gold, silver also began its rise although it was constantly in the shadow of the more familiar yellow metal. The Hunt corner was giving the impression that silver was also an anti-inflationary metal although there was little evidence to suggest that any factors besides the Hunts and their Saudi investors were influencing its price. Gold could not be manipulated and was the favorite noncurrency asset of central banks around the world. The Hunts' relentless buying gave the impression that unseen forces became interested in silver although it was mainly a ruse designed to entice other traders into buying. Many professional metals traders did not share the enthusiasm for silver and as the metal finally peaked in price they would lose substantial sums of money in the process by being short. The inexorable price rise cost them too much and the traders were forced to liquidate short positions that would have been viable in any other market.

The most serious run in silver began in summer 1979. The Hunts and their cohorts placed substantial orders at brokers amounting to over 40 million ounces and the price reached almost $11. Most of the buying came from the International Metals Investment Co. (IMIC), owned primarily by the Hunts and the Saudis. The company was located in Bermuda and the CFTC made inquiries in order to determine who owned it. Even after discovering that the Hunts were principals, the CFTC was still at a loss regarding the best course of action. The price rise and the enormous positions caused the COMEX to raise its margin requirements but that action did not stop the speculation. When a trader buys a contract on margin and the price increases, the trader is able to invest the paper gain in more contracts, again on margin, a perfectly legal process in the markets known as "pyramiding." The risk factor is a separate issue, however. If prices should drop, the positions can easily cost the trader substantially, if not wipe out the positions entirely.

The size of the positions made one of the brokerage firms, Shearson, so nervous that it forced the Hunts to move their accounts elsewhere. The firm had good reason to worry about the risk involved because it was one of the firms that had absorbed a weaker firm during the backroom crisis earlier in the decade. When news that the Hunts were behind IMIC, the price of silver sharply increased again. It was becoming apparent that the corner was of historic proportions. Even some of the CBOT pit traders became nervous at the prospect of a few individuals having such influence over the market and grain traders were afraid of the spillover that a corner in the silver market might have on their own markets. Read Dunn, a Mississippian who served as one of the CFTC's commissioners, recalled a meeting he had with Warren Leibig, one of Chicago's largest and most influential grain traders. Leibig told Dunn that "we would rather see the silver market closed than have that happen." Dunn's reaction was disbelief. "It was astonishing. I, a federal regulator, was actually being encouraged to do something by these erstwhile laissez-fairers."[26] The concern, however, was not entirely about the integrity of the markets. Silver was primarily traded in New York on the COMEX, located in the World Trade Center. It was traded in Chicago as well but to a much smaller extent. A massive corner would only pique the interest of Congress and no one in the futures markets during the late 1970s wanted anything more to do with regulators.

Dunn and James Stone, the CFTC chair and a former economics lecturer at Harvard, discussed alternatives to control the market, settling on the simplest course of action—imposing position limits. They passed their concerns about the market to Robert Wilmouth at the CBOT who in turn, passed them to the Hunts. What was not clear at the time was that the Hunt children had again become commodity traders—this time in silver. Despite their assurances, the CBOT imposed position limits stating that no trader could have net positions of more than 600 contracts, long or short. The simple yet effective new rule for silver hit the Hunts hard because it impinged on their market positions. Nelson Hunt took the new rule especially hard and struck back at the pit traders, or locals, on the CBOT floor. "The fact of the matter is," he fulminated, "that the hometown boys who run the markets don't want anybody from out of town to make money in their markets."[27] He was probably partially correct but free-enterprise capitalism did not imply that markets could be manipulated by substantial investors having some of the world's deepest pockets.

The COMEX also imposed position limits on silver for the first time. The exchange allowed no positions of more than 500 contracts net, long or short. The CFTC did not act, preferring to leave the decisive actions to the exchanges themselves. Stone noted that the agency did not have the legal authority to impose limits retroactively and decided to let the exchanges determine the fate of the Hunts' positions. That lack of decisiveness would be a source of great criticism after the silver debacle finished. For his part, Nelson Hunt seemed indifferent to the wishes of the CFTC. If he and his brothers—W. Herbert, as well as Lamar (now also actively speculating in the silver market)—had been forced offshore, their ability to continue accumulating silver would have been made easier. As a result of the actions by the exchanges, *The Economist* commented, "Nelson Bunker Hunt will not be able to corner the silver market by amassing a huge position in silver futures."[28] But that missed the point, for the Hunts had already cornered the market.

Even in the face of strong opposition, the corner continued. Nelson Hunt took delivery of 1,200 contracts in December 1979, and his Saudi counterparts also took delivery of contracts. By late December of that year, the price was almost $30 per ounce and rising. The profits from the accumulation were beginning to emerge since the buying originally began with silver at $4 per ounce. No one could be sure of the Hunt brothers' total position at the time. The CFTC estimated that they held more than 200 million ounces at the beginning of 1980. Of that they held half the COMEX stock and 70 percent of the Chicago stock. Yet, simple questions continued to be raised. Some at the CFTC actually continued to wonder whether the operation was a genuine corner. That was an academic point to CFTC Commissioner David Gartner, who snapped, "Irrespective of their intentions, if they're cornering the market, they're cornering the market and that's manipulation." Read Dunn did the sums again when silver rose to $37 per ounce and figured that the positions were worth $2.2 billion in New York and $800 million in Chicago. When he wrote the numbers down, he remarked in his Southern drawl that "my pencil gets a shakin'."[29]

One problem that the Hunt brothers and the Saudis encountered with their silver-buying program could not have been anticipated because of its extraordinary nature. In October 1979, Paul Volcker, a veteran central banker, took over the helm as chair of the Federal Reserve Board, appointed by Jimmy Carter. His emphasis on controlling inflation was to center on the money supply rather than on interest rates, fully realizing that by tightening the supply of money and credit, interest rates would rise as a result. This was the beginning of a five-year battle to reduce inflation and bring interest rates down to reasonable levels. The effect it had on the financial markets was at first severe because it made credit more restrictive.

Credit became even more restricted the following March when the Carter administration and the Fed imposed special credit controls on banks and financial services companies in another attempt to reduce inflation. As a result of both measures, credit was more difficult to obtain. Lending by banks and brokers to the Hunts to fund their margin positions would become more expensive and then almost impossible. The price rise in silver in late 1979 was the last hurrah for the metal before it slipped drastically in price.

In late 1979, the Hunts ventured outside the silver market and bought a 3 percent stake in the New York brokerage firm Bache & Co. What appeared to be an independent investment quickly began to look like another ploy, however. Bache & Co. was a large broker in the futures markets, with many orders passed through it. The firm was revealed to have loaned the Hunts over $200 million in margin funds so that they could continue to accumulate. But the ploy still was working successfully. Silver finally hit $50 per ounce in late January 1980, although it could not be maintained. It was the highest price ever recorded.

Some attention was diverted from silver when the CFTC

ordered a temporary halt to grain trading in January because of President Carter's curtailment of grain shipments to the Soviet Union. The CBOT and other grain exchanges protested vigorously about the infringement to free-market capitalism but the CFTC took the president's lead and called the halt. Critics of Stone and the CFTC were not mollified by the move and cried foul. Stone's supporters took heart from the actions, however. They noted that the chair had been able to increase the CFTC's budget by 14 percent and had added 10 staff members to its admittedly small group. One of Stone's stronger suggestions for regulating the markets was the subject of much derision from the futures industry. In 1979, in response to the rumors of Saudi support for the Hunts' corner, the CFTC tried to implement tougher rules for foreigners who traded in the U.S. futures markets. One of the commission's ideas was to require foreigners to designate a U.S. representative responsible for disclosing, if requested, its clients' positions in the markets. This move was reminiscent of the Soviet grain short sales 50 years before. The futures industry would have none of it, however. David Harcourt, chair of the London Commodity Exchange, remarked that "the essence of a free market is that everyone trades in his own right and that business is confidential."[30] Critics with no vested interest in the argument simply saw the ideas as tangential to the issue. If the Hunt family was cornering the markets, it—not its supporters—should be confronted.

The situation was a no-win one for both the Hunts and the CFTC. The agency appeared incapable of dealing with the Hunts who cried that capitalism was being attacked at every opportunity by an interfering government. Again, it was the exchanges that initiated the action that brought the silver bubble to an end. After the price hit $50, the COMEX initiated a temporary rule that allowed further trading for liquidation purposes only so that new net positions could not be established. While the action seemed sensible, it was somewhat late and only opened the exchange to charges of protecting its own traders first. The effect was immediate. Silver began to tumble.

By March 1980, the Hunts' positions were unraveling, and the corner was finished. There was little doubt that the world's wealthiest family was able to absorb any losses but that naively overlooked the matter of margin calls. What was owed to whom would become a matter of concern for, as in the De Angelis affair, dozens of banks were involved in the United States and abroad. The pyramiding of contracts on top of each other was causing the pyramid to collapse from the top down and it was unclear who was supporting it. Then, in mid-March 1980, a margin call from Bache & Co. to the Hunts' account was not met and the brokerage firm had to meet part of it from its own resources to avoid a collapse. Another obligation—one to the Englehard Metals Co.—could not be met either but the world's largest metals trading company was not to be "bunkered" by the Hunts, as *The Economist* described their general market tactics. Cash was now needed and it was not forthcoming.

The Hunts' problems were so large that they recalled Mark Twain's famous adage: "When you owe a bank $1 and cannot pay, you have a problem. When you owe them a million and cannot pay, they have a problem." Fast-forwarding the adage to the 1980s made the problem even more urgent. At first glance, the Hunts apparently owed anywhere from $800 million to $1 billion that they could not pay back. Eight brokerage houses were in financial difficulty because of the futures dealings and banks were refusing new credit to the brothers because of the tight credit conditions imposed by the Fed. Compounding the problem was that the CFTC was not clear about the extent of the problem either.

The silver affair peaked on March 27, 1980, better known as "Silver Thursday" in the markets. The price touched a low of $10 before closing at $15, a full $35 per ounce off the all-time high. The price bounce was enough to save Bache & Co. and the other brokers who dealt with the Hunts although their losses were substantial. They all closed their long positions at the higher prices, avoiding serious losses in the process. Englehard Metals Co. demanded cash for the contracts sold to the Hunts, claiming that it would settle for nothing less. Finally, it accepted 20 percent of their Beaufort Sea oil holdings. Apparently, the Hunts were indeed short of cash and many more creditors waited impatiently for settlement.

The issue finally was settled when an international group of banks made a huge $1.1 billion loan to the brothers. Technically, it was made to one of their more successful companies, the Placid Oil Co. A condition of the loan, one imposed by Paul Volcker, was that the brothers refrain from speculating in the futures and commodities markets until they repaid the company. It had been collateralized several times over with some of the best energy-related properties in their portfolio. Most remarkable was the fact that the full extent of the brothers' holdings was still not revealed and that they had been able to borrow their way out of further trouble. But none of the troubles seemed to bother the Hunts, who claimed with a considerable amount of hubris that they were victims, not the perpetrators, of the affair. Both Nelson and W. Herbert told senate and congressional committees investigating the debacle that they were simply investors who had been caught in unfortunate circumstances.

The brothers appeared before the House Commerce, Consumer, and Monetary Affairs subcommittee headed by Representative Benjamin Rosenthal, Democrat of New York. They told their lamentable story of a simple investment gone awry and complained about undue government and exchange interference. A former employee, William Bledsoe, then appeared, making statements that contradicted the brothers. In 51 pages of testimony, Bledsoe, an executive of one of the Hunts' subsidiaries for 15 years, gave a comprehensive account of how the brothers mounted the silver operation from the beginning, including trying to convince the Shah of Iran to join them. "As I saw it at the time," he stated, "the Hunts were making a concerted effort to manipulate or control the world's supply of silver."[31] The brothers did not take news of his testimony lightly, suing him at the time for embezzlement and breach of fiduciary responsibility. In one particularly damning bit of testimony that rang familiar, Bledsoe told how Nelson put his son and daughters into oil drilling deals to shelter income made from soybean trading in 1977 and 1978 even though the drilling contracts had already closed. Rosenthal became so incensed by the testimony that he asked the Justice Department to examine the testimony of the brothers for possible perjury charges.

## *AFTERMATH*

The silver fiasco ended noisily for the Hunts and the CFTC. The agency came under intense fire for its handling of the affair and the fiasco was particularly unfortunate for it because its mandate was due for renewal in 1982. The agency's detractors took every opportunity to assail it as weak, behind the times, and ineffective when dealing with major problems.

The criticism did not stop there. Old criticisms of the commission never stopped, even during the silver crisis. At congressional hearings in February 1980, during the height of the silver crisis, representatives of the Treasury, the Fed, and the SEC told the subcommittee that oversees futures trading that the CFTC allowed exotic financial futures to grow too quickly, raising the question once again of who should regulate futures on Ginnie Mae bonds, Treasury bonds, and Treasury bills. Stone, who also testified before the subcommittee, never had the opportunity to respond because the other agencies raised the issues after his testimony had been completed. Mindful of the silver problem at hand, a Treasury official urged Congress to consider whether the CFTC had adequate resources to regulate financial futures, knowing full well the answer would be only a qualified yes at best.

Echoing the concerns, Senator William Proxmire, Democrat of Wisconsin, began drafting legislation to transfer the authority to regulate over a dozen futures contracts mostly to the SEC as well as a few other agencies. Proxmire also wanted to allow the Fed to set the margin requirements for futures markets in the same way it set them for Wall Street securities accounts. The CFTC demurred. However, as a peace offering Stone stated that he could countenance the margin power being given to the Fed. The one ally that the CFTC had at the time was Senator Herman Talmadge, Democrat of Georgia, who strongly opposed any threat to the commission's powers. Clearly, the silver fiasco had left the CFTC weakened and in serious danger of being dismembered before it could establish any lasting legacy.

As with many good dramas, the futures markets' battle with the CFTC and with their public image would continue well into the next decade. The clashes of the 1970s proved only the beginning of a continuing rift between the markets and their critics. However, one clear fact that emerged from the 1970s wore heavily on the regulators. After the silver fiasco, the Hunts walked away from the debris they left behind relatively unscathed. Even Arthur Cutten in the 1930s had more troubles with regulators before he emerged victorious in his battle with the Department of Agriculture. After 40 years and 2 regulatory bodies, the markets were still one step ahead of regulators.

The Hunt brothers went on to other ventures after the silver fiasco faded. In 1981, at an investment seminar in California, Nelson stated, "The most important thing to have is a spiritual environment in this country which will mean we can keep the money we make. Just making money doesn't mean much when the system is going to collapse."[32] Although his remarks were out of tune with the times, it was clear that he was still pining for the sort of capitalism preached decades before by pit traders who had also mounted their own successful corners. The question was whether futures markets were moving away from the big trader mentality and closer to a more modern system that would value stability and integrity.

## *NOTES*

1. New York Stock Exchange, *Fact Book* (New York: New York Stock Exchange, 1984).
2. New York Stock Exchange, *Demand and Supply of Equity Capital* (New York: New York Stock Exchange, 1975).
3. *Washington Post,* February 28, 1977.
4. *New York Times,* September 26, 1973.
5. Leo Melamed, *Leo Melamed on the Markets* (New York: John Wiley & Sons, 1993), pp. 56–57.
6. Ibid., p. 108.
7. Ginnie Mae certificates had one feature attached to them that made futures trading cumbersome if not impossible. They could be redeemed whenever mortgage holders decided to pay back their mortgages. As a result, they were contracts that could never substantially rise in price (called a "par cap" in futures parlance) and eventually had to be discontinued.
8. *Financial World,* August 20, 1975.
9. Stephen Fay, *Beyond Greed* (New York: Viking Press, 1982), p. 74.
10. *Business Week,* May 16, 1977.
11. Fay, *Beyond Greed,* p. 76.
12. *Washington Post,* October 25, 1977.
13. *Washington Post,* February 11, 1978.
14. Interview published in *Euromoney,* October 1985.
15. Bob Tamarkin, *The MERC: The Emergence of a Global Financial Powerhouse* (New York: HarperBusiness, 1993), p. 237.
16. *Business Week,* June 7, 1976.

17. *Washington Post,* March 4, 1977.
18. *The Globe and Mail,* January 27, 1978.
19. *Business Week,* September 20, 1976.
20. Quoted in *Barron's,* November 14, 1977.
21. Patricia A. Dreyfus, "Commodities Futures for the Small Investor," *Money* (May 1979).
22. *Commodity Journal,* January/February 1981.
23. *Globe and Mail,* March 23, 1979.
24. Fay, *Beyond Greed,* p. 63.
25. Ibid., p. 71.
26. Ibid., p. 132.
27. Ibid., p. 138.
28. *The Economist,* January 19, 1980.
29. Fay, *Beyond Greed,* p. 152.
30. *Business Week,* January 21, 1980.
31. Quoted in the *New York Times,* June 11, 1980.
32. Quoted in Fay, *Beyond Greed,* p. 285.

# CHAPTER 6

# CHICAGO FOLLIES

T HE 1980s DID NOT BEGIN ON A STRONG NOTE FOR futures markets. On the one hand, their collective ambivalence toward the CFTC and their continuing problems coping with a more open investor-oriented environment seemed to underline some fundamental weaknesses. On the other hand, new products and bold attempts at further innovation amply demonstrated an attempt to cope with the new financial environment of the 1980s. The question still not answered after over 100 years of turbulent history remained the same as it was after the Civil War. For whom were the futures markets dealing—the public or themselves?

Complicating matters were the new derivative products being developed away from the pits at investment banking houses mostly in New York and London. The swap market was born in the early 1980s and was quickly destined to become the largest financial market ever devised in terms of dollar-volume turnover. Because of their very structure, futures markets were helpless in the face of swap development. Pit traders could not assume offsetting risk traded in the market by banks and multinational corporations. Swaps were designed for corporate and governmental clients, which ordinarily entered transactions of $50 million or more. One single client of the swap market often had outstanding obligations that would dwarf the Hunt brothers' total exposure in the silver market. Clearly, this was not a market that could be maintained in the pits.

Options also made great strides in the 1980s, with more puts and calls being created on common stocks. The idea also became popular in other financial instruments. For instance, commodity options finally became legitimate in the early 1980s after years of being off limits in the domestic markets. Even with SEC regulation, however, the share options market still managed to suffer an embarrassing scandal that underscored basic weaknesses. The 1980s proved to be the watershed for the derivatives markets in general although it would still not be clear by the end of the decade that they had come of age. One scandal followed another and matters were not helped by the markets' oblivion to events surrounding them.

Market developments still occurred with great speed. The debate continued over the nature of futures regulation and the mood continued to be ugly when the CFTC was mentioned. In summer 1980, the *Commodity Journal* stated emphatically, "On today's commodity futures markets, the opportunity exists for price manipulation for the benefit of a few traders. This type of opportunity existed in the stock market over a century ago, but latter day efforts at manipulation are more refined and far reaching in their effects . . . the Commodity Futures Trading Commission has done little more than wring its hands."[1] *Fortune* made a similar remark, stating that "the entire U.S. commodity market has for years operated pretty much as the stock market operated in the days before the crash in 1929 . . . the case for self-regulation has always turned on the argument that the commodity pit was too exotic and complex to be presided over by outside referees."[2] The financial community was unhappy about the Hunt brothers–related silver fiasco, but opinions clearly differed over how the market regulation issue would be settled. Regardless of the debate, almost nobody expected to find FBI agents mixing with traders in the pits within several years.

The old debate about regulation had an institutional side that worried the futures exchanges. Market officials realized that the true measure of success for the new financial futures would be their use in institutional debt management. Investors holding bonds could use futures to hedge their positions, both long and short. However, these investors were pension funds and insurance companies. Regulators would have to be convinced that the markets had enough integrity to be used by fiduciary investors. Clayton Yeutter of the CME stated flatly that the intense, divisive focus on the markets hurt their image so greatly that it would discourage the use of futures for debt management. James Stone echoed that remark but added an element of warning, stating that events like the silver debacle could cause a 1929-style crash in the financial system. It was felt that stricter controls would be needed to avert future disaster. The CFTC's critics were not mollified, however, finding it strange that the CFTC chair would make such remarks in public. Obviously, who governed these markets was still a contentious issue.

Speculation was at the center of the debate, as it had been for over 100 years. Scalping among pit traders was often confused with price manipulation, since the activity was so frenetic that outsiders could never be sure about its goals. However, it was no longer considered immoral or excessive. The more pit traders (locals) who occupied a trading pit, the more liquidity the market possessed. Replying to the controversy concerning the number of new financial futures contracts being introduced, David Gartner, a CFTC commissioner, stated that they were the natural outgrowth of the inflationary environment and constituted a constructive method of keeping a lid on volatility in the economy. Futures trading was essentially a zero-sum activity; it created no money or credit. In other words, futures traders either won or lost but did no harm to the economy. The fact that their winnings or losses were theirs alone constituted a valuable function for the markets.[3] Although this condition was certainly true of a certificateless trading market in general, it overlooked the fact that rampant speculation continued to underscore the weaknesses of futures markets in their decades-old quest to be taken seriously. The New York stock market had been tamed decades before. Why was it that futures markets could not follow suit?

A self-regulatory industry group evolved late for the futures markets. In 1981, the industry finally got the National Futures Association (NFA) as its official body to take some of the oversight pressure off the CFTC. Technically, the NFA was a Title III organization under the Commodity Futures Trading Act. Its original sponsor was the ubiquitous Leo Melamed, who saw it as an organization that initially could come to grips with the rash of nonmember brokers springing up around the country. Not being members of a futures exchange, these brokers could be regulated only by the CFTC. Everyone in the industry realized that the commission was already stretched beyond its meager capacities with stock index futures and futures options so it was hoped that the NFA could keep nonmember brokers in line to avoid a new crisis. The CFTC agreed and approved the new organization in September 1981.

Selling the new organization to the futures industry was more difficult than selling it to the CFTC and Congress. Change came slowly on the futures exchanges, especially the CBOT. The matter of broker licensing exams was a case in point. Until 1981, exams and licenses were not universal. Several exchanges required commission merchants to take and pass the National Commodity Futures Examination but doing so was not uniformly required in the industry. The CFTC pro-

247

posed that a standard proficiency exam be established but some of its own commissioners were not in agreement, suggesting that it was not within the commission's ambit. Commissioner Bob Martin stated that the CFTC could find "other and better" uses for its time and resources. The CBOT agreed, not wanting to add more regulatory woes and requirements to its agenda. It was proposed that the NFA take up the gauntlet once it became better established. Melamed put it succinctly by saying, "In an emotional speech, I lectured the CBOT board and its skeptical membership that our industry must grow up. That it was far smarter to police ourselves than have government do it to us. NFA, I promised, would safeguard the integrity of the futures industry without ever stepping into the province of futures exchanges or interfering with the hallowed rights of its floor members."[4] The NFA became the futures industry's version of the National Association of Securities Dealers (NASD), the government-inspired self-regulating body overseeing the stock and bond markets.

## SWAPS

One of the more intriguing markets to be developed in the twentieth century began to take shape in the late 1970s. High interest rates caused many companies to have high-interest-rate bonds and bank loans on their books. Many of these were floating-rate obligations, in which the interest rates were adjusted periodically to reflect current market conditions. At the time, credit markets loaned money at fixed rates to more-creditworthy companies only. The markets loaned money to less-creditworthy companies at floating, or variable, rates. The latter practice created a problem in which financially weak companies were saddled with rising interest rates.

At first glance, it seemed that swapping interest-rate payments between two parties was ideally suited for the futures markets. It was a natural horse-trading technique that combined elements of speculation with asset management. However, the markets never entered into competition for the new products and they quickly evolved to, and remained with, the large commercial and investment banks. The reasons for swaps development underscored the natural weaknesses of the futures market in developing debt-management techniques. The markets' history and their basic structure did not allow for trading on the scale that would satisfy a corporate treasurer. The sums involved were too large.

In the late 1970s, Salomon Brothers began experimenting with a trading scheme allowing companies to swap interest payments with others. In this scheme, a company paying floating rates would swap with another company paying fixed rates, and both companies would agree to the swap if the new rates suited their financial needs. Salomon, as the arranger, gained a fee for its efforts. Originally, savings and loan institutions were the first to take advantage of the new concept but within only a few years hundreds of companies of all sorts were participating. The swap market was born and included swaps of all sorts, not just fixed for floating rates.[5]

Almost from the beginning, the amount involved in swaps was far in excess of anything the futures markets were capable of handling adequately. If two parties decided to swap interest payments of different sorts on a principal amount of $100 million, they would simply calculate what each owed the other for an interest period based upon a preset formula and net the difference between them. One party owing 6 percent on floating interest and another owing $5\frac{3}{4}$ percent on $100 million would see only $250,000 actually change hands in the transaction. The amount of credit risk was another matter, however. Each party had a liability to the other of the total $100 million, although it was understood that only cash flows changed hands. No futures trader could assume a potential liability that large from a counterparty, regardless of the nature of the swap. Only financial institutions could deal in the market which exploded in the early 1980s.

Swap trading originated in part because of the need in banks to find another profit center after they had retracted lending to developing countries in the early 1980s. As their loan-loss portfolios sagged under the weight of poorly performing loans, banks needed to raise new capital. Loans required a percentage of their outstanding principal amounts to be set aside as capital (equity or debt raised from the market or retained earnings). However, banks discovered that swapping was a way to earn money by trading rather than by making loans and required no capital to be set aside. As a result, many banks quickly embraced swaps as a savior at a time when their financial ratios were under severe strains.

In the early years, swaps began as structured deals. Two parties borrowed large sums of money and then swapped interest payments with each other. Soon, it became obvious that a market existed for traders who wanted to pay one sort of interest while receiving another sort without entering a structured deal. When that side of the business was developed, customers could call a swap dealer and enter into an agreement to exchange payments. The swap market was officially born, closely resembling a secondary market similar to the foreign exchange market. In the late 1970s and early 1980s, it was still an embryonic market understood only by corporate treasurers. Once its virtues were better understood, however, it became the fastest growing financial market ever witnessed.

The method of counting the amount of swaps outstanding was the same as that used for futures market turnovers. The amount of the swap, as with the dollar volume of futures contracts, was used for reporting purposes. Regardless of how the numbers were totaled, they were impressive—even staggering. By the end of the 1980s, over $3 trillion of swaps was outstanding. About one-third of that amount was attributed to currency swaps, where two parties exchanged principal amounts of currencies rather than interest payments. The currency swap business became so large that it dwarfed the currency futures trading on futures exchanges, severely limiting the ability of the exchanges to grow. As a result, currency futures trading remained mostly a retail activity for the contracts were for relatively small amounts.

As the 1980s progressed, the number of swap variations became increasingly complex. They ranged from plain-vanilla swaps (fixed for floating interest) to currency swaps and commodity swaps. Commodity swaps, in particular, cut into the futures markets business and were so large that they required a bank, rather than a clearinghouse, to guarantee them. If the guarantor bank felt uncomfortable with the exposure from a swap, it could always swap the exposure with another bank in the market. With the advent of swaps, it became clear that futures markets had limitations that did not satisfy corporate treasurers and multinational traders such as hedge funds. Futures could benefit indirectly, however, when some of the large commodity swaps actually were exercised into futures contracts.

Borrowing a concept from the options markets, banks also began creating foreign exchange (forex) options and options on interest rates. These were very large contractual amounts designed individually for each customer and priced by using formulas similar to the Black–Scholes model. A corporate customer could buy a call on interest rates or a currency and the bank would agree to provide the funds if the option was exercised. The premium charged became a valuable source of revenue for the banks, which could then lay the risk off in the forex or swap market if necessary. Unlike exchange-traded options, these large puts and calls were designer options created specifically for the customer. Clearly, they represented amounts that the option market for currency futures could not accommodate when it began in 1982. Borrowing another concept from options, banks also created "swaptions," options that could be exercised into swap agreements. Clearly, second-generation derivatives of that nature appealed only to professional hedgers and money managers.

## OPTIONS ON THE FUTURE

Of all derivatives instruments traded in the pits, commodity options had the most checkered history. There was demand for them again in the 1970s after the introduction of financial futures but the 1978 CFTC ban was necessary to ensure that a decent market could be developed. Finally, in 1981, the CFTC relented and approved a three-year pilot program that would reintroduce commodity options for general use on futures exchanges.

Trading began in 1982. The CBOT began trading options on Treasury bond futures and the New York Coffee, Sugar, and Cocoa Exchange began trading options on sugar futures. The COMEX followed with options on gold futures. The exchanges argued successfully that options on futures allowed traders to limit risk rather than be exposed to the entire futures contract. The timing of the announcement, however, struck some observers as strange. One reason that the CFTC banned options in 1978 was that it did not have the staff necessary to monitor a new market successfully. In reality, its staff had never been large enough to forge ahead but it nevertheless always managed to hold its own in the past. The legitimate London commodity options market never had a default, a fact that American regulators and exchanges were aware of. Therefore, the CFTC relented and, in the name of progress, allowed the market to proceed.

The Philadelphia Stock Exchange opened a market in foreign currency options, following the lead of the European Options Exchange (EOE) in Amsterdam. The Philadelphia Stock Exchange was clearly looking for new business, for at the time it traded only about 12 percent of American share options. Since it was a stock and options exchange, it submitted its proposal to the SEC, its approval process dragging on for more than a year as the SEC and the CFTC squabbled over jurisdiction. The SEC finally approved it because, as stated by *The Economist*, it was satisfied that nobody was big enough even to attempt a corner in foreign currency"—that "nobody" a not-so-oblique reference to the Hunts. But, as it went on to note, "One scapegrace working for a central bank could have a field day in the options market if he got advance word of a devaluation. On the whole, as W. C. Fields said, he'd rather be in Philadelphia."[6]

Regardless of the advances made by the exchanges, critics refused to be impressed. The markets were still considered cowboy markets, an image that was not changing for the better. Even in the late 1970s, the CBOT-mandated commodities broker licensing exam had an extremely high pass rate and was given to applicants within an hour of an intensive crash course in futures trading given by the brokerage houses. Often, licenses were issued without the applicant actually having taken the exam. Even disclosure about risk factors in futures investing was opposed by members of the futures industry. A CFTC requirement that attempted to impose "increased suitability burden" on futures commission merchants was opposed. The idea was to have brokers give customers risk-disclosure statements when they opened trading accounts. Part of such statements included giving the CFTC information on the customers, something many brokers objected to. The *Commodity Journal* stated unequivocally that "the futures business in the U.S. has not moved beyond the philosophy of the purveyors of Indian Snake Oil." Citing boiler-room tactics used in the market, and the use of confusing, technical sounding jargon used to mask wheeling and dealing, the journal accused the industry of "keeping the subject complex enough to keep the public unaware of what is happening."[7]

By 1982, the argument had been heard hundreds of times and was becoming common. However, this was also the year for the CFTC to be renewed. The sunset clause again was shining and the question of whether Congress would renew the commission's mandate was raised. Philip M. Johnson replaced James Stone as chair when the Reagan administration took office. Johnson was a highly regarded commodities lawyer who practiced in Chicago before joining the commission. He quickly adopted many compromises to ensure that the commission survived, working out a deal with SEC Chair John Shad to keep financial futures within the ambit of the CFTC and stop the bickering between the two agencies. Stock index futures were in particular a sticky point between the two agencies.

The Kansas City Board of Trade began trading stock index futures in February 1982 based upon the Value Line index. The contract was the first cash-only settlement contract traded on a futures exchange. Based upon the underlying index, the contract's price moved up and down with the index but could obviously not be physically delivered, given the index's complexity and the way in which it was weighted. Settling in cash was the only way to logically deliver. The SEC could not actually claim that the instrument was within its ambit, because of the cash settlement; hence the CFTC could comfortably claim jurisdiction. Other exchanges quickly designed their own stock index futures. The Chicago futures exchanges adopted the Standard and Poor (S&P) indices while the New York futures exchanges naturally adopted the NYSE index. Not all of them would survive the decade, however.

Because of intense lobbying by Johnson and James Stone,

who remained a CFTC commissioner after his position as chair had expired, the CFTC survived and was renewed for another four years when President Reagan signed the Futures Trading Act of 1982 in January 1983. Johnson then resigned as chair and Stone followed with his resignation as a commissioner. Both returned to the private sector but shortly before they left the agency they took part in a first-time meeting between the SEC and the CFTC to discuss stock index futures, surveillance, and information sharing. The two regulators began to bury the hatchet, for it was clear that the CFTC was now almost a permanent fixture in the commodities markets.

## ON THE HEAD OF A PIN

Since options and futures trading do not confer ownership of the underlying commodity or financial instrument, the number of buyers and sellers is theoretically unlimited. If a trader wants to buy a futures contract and another decides to sell one, then a new position is created. An unlimited number of contracts can be created in this manner. The only limiting factor is position limits, which restrict the amount of contracts that any one trader can hold. If there are enough traders in the market, theoretically the amount of open interest will be infinite, although in reality, it is limited by usual supply-and-demand factors.

The same is true of options. Call sellers can sell as many contracts as they like as long as they do not exceed position limits. In theory, the number of options outstanding could exceed the actual number of shares in existence. If all the calls were exercised, a serious problem could develop because of insufficient available stock. The problem existed only in theory—until 1981, at which time a takeover deal proved that the number of options that can be fit on the head of a pin is indeed limitless.

In what proved to be the largest takeover deal to date, E. I. DuPont offered $7.3 billion for Conoco, at the time the ninth largest oil company in the country. Part of the deal was motivated by DuPont's desire to ward off an attempt by Seagram of Canada to acquire a 40 percent stake in the company. The deal was sealed on August 5, 1981. Two weeks later, a major disturbance rattled the options market when it was discovered that many call buyers had instructed their brokers to exercise options and take delivery of Conoco stock. Previous purchases of the stock by Seagram and DuPont took all the existing shares out of the market and the Options Clearing Corp. (OCC), which settles trades for the options markets, was short 2 million shares for delivery. It soon realized that it was faced with a major problem that would test the integrity of the market. If delivery could not be made, the popularity of options would quickly collapse. As a result, the call holders were paid in cash rather than in stock. The price was $92 per share, or $9,200 per option. The total bill was $184 million.

The settlement became the first forced cash delivery in the young options market. Inadvertently, it became a litmus test for the strength of the OCC, which met the cash obligations and added some stability to the market in the process. However, it was not an experience that both the OCC and the SEC wanted to see repeated. Clearing corporations were funded by members of the various exchanges and represented a significant cost for trading members. In a sense, the clearing corporation was picking up the tab for the excesses of the pit traders who created too many options to begin with. Paying cash was the only practical way to end the problem but further problems of that nature would only scare away money and fund managers who were required to deal in established markets of good standing.

Financial futures and options were the bread-and-butter of the markets by the mid-1980s. Volume on the futures exchanges increased steadily every year, although it was not an across-the-board rise. Financial futures were in the vanguard while agricultural commodities slipped in trading volume. In 1985, agricultural volume declined about 25 percent while financials rose by the same percentage. The slowdown forced the MidAmerica Commodity Exchange to request the CBOT to absorb it as a subsidiary and both exchanges rapidly approved the plan. Making matters worse, the decline prompted traders to trade agriculturals even more frequently than in the past. The results sometimes bordered on the catastrophic.

A favorite ploy of pit traders always involved trading off the back of natural disasters or political events. The Chernobyl incident in the Soviet Union in 1986 was but one example. After the nuclear plant had melted down, futures traders spied opportunity, hoping to cash in on fears and potential future trends. The disaster was tailor-made for traditional agricultural and metals traders. The United States had a huge surplus of corn that year and traders quickly pushed up the price in the hopes that the Soviets would need to increase their overseas purchases. Oil futures rose under the assumption that nuclear power would give way to oil-fired generating plants. Gold looked bearish since traders assumed that the Soviets would sell part of their large domestic stock to pay the bills associated with the disaster. Most of the activity, however, was short-lived. Within a couple of weeks following the disaster, most prices stabilized and no long-term trends developed.

Gold was the most difficult commodity to predict with any reliability. In 1985, a trading firm in New York closed its operations after three locals sold gold short in March. The sale was large by COMEX standards. The three locals shorted 1.2 million ounces, only to watch the metal then rise by an unprecedented amount—$35.70 in one day. The ensuing $28 million loss ruined them. The firm that had cleared their trades, Volume Investors Corp., also defaulted. It, too, was forced to close its operations. Customers of the clearing firm found that their funds were being used to cover traders' losses, an activity that was a clear violation of futures trading laws. The event sparked new rules from the CFTC and the usual howls of protest from the futures industry.

The Volume Investors affair was an acute embarrassment for the COMEX. Several of the principals in the firm were individual seat owners and they continued to trade for themselves after the firm closed. One of the principals, Owen Morrissey, was among the leaders of the COMEX whose picture appeared on the cover of the COMEX's annual report from the year before. Another of the principals, Charles Federbush, was a member of the COMEX governing board. He was frank about the collapse of Volume Investors and its effect. "What the Volume situation did," he confessed, "was to magnify the weaknesses and the strengths of the exchange. Unfortunately, there are not many strengths. When something happens here, nobody cares about the institution."[8] The COMEX had experienced its share of problems since it was founded in 1933, one of which was an affair involving the Hunt brothers. However, when the Volume problem emerged, the COMEX did not attempt to solve it in the usual Wall Street or LaSalle Street manner.

At the same time that Volume Investors failed, a Chicago brokerage firm called First LaSalle Services also failed. The company found itself involved with a failed New Jersey money market firm, which, in turn, left it insolvent. As a result, the CBOT transferred First LaSalle Services' funds and customer accounts to other exchange member firms so that business could continue. The COMEX did not do the same with Volume Investors; it allowed the firm to fail and have its funds tied up in bankruptcy proceedings. Clearly, the Chicago operation was best-suited for market confidence and integrity. When asked why the CBOT chose a path different from that of

COMEX, a COMEX official sniffed, "Clearly they have more experience."[9] The intercity rivalry could not be subdued, even in times of crisis.

The COMEX offered cash to compensate the firm's investors. Within six months, they had received about half the $14 million lost when the firm closed its doors. Morrissey and Federbush offered to put up $4 million between them as compensation but later withdrew the offer. Morrissey was suspended from the COMEX at the end of the year. The bailout was not without risk to the exchange because it assumed the firm's liability to customers. Traditionally, that was the function of a clearinghouse. The NYSE bailout of its own member firms in the early 1970s employed solvent firms to assume the accounts of failed members. The COMEX could only hope that the problem would not repeat itself because it could again find itself in the role of partial guarantor of its member firms.

Despite all the notoriety of financial futures, agriculturals still made the news on more than one occasion. The speculation erupting periodically in the grain pits still upset farmers much as it had in the nineteenth century. Speculation in soybeans was suspected in 1983 when prices began to gyrate, sparking calls for an audit trail of pit trades to establish who was behind the trades. Farmers still protested prices in general and over 100 gathered outside the two major Chicago futures exchanges to protest, charging that speculation was at the heart of the problem. The CFTC did not concur, however. Kalo Hineman of the commission stated that past studies never convincingly demonstrated that speculators caused low farm prices. However, commodities prices were low during 1985. The Commodity Research Bureau's index of 27 commodities stood at a seven-year low although it did manage a slight rebound by the end of the year. As in the past, low prices caused the farm sector to complain about the exchanges.

Within a few years, they would have some tangible proof that their suspicions were correct.

## SWAP SHOP

The swap market grew so quickly in the 1980s that it was only a matter of time before a major problem occurred. Banks were creating swaps with customers at a furious pace. Entities ranging from corporations to governments were active in the market, hedging currency, interest rate, and commodity exposure. Less-obvious bank clients were local government authorities, who nevertheless took to the market with relish. The two major swap fiascoes receiving the most publicity were by municipal governments—one in Britain during the 1980s, the other in California during the 1990s.

The British case was the best example of the old market adage "know your customer." In the futures markets and the stock market, that adage is enforceable because trading is done on an exchange and brokers need to know the financial profile of their clients. If a client deals with more than one broker, information about excessive trading should eventually filter back to the exchange and the clearinghouse that stands behind it. Centrally located markets have an advantage over OTC-style markets by knowing about clients who trade with multiple brokers. Although regulators were less than effective in dealing with Tino De Angelis and the Hunts, their respective activities in the market did surface before their finances began to unravel. In the bank market, the unraveling could occur quickly, without anyone aware that a problem even existed.

When customers deal with banks in the forex or in swaps, the transparency picture changes. The deals are private— between customer and bank—so no one else necessarily knows of it. Customers can, in theory, deal with as many banks as desired, a situation that would never be discovered unless a problem arises. When a problem does arise, it usually is of enormous size. That is exactly what occurred in 1987 in the London municipal borough of Hammersmith and Fulham. In this case, banks clearly had no idea who their real counterparty was.

The borough council was run by the Labour Party. Because the Westminster government was Conservative, led by Margaret Thatcher, some local tensions simmered below the surface. In 1987, a routine audit by an accounting firm discovered that the local government had entered into £110 million ($165 million) worth of interest rate swaps and other derivatives exotica. Unsure of the market and their accounting stature, the auditors reported the problem, beginning one of the decade's great financial debacles. The problem did not stop with the audit, however. Within two years, the portfolio had grown to £6 billion. The questions raised by its size were obvious. How did a municipal government with an annual operating budget of £85 million become entangled in swap trading worth that much?

Over a two-year period ending in late summer 1988, Hammersmith and Fulham engaged in a staggering 592 transactions worth a nominal £6 billion. Even after the transactions were discovered, over half of them remained on the books in 1989 because it was difficult to unwind them without affecting the market and losing money. As the courts soon learned, the swap portfolio had been constructed by members of the borough's financial team without any of its elected officials knowing about it. This was the worst example yet seen of what became known as "rogue trader" mentality in the markets. One or more traders assumed swap positions causing financial calamity for their employers and constituents without anyone knowing of their actions. Many rogues would be discovered before the century was finished.

The investigation that followed revealed that many local

government authorities engaged in the practice. Many also brokered, or fronted, for others whose creditworthiness was less than desirable. Many of Britain's local authorities were run by fringe elements of the Labour Party whose politics were diametrically opposed to the more conservative bankers with whom they dealt. The reputation of Hammersmith and Fulham was much stronger, however, and it began fronting for the far left wing local governments. The increase in swaps reflected the brokering. Had the banks known who the counterparties were, they would not have dealt with them. So, Hammersmith and Fulham filled the void. However, between 1987 and 1989, a market problem arose that led Hammersmith and Fulham to rethink its position in the market.

The borough had arranged to receive fixed-interest payments in return for floating payments. Unfortunately, British interest rates rose, making the strategy very expensive. The payments made on the outgoing swaps were now due to rise substantially, negating any positive cash flows experienced before. Rather than face the music, Hammersmith and Fulham, the largest municipal swapper in Britain, simply decided to walk away from the deals. It claimed that it did not have authority to deal in swaps in the first place and therefore was not responsible for them after the fact. This "orphan" defense did not seem to stand a chance. We cannot be sent to prison for murdering our parents, the children claimed, because we are orphans. The banks seemed to be saved from loss if not embarrassment.

To the surprise and dismay of the 70-odd banks that dealt with Hammersmith and Fulham, Britain's high court agreed with the borough. In 1989, it ruled that the power to engage in swaps was *ultra vires*—that is, beyond Hammersmith and Fulham's normal powers—and ruled them null and void. Many of the banks, which had already been through a couple of rounds of tortuous debt renegotiations with developing countries, were astounded, for they had no recourse and would have to absorb their portion of the losses. Avoiding the obvious politics of the issue, *The Economist* said simply that the "ruling handed down by Britain's high court on November 1st is damaging London's reputation as a financial center." The issue went deeper, however. Apparent to many critics was the fact that the local Labour Party–run government, no particular friend of market capitalism, simply walked away from the deal when it suited, leaving the capitalists to clean up their mess. The *Wall Street Journal* predictably was more harsh. It commented that "the council officials said, awfully sorry, we didn't have the legal authority to make these agreements. And the court agreed to this heads-I-win–tails-you-lose rule and voided the swaps (while calling them a useful tool) despite broad statutory power for councils."[10] Adding insult to injury for the banks involved, the high court ordered the banks to split the auditors' costs with Hammersmith and Fulham.

The court decision was appealed but allowed to stand when the House of Lords affirmed the decision. The Labour Party, in the minority in Parliament at the time, quickly eschewed any sympathy for Hammersmith. Marjory "Mo" Mowlam, the Labour Party spokesperson for the City of London (Britain's financial district), said the House of Lords' decision was "not sensible" and could damage London's financial standing before she set out to attack London's system of self-regulation as inadequate. However, the damage was done. The banks were forced to absorb over £1 billion in losses. The affair prompted moves toward international banking regulation even before the case was finally decided and the banks learned a valuable lesson about dealing with customers. Ironically, the decision and outcome were the exact opposite of the next major swap debacle, this one in California during the 1990s. In this case, U.S. law applied and the results differed substantially from those of the British case.

All of the financial markets entered another brave new world in the mid-1980s. Futures volume rose along with stock market volume. Stocks were also beginning to be treated much more like futures than at anytime in the past. Buying with the intent of holding for the medium or long term faded in popularity as scalping and day trading became more popular with investors. In this fast-moving world, the flow of information became crucial to successful short-term trading. Accompanying the trading was manipulation using false information leaks to move futures prices. Although this was certainly not a new practice, the increased number of pit traders on the floors of the exchanges made the practice very difficult to detect.

Traders had always bought and sold on rumors, tips, gossip, and real news but realized that financial futures contracts were extremely susceptible to leaks. At the end of September 1989, a rumor began to spread in the Chicago pits that the retail sales figures for the previous month, as reported by the commerce department, would be exceptionally strong, rising by 2.5 percent. If true, news of that sort would force bond prices down and the stock market as well, especially since traders expected the Fed to react to such news by raising interest rates. When the rumor was leaked, the Dow fell by 86 points, about 3 percent of its value at the time. Bond prices weakened and short sellers of bond and index futures turned a quick profit. When the actual news hit the press, retail sales did increase but only by 0.8 percent. A CFTC official commented that regardless of whether the rumor was inadvertent or planted, the commission would never discover the truth behind the leak. "We've not been very successful in finding sources of these rumors," the official confessed.[11] Yet damage could be done by just a hint. "Even if you're smart enough not to believe it, you get whipsawed," remarked a trader. Although rumormongering was nothing new in the markets, the spillover from futures to the stock market showed how close the two markets had become since the introduction of financial futures.

## WITCH HUNT?

When stock index futures were first introduced on the futures exchanges, no one could have foreseen the problems that the contracts would pose. The futures markets always had a link to the stock markets but it was usually indirect. The old CBOT experiment with trading stocks did not prove particularly successful even when the stock markets were on the rise after World War II. However, stock index futures would drag the futures markets into the equities arena in the 1980s with great fanfare and a large dose of sour grapes.

A year before the stock market collapse of 1987, trading in index futures was frenetic. Along with other financial contracts, the futures pushed agriculturals into second place in terms of volume turnover. Fears of rising interest rates caused many traders and money managers to actively trade the S&P 500 index futures contract, using it as a surrogate for the stock market. In only two days in September 1986, over $36 billion in index futures traded in Chicago. At the time, most market participants felt that the trading was a healthy sign for the stock market. "A good deal of equities which would have been sold on the NYSE are now being hedged rather than liquidated directly," said Richard Sandor at Drexel Burnham.[12] If hedgers could use the market to lay off risk, it seemed logical to think that index futures trading would take some pressure off the stock market. Much of the trading was attributed to portfolio insurance, a newly developed technique. Fund managers sold index futures short to protect the value of their actual stock portfolios. This practice was first introduced in 1985, only a year before the extreme turbulence began. Price swings were not confined to the futures markets alone, however. They began to spill over into the stock market. One well-known trader was reputed to have lost $10 million on index futures in a single day. Five members of the CME lost so much money on the same day and so desperately needed to raise cash that they had to sell their seats before the end of the day.

The volatility subsided but reappeared the following year with more devastating results. The stock market collapse of 1987 demonstrated how much the new financial environment differed from the old. In the past, the stock market moved separately from the other markets, which often benefited from the market's retreat. In 1987, there was too much cross-listing between markets and financial products to expect a stock market slide to be confined to equities only.

When the market indices began to drop precipitously on October 19, 1987, most of Wall Street seemed unprepared for the rout. A hint came when Alan Greenspan and the Fed raised interest rates late in the previous summer after Greenspan had first taken office. The drop in interest rates that occurred in 1984 from previously high levels produced a prolonged stock market rally and bond rally and a sharp drop in the value of the dollar on the forex markets. A subsequent rise in interest rates had a collateral effect in the markets. Short-term interest rates were an important component of the Black–Scholes model and many other calculations used to value options and futures. Ordinarily, derivatives followed their underlying instruments, relying on them for their direction. Would 1987 prove an exception?

The damage on Wall Street was severe. The major market averages dropped 21.5 percent on October 19 (on what was to be called Black Monday), and in sympathy, the world's other equity markets also dropped precipitously. The American market slide was actually mild when compared to the drops in Australia (−58 percent), Hong Kong (−56 percent), and Mexico

(−38 percent). Of all the major markets, Japan had the slightest drop (−12.5 percent) There was immediate debate concerning the origin of the drop and the mechanisms that transmitted it quickly around the world. Other U.S. markets also felt the pinch. The junk bond market began a lengthy slide, eventually leading to massive defaults that, in turn, led to crisis in savings and loan institutions, many of which were heavily invested in junk bonds. Since the economy in 1987 was in tolerably good shape, the inevitable question was asked. What caused the stock market collapse?

The damage spread far beyond the confines of Wall Street. The drop in the major indices brought a temporary end to the bull market that had begun in 1983. The strong market would recover and was destined to continue well into the 1990s. However, the derivatives markets were about to pay a price for their success. The Chicago markets quickly entered the debate over the causes of the stock market collapse. They soon discovered that trading financial futures was not without political risks. Wall Street was a favorite in Washington at the time and was crying foul.

By 1987, options existed on most of the well-traded stocks as well as on futures contracts. The latter existed on stock indices such as the S&P 500 index—the most widely used market measure—in addition to the interest rate instruments and foreign currencies that had been introduced in the 1970s. Arbitrage existed between the markets and buy-and-sell orders were entered either on the basis of fundamental investment decisions or the fact that a stock or one of its derivative instruments was out of line with the market. Fundamental economic reasons were not the only forces behind a stock's rise or fall in price.

In addition, matters became confused by the "triple witching day," the one day within a particular month when options, futures, and futures on options all expired. Because 95 percent or more of derivatives were never delivered, outstanding positions had to be closed by pit traders so that delivery would not be triggered inadvertently. Arbitrageurs also took advantage of any minute price discrepancies during the last hours of trading. As a result, prices could swing wildly on triple witching day, which demonstrated that the markets had become much more closely integrated than previously thought.

The computer was another culprit in the 1987 stock market collapse. In a process called "program trading," analysts, by using quantitative arbitrage programs, devised formulas telling a computer when to enter buy-and-sell orders automatically. A program that suggested an inexpensive option might enter an order to buy the option and sell the stock at the same time. If the same were true of other widely held stocks, the program might also dictate a sell order in index futures simultaneously.

Portfolio insurance also figured into the market equation. Many institutional portfolio managers sold stock index futures short, hoping to hedge their portfolio values. In theory, the gain on the futures would offset the loss on the actual stock portfolio. However, the strategy did not work on October 19, 1987. The futures markets saw a constant flow of sell orders on that day and the arbitrageurs picked up the signals and continued to sell stock. Portfolio insurance failed its test in the first bear market encountered since its creation in 1985.

The performance of the portfolio managers angered the pit traders, who complained that all the short selling did not bring the inevitable bids for buying to cover at reasonable prices. "They were looking to the big locals to take the other side of the trade," said one Chicago pit trader in reference to the portfolio managers' selling. "But nobody wants to stand in the way of a freight train."[13] In other words, there were more sellers than buyers and the selling was massive. Many traders and commentators wrote off the incident to new, untested concepts and to new futures and options markets that had never before experienced anything like them. "The instruments are there," commented another Chicago trader, "but you better know how to use them or you'll get run over." Traders recognized this as a professional trading hazard. However, the public simply saw it as a drop in stocks and in market indices, indicating that something was fundamentally wrong.

Many commentators and analysts immediately began to criticize the derivatives markets for their role. Program traders admitted that their computer models entered sell orders automatically and that a triple-witching-day effect had occurred although Black Monday was not a triple witching day. To make matters worse, many of the securities firms employing program trading used it for their own proprietary trading so it appeared that they were doing something opposite of what they were advising their clients to do. Fringe critics maintained that because some of the program traders, such as Lehman Brothers, had traditionally Jewish names, the whole affair was a Jewish plot to destroy Wall Street and the economy. Remarks like that, not heard since the 1920s, were symptomatic of fear and confusion at best.

The Chicago futures exchanges in particular claimed that they were being singled out for unfair criticism. Wall Street blamed the derivatives markets for its troubles and that pointed to LaSalle Street. The futures business realized that it had a fight on its hands. Program trading and the murky world of derivatives trading were coming under fire. The president of the Futures Industry Association put it in perspective when he complained that the "NYSE was an 800-pound gorilla that was motherhood and apple pie in the eye of Congress."[14] Wall Street had powerful friends in Washington. Many members of the Reagan administration were Wall Streeters. It took only a matter of days before congressional hearings were called to examine the market collapse. Wall Street was being blamed for the problem but not with the usual political vehemence of previous years. Others, too, were suspected. Wall Street pointed a figure toward the Chicago exchanges.

The rivalry between Wall Street and LaSalle Street quickly came to the surface. John Phelan, NYSE chairman, imposed a ban on program traders having access to the automated execution system at the Big Board. Within two weeks of the stock market collapse, Representative Edward Markey, Democrat of Massachusetts, called hearings of the House Telecommunications and Finance Subcommittee. That was especially worrisome to LaSalle Street for Markey had acquired a reputation as something of a flamboyant publicity hound—one who liked to call hearings during times of national distress. The SEC was already investigating the NYSE and the futures markets' roles in the stock market collapse. "We are concerned that the regulators might get carried away," claimed CBOT Chairman Karsten Mahlman. The futures markets knew that their collective reputation was not strong in Washington. Wall Street disliked pit traders for having developed the options and the index futures markets and the public was ready to denounce anyone who might be blamed for the precipitous decline in stock values.

Initially, word spread that legislation would ban program trading entirely. Cooler heads prevailed, however. The market continued to swing after Phelan's ban on program trading and futures traders took note. "The most volatile trading occurred when program trading was non-existent because it's been banned," claimed one trader. Specialists on the NYSE were having a difficult time matching large orders after Black Monday. The auction market system was being called under question again, as it had been in the past, for not providing a liquid market when sell orders began to pour into the exchange. The Reagan administration acted quickly, calling for a commission led by Nicholas Brady to investigate the market rout.

The Brady Commission studied the markets' problems. One of the problems that it tackled early in its investigation was the matter of the two regulators—the SEC and the CFTC. The commission favored the idea of recommending a market-coordination agency. Phelan also favored the idea, although he acknowledged that it probably would not work because of futures industry opposition. Skeptics abounded, knowing the history of conflict between the two regulators and the general abhorrence on both LaSalle Street and Wall Street of adding another layer of bureaucracy. Edward Markey personally felt that the White House would back away from the Brady report, especially if it offered any radical proposals for monitoring the markets. He did acknowledge that "the regulatory structure does not adequately reflect the markets," and James Stone, a former CFTC commissioner, added that "some people fear that the Brady recommendations will drive business abroad . . . [but] the proposals in the Brady report will make the markets more stable and honest. That will attract business, not repel it."[15]

The futures industry vigorously opposed the idea of adding another layer of regulation or enhancing the SEC's power. The CME organized its own committee to study the futures exchanges' role in the collapse and naturally concluded that financial futures trading was an inescapable part of the financial markets. Dozens of studies appeared, sponsored by various interest groups hoping to influence the Brady Commission's final report. One suggestion gaining popularity at the time was even more vehemently opposed by the futures industry than the idea of another regulator. This concerned the matter of "harmonization" of margins between the stock market and the stock index futures markets. In theory, if the margin requirement in the stock market were 50 percent, the margin requirement would be the same—50 percent—in the stock index futures markets. In reality, however, the margin requirement of the stock index futures markets was only a fraction of that. Futures industry officials realized that adapting the proposal would mean the rapid demise of the index futures business. Leo

Melamed recalled how he began meeting with John Phelan of the NYSE for individual sessions and insisted that CBOT officials, traditionally antagonists of the NYSE, be included in future meetings at every opportunity. The markets needed to put on a united front if they were to fend off further detrimental regulation. "He was damn well going to prevent blame from ending up on the specialists' doorstep, and I was ready to die before I would allow the futures markets to become the culprit," Melamed recalled, adding, "Under no circumstances did either of us want government intrusion into the marketplace."[16]

The Chicago exchanges proposed their own reforms for warding off more draconian measures. The CME suggested forming an intermarket committee composed of securities and futures regulators and exchange officials that would coordinate actions affecting the markets. The CBOT went further by offering the NYSE the use of its computerized tracking system by which trades could be tracked for quickly detecting trading abuses. To Phelan, the CBOT wrote, "Once the New York Stock Exchange is able to generate such information, we can jointly move forward to provide the sort of inter-market coordination which the Brady task force so forcefully endorses."[17] The proposals came in the face of stern talk from the SEC. Chair David Ruder told the Senate Banking Committee that his agency should assume regulation of the stock index futures market.

The flurry of activity prompted the leaders of futures and stock exchanges to begin meeting informally to discuss how to prevent another stock market collapse. No futures executive would have imagined being at that sort of meeting 10 years before. Meeting at the offices of the SEC on an ad hoc basis were Phelan and Melamed, as well as David Ruder of the SEC and Kalo Hineman, then acting chair of the CFTC who was also at the time chair of the CME executive committee. Asked why Melamed represented the futures industry rather than other CME or CBOT officials, an SEC spokesperson stated that it had been Hineman's decision to include him.[18]

The Brady Commission reported to the president on January 8, 1988. Its major recommendation was that a "circuit breaker" be instituted on stock exchanges so that the market could be closed temporarily if prices started to fall rapidly. The halt would apply to all equity-related products. The commission also suggested that the Federal Reserve fill the role of intermarket agency, something that Alan Greenspan would disavow as impractical. Uniform margins were also recommended, a suggestion that the futures markets eventually defeated. The Brady Commission then was replaced in March 1988 by the Working Group on Financial Markets, which was charged with making specific recommendations to deal with the problems outlined by the Brady Commission. The group consisted of Alan Greenspan, chair of the Fed; David Ruder, chair of the SEC; Wendy Gramm, chair of the CFTC; and Glenn Gould, an undersecretary of the Treasury.

The group recommended that the NYSE use a circuit breaker and its recommendation was carried out quickly. The idea was borrowed from commodity futures markets where limit movements had been in place for decades. In this case, the entire NYSE would be placed under a limit movement if the major market indices declined by specific percentages. The exchange would remain closed until orderly trading could be resumed. The group clearly had the 1929 stock market crash in mind. With the stock market collapse, the backrooms of many Wall Street firms had a difficult time coping with the flow of sell orders—a phenomenon that was repeated in the late 1960s when market volume rose. Trading halts would give floor traders and order processors time to sort out their books so that they could keep abreast of the market. Any lingering discussions within the group about market coordination died quickly, leaving the circuit breaker as the major recommendation to be adopted.

The harmonization issue did not die completely. Congress continued to debate the issue of whether the Fed should assume regulation of index futures margins. Representative Jim Leach, Republican from Iowa, was heartily in favor of harmonization, whereas Merton Miller of the University of Chicago opposed the move. The issue was finally resolved in favor of the futures exchanges and the Fed did not enter into the picture. The fallout from the 1987 stock market collapse ebbed away very slowly, however. It became apparent that the NYSE was blaming the Chicago markets for the problem and some saw the charge as a way of deflecting attention from the NYSE's own structural problems. Referring to the NYSE's specialist system, *The Economist* remarked, "New York blamed Chicago's trading in stock index futures for the crash, with no clear evidence to hand, so as to divert attention from New York's own trading methods."[19] Leo Melamed remarked, "We were busy trying to defend ourselves against demons that did not exist. Now we are going to serve the needs of the investing public and we are going to grow."

For their part, the futures markets escaped another boondoggle. The CFTC remained firm in its place as their regulator and stock index futures remained within their realm. Once again, the regulatory spotlight had cast a harsh light on the futures markets yet they emerged unscathed. All the attention gave the impression that they could do no wrong in the marketplace and were the rightful heirs of the "go-go" stock market of the 1960s and 1980s. However, the hubris displayed by some futures traders eventually led to troubles beyond imagination. Unlike the onion trading ban of the 1950s, this particular problem would make the front pages around the world.

### WHERE THERE'S SMOKE

Although the 1980s witnessed the beginning of the largest bull market in stock market history, the decade was also one of a strong bull market in commodities. Inflation and high interest rates pushed commodities prices higher and traders cashed in, often making large fortunes. Many large commodities traders were flush with cash and sought merger partners outside La-Salle Street. Some individual traders became the best known conspicuous consumers of the day.

In 1981, Philipp Brothers, a large commodities trading firm, purchased Wall Street investment bank Salomon Brothers for $550 million, giving the 70-year-old firm a much-needed infusion of capital. Shortly before, Philipp had separated itself from Englehard Industries, which was closely involved with the Hunt brothers. Salomon returned the compliment several years later by absorbing Philipp Brothers in a reverse buyout. Also in 1981, Goldman Sachs purchased gold trader J. Aron & Co. in a clear attempt to diversify some of its operations by becoming more commodities-oriented. Deals such as these brought the different cultures of Wall Street and LaSalle Street closer together than ever before, although the frenetic trading environment of the commodities world often did not blend in well with Wall Street's more staid atmosphere.

Individual traders fared extremely well by anyone's standards. After the 1987 stock market collapse on Wall Street, Paul Tudor Jones, a New York investment manager who managed commodities funds, was, according to *Financial World* magazine, the highest paid Wall Street executive. He was estimated to have earned between $80 and $100 million for the year, placing him ahead of George Soros and Michael Milken. The amount was so high for the time that *Financial World* claimed Jones "could hail a New York City cab and tool about the continent for over 11 years straight," with the meter running.[20] His previous track record with managed commodities funds was impressive. Since 1982, he only lost money in 5 of the 41 months that had elapsed. However, the title of heir apparent to the classic traders of years past went to Richard Dennis, a trader who

275

bought a seat on the MidAmerica Commodity Exchange in Chicago after graduating from college.

Beginning his commodities career on the CME as a runner while still in his teens, Dennis was a principal in a two-person trading operation. He was a typical local on the exchange floor, having been born, raised, and educated in Chicago. His notoriety came when he went long on Treasury bond futures just before the bond market's upward price swing in 1982. The market began to react favorably to Paul Volcker's inflation-fighting tactics at the Fed and bond prices rose sharply. Anticipating the move, he acquired 2,000 bond futures contracts that appreciated by about $13,000 per contract before he sold. When added to his other trading profits for the year, the amount that Dennis amassed in 1982 alone was about $50 million. His success, with which the markets and the financial press were impressed, helped illustrate how much the markets had changed over the years.

No futures trader could claim unblemished success in the pits, however. Dennis later lost a reputed $10 million in the stock index futures turbulence in 1986. But his legend had been made for his success in the markets led other traders to emulate him. As a result, he began trading managed accounts for others who paid him one-third of their trading profits beyond the Treasury bill rate as compensation. At age 33, he became a legend on a street both accustomed to and hungry for folklore. He did not, however, mount a corner. When he wanted to sell his positions, he was able to do so because the market had enough liquidity to absorb his contracts. His trading philosophy was no secret. He sold his positions just when others began to take notice, adopting a contrarian position on more than one occasion. Although not a new philosophy, the openness was refreshing. Old-style corners were secretive affairs using duplicity and false information to accomplish their ends. The new breed of trader used instinct, as did its predecessors, but the market could not always be manipulated with faulty information. Unfortunately, this generalization could not be made throughout the 1980s although the information flow was greatly improved.

Despite the great strides that futures markets had made over the years, old habits and perceptions did not die easily. Young traders making tremendous sums of money drew attention from regulators and the press. Before long, the old investigative adage would again become operative. It was felt that when a lot of smoke is detected, a fire must surely be somewhere on the trading floor because a skeptical public found it hard to imagine how someone as young as Dennis could make so much money. What was not anticipated at the time was that the conspicuous consumption displayed by commodities traders would attract attention of the most unwanted kind.

How efficient and fair could the futures markets be, detractors asked, when it apparently did not take much skill to make unheard of sums of money? Many pit traders were reputedly worth millions in the 1980s, although not on the scale of Dennis or Jones, and many seemed to base their trading strategies on psychological factors requiring one to read the prevailing trends not in the economy but in the pits. If making money was confined to the pits, then the industry appeared to be operating on knowledge of inside information rather than outside influences. While the markets had done much to improve their image, the occasional tawdry incident still occurred, inviting attention. In 1985, after a year-long investigation, 34 people were arrested on charges of selling cocaine on the streets around the Chicago markets. Their customers were pit traders. In addition, rumors were rampant about prostitutes being invited into the exchanges at lunchtime for private conferences in traders' offices. Traders' activities were always notorious but when the average commodities trader was making more money than his or her Wall Street counterparts, eyebrows were raised.

Indiscretion, though, was not at issue but price rigging and manipulation were. By 1986, both issues were again under investigation—this time secretively.

## MOLES IN THE PITS

The decade of greed caught the futures markets by surprise in more than one respect. Unknown to the markets, a secret investigation was begun in late 1986 into the activities of pit traders on the major futures exchanges in Chicago. Reacting to complaints from major commodities firms and processors, the FBI began an undercover operation that would last two years and result in numerous criminal charges made against pit traders. The exchanges maintained that the whole operation was simply a sting—operating under false assumptions—but by the time the information was made public, a substantial case had been made. The investigation coincided with revelations about insider trading on Wall Street that rocked New York.

The Wall Street scandal was easier to understand than the futures investigation. Because of the nature of the boom in mergers and acquisitions occurring at the time, most investors were able to appreciate how investment bankers were able to cash in on their inside knowledge of deals in the making. To have advance knowledge of a deal having the potential to cause a stock price to rise, someone working on the details would have to leak information to traders or investors who could make money with the information. In theory, the same could happen in the commodities business if someone had advanced knowledge of an enormous grain deal although keeping such deals secret was difficult. News was not censured in the commodities markets, only price manipulation and collusion. Moreover, it was not illegal to trade on nonpublic information. Because futures contracts were not securities, insider trading laws did not exist in the futures markets. If a problem arose in the futures markets, it would be found in the pits where the rules of the exchanges, as well as federal regulations, could be enforced but only with great difficulty. Trades occurred so frequently and so fast that recordkeeping occasionally presented a problem. Monitoring the pits was necessary but often impossible.

The Wall Street insider trading scandal certainly had all the elements of intrigue necessary for a good novel. In 1986, the Justice Department filed charges against Ivan Boesky, a Wall Street arbitrageur, claiming that he used inside information when determining which stocks to buy. Boesky operated his own firm and arbitrage fund, financed by Michael Milken and Drexel Burnham Lambert. He received inside information from Dennis Levine, a corporate finance specialist working for Drexel Burnham. Levine also traded on the information and made millions. Levine was arrested first and divulged information about Boesky. Boesky then pleaded guilty and received a $100 million fine, the largest ever recorded on Wall Street, and a prison sentence. Levine also received a prison sentence but neither man was the real object of the probe.

Both were small fish compared to the case that was mounted against junk bond king Michael Milken, whose operation at Drexel Burnham was revolutionizing the way Wall Street financed companies with poor credit ratings. Since the late 1970s, Milken had become a Wall Street legend, and his underwriting and trading of junk bonds vaulted Drexel from relative obscurity to the very top of the Wall Street league tables for underwriting corporate securities. The firm and Milken made so much money that the press dubbed the 1980s as the "decade of greed." Corporate finance specialists and top-notch traders became known as "masters of the universe" for their unfailing ability to make money at every turn. After Boesky provided information against Milken, the Justice Department charged him with over 100 counts of fraud under the Racketeer Influenced and Corrupt Organizations (RICO) Act. Milken was sentenced to 10 years in prison but served a much shorter sentence. The old adage about smoke and fire was once again about to be invoked, this time in a different locale. As it turned out, it was not difficult to prove that when there was that much money, serious improprieties followed.

Supporters of the futures markets later claimed that success on Wall Street emboldened the Justice Department to proceed against LaSalle Street. However, the amount of ostentatious wealth being created on both streets helped provide a guide for regulators. For example, Ivan Boesky drove a pink Rolls Royce convertible and investment bankers and futures traders sported expensive watches and automobiles. Wall Street was traditionally known for merger activity and large sums were always associated with the fees attached to merger-and-acquisitions deals. The DuPont–Conoco deal in 1981 alone generated several hundred million dollars of investment banking fees. In one sense, payouts to investment bankers working on deals of that nature was understandable but enormous payouts for pit traders was another matter. Floor traders on the stock exchanges made handsome livings but nothing compared with the mergers-and-acquisitions bankers. How was it possible that futures traders could make as much if not more in a business traditionally associated with smaller commissions for dealing with client orders? Obviously, the compensation had to come from scalping and position trading in the pits and that is where the investigation was centered.

The pits developed an even faster reputation in the 1980s. New members admitted that when many of the exchanges were enlarged, they were after fast profits and a fast lifestyle. In that respect, they were no different from their Wall Street counterparts. However, a strong element of braggadocio mixed with hubris still imbued many pit traders. When asked why he valued money above all else, one trader admitted that "people talk about freedom in this country. But it's really security they're talking about. There is no security at the Board of Trade. You're looking at capitalism in its purist form." Traders had to make their fortunes and leave because the exchanges did not value older members or offer pension benefits. Also, the pits were more crowded than they were in years past. As a result, traders made more errors when sending hand signals or crying out at prices thereby adding to the confusion and pandemonium. Nevertheless, opportunity could still be found. "The trading floors are the last bastion of true independence," another trader ventured. "But with that ability to be independent, there's a lot of opportunity to go astray. The circumstances don't make a man what he is, just expose him to more opportunity.[21]

A complaint from the agribusiness giant Archer Daniels Midland (ADM) brought the Justice Department to the pits beginning in late 1986. The company was headed by Dwayne Andreas, a 70-year-old domineering chief executive with no fondness for the CBOT. That ADM held a seat on the CBOT did not soften Andreas' criticism of the exchange. "It's really gotten to be a gambling den up there," he complained, adding that "the prices on the Chicago Board of Trade bear no resemblance to reality, to the true prices anywhere outside Chicago."[22] Orders were not being executed as quickly as possible or at prevailing prices. Pit traders appeared to be dealing for themselves first and their customers second. The company owned its own trading subsidiary, which operated on the floor of the CBOT, and the Justice Department suggested that it use its own agents to trade for the firm, allowing it to discover any illegal activities firsthand. Archer Daniels agreed and the plot was laid for the first undercover operation to ever be conducted on an exchange.

Conducting a covert operation was not an easy task. The pits were manned mostly by the locals who all knew one another and who did not admit outsiders to their ranks easily. "A new guy comes in and he finds that everybody has his own clique," a CME trader commented, "and the new guy has to work himself in." To avoid suspicion, the FBI, which conducted the operation, had to plant several traders into the clubby confines of the exchanges without being suspected. An even greater problem was teaching the techniques of trading to undercover agents who knew nothing about futures exchanges.

The FBI selected four agents to infiltrate the exchanges, two at the CBOT and two at the CME. The New York exchanges were not included in the initial operation. To make the agents as inconspicuous as possible, the FBI had to buy them their own exchange seats, rent offices for them, and provide expensive automobiles and wristwatches. The FBI also rented expensive apartments and health club memberships for the four agents so that they would appear to be normal floor traders indulging in their usual extracurricular activities. When the four began trading at different times in 1986 and 1987, they appeared and acted no different than anyone else in the pits.

Their backgrounds had to be credible when they were checked by the exchanges. The FBI "backstopped" the four, giving them fictitious backgrounds that would be confirmed, if questioned, by former employers and colleges. The CFTC provided training in the ways of the pits along with ADM. The operation was so secret that the chair of the CFTC, Wendy Gramm, initially did not know of its existence. Officials of the exchanges were not aware of the operation either. When in December 1986 the first agent ventured into the pits his cover was complete, and within a few months, all four were accepted into the traders' fraternity. Of course, no one knew that the agents wore tape recorders and made detailed records of trades. The evidence they gathered would not surface until 1989.

Initially, all four agents moved into the financial futures pits on both exchanges. The two operations were known by their nicknames—Operation Sourmash at the CBOT and Operation Hedgeclipper at the CME. As the agents became familiar with the pits and their compatriots, the inevitable question arose. What would happen if the agents themselves were involved in illegal trading? Since they were trading with taxpayer funds, the issue proved sticky. An FBI official discussed the problem, saying, "We're prepared to rectify any customer losses. I can't have my people involved in illegal trading. They only have to appear to be involved."[23] Clearly, the FBI would be liable for an open-ended loss if agents' trading in the pits got out of hand.

The customers allegedly being cheated by the CBOT and the CME ranged from large food-processing firms, such as ADM, to the commodities trading houses themselves, such as Drexel Burnham, Shearson, and Lind–Waldock & Co., a large Chicago discount futures broker. Small-scale retail investors were also involved although most did not realize it until after the fact when they read about the transactions in the newspapers. Problems occurred when such investors used independent floor brokers to execute trades for them during the course of a trading day. Their complaint was that they were not receiving good, clean prices on the trading executions. The violations with which pit traders would be charged were of three types—front running, knowingly not getting a customer the best price, and prearranging trade prices between traders themselves.

When two or more traders prearranged a price, they simply agreed in advance to the customer-assigned price, which usually was not as beneficial as the executed price. Alternatively, they could assign the customer the worst price received in a sequence of trades, keeping the best price for themselves. Front running was, however, almost impossible to detect. A broker would receive an order from a customer to buy a large amount of contracts. Before entering the customer's order, the broker would enter one for him- or herself. After entering the customer order and watching the price rise slightly, the broker would sell his or her position. The scalping profit would come off the back of the customer order and the customer would not necessarily get the best price. This method, it was widely suspected, was one of the most commonly used in the pits. Even keeping track of orders by computer did not necessarily help detect the problem. The exchanges were divided over the use of camera and computer surveillance. The income made by small fractions skimmed off a price had the potential to soon become substantial because of the enormous volume that the exchanges were recording at the time—a phenomenon that explained how many brokers and traders were able to afford their affluent lifestyles.

At the heart of the matter was the market system itself. In many ways, it invited abuse. Pit traders operated in a dual-capacity-type system not unlike that used by specialists on the stock exchanges. Floor traders could trade for their own books or simply broker customer orders with the market makers in the pits. When the two came in conflict, as was often the case, it was natural for floor traders to keep the price advantage for themselves. When the smoke cleared from the scandal, the exchanges moved to eliminate dual trading on some contracts under certain conditions so that impropriety would not be assumed.

A Chicago grand jury convened in winter 1989 to investigate the charges of fraud and abuse. At the same time, the CFTC released a report critical of the CBOT, claiming that the exchange's computer-surveillance program was inadequate to deal with potential trading abuses. The CFTC needed to be vocal in criticizing the markets, especially those in Chicago, for its renewal was due again in 1990 and Congress would take the surveillance program into account when renewing the agency's mandate.

The undercover operation finally surfaced in 1989 and

specific charges were leveled in early August of that year when the Justice Department filed charges against 46 brokers and traders. Another 100 indictments were being prepared. The investigation struck Chicago hard and many in the futures industry were both indignant and angry over the way in which the investigation was conducted. One Chicago trader hanged himself before a second round of charges was filed. Wendy Gramm, chair of the CFTC, defended the techniques used, reasoning that "the charges involve violations that could not be detected by commission oversight alone."[24] The New York exchanges also fell under investigation that summer by the CFTC, not the FBI. In a separate action, the COMEX and the New York Merc were raided and searched by agents from the CFTC and the postal service.

The New York investigation centered on the silver and gold pits at the COMEX and the crude oil exchange at the New York Merc. A total of 47 subpoenas were served on traders. Wendy Gramm told Congress that the action resulted from an extensive CFTC investigation. The commission could not file criminal charges against traders because the commodities and futures acts did not give it the authority to do so. However, other agencies invited into the investigation did have such authority and exercised it. Senator Patrick Leahy, Democrat of Vermont and perhaps the most recent fly on the markets' wall, described the CFTC's initiative as "indicating that concerns about floor trading practices are not limited to Chicago but rather are industry-wide."[25]

The complaints in New York were similar to those filed in Chicago. In addition to front running, the New York traders were charged with illegally manipulating trades to avoid paying taxes as well as with improperly paying off officials at other firms to absorb their trading losses. These activities could only be practiced by insiders. "Insiders have advantages in terms of trading," remarked a securities lawyer familiar with the commodities exchanges, adding, "That's the source of long-standing complaints. These markets are not fair, open markets operated for the benefit of the public."[26] The futures markets could not stand next to the stock exchanges in terms of openness or integrity. Many floor traders in New York acknowledged that there existed a great deal of serious fraud in the pits that was simply "winked at" by other traders who were well aware of the sorts of practices used by their colleagues. New York also had an advantage in this respect since four of its markets all occupied the trading floor at the World Trade Center—the COMEX, the New York Merc, the Coffee, Sugar, and Cocoa Exchange, and the New York Cotton Exchange.

### SALLY LASALLE GOES TO JAIL

Not even the trading scandal could dampen the sense of humor in Chicago. In summer 1989, a comic book entitled *Chicago Follies* appeared for sale on the street around the exchanges. The heroine of the satire was Sally LaSalle, a neophyte trader who was unwittingly duped into the trading scandal by an evil trader nicknamed "the Lizard." The FBI hauled her off to jail as she exclaimed innocently, "Oh God, no!" At $3.95, *Chicago Follies* was a huge success, illustrating that the innocent were taken away with the guilty.

Needless to say, the scandal was considered a huge mistake at the futures exchanges. Traders considered it a sting operation along the lines of the Abscam scandal of several years before. Most observers concluded that the benefits of the exchanges far outweighed their drawbacks. There was consensus that "boys will be boys" and that trading should continue without fear of government interference. The exchanges portrayed themselves over the years as the last bastions of free-market capitalism and it was felt there was no reason to adopt another position.

The indictments did, however, bring a number of guilty pleas from the traders. Many such traders came from the foreign currency pits at the IMM. When the indictments were first announced, they caused quite a commotion in Chicago. They were sought by U.S. Attorney Anton Valukas who, almost from the beginning of the process, invited comparisons with his counterpart in New York—Rudolf Giulliani, who brought charges against the inside traders on Wall Street. Valukas was criticized for seeking higher political office, as was Giulliani. When the indictments were first announced, even members of the grand jury itself requested permission to attend the news conference announcing them. Chicago was abuzz with rumors about who might be next in line to be charged and the exchanges were in a state of turmoil and excitement.

The original charges brought against currency and soybean traders amounted to 1,275 pages against 46 defendants on 608 counts. Naturally, some of the charges appeared more substantial than others. Almost from the beginning, it was clear that the exchanges did not believe the gravity of the charges, although it was clear that some of the traders would be found guilty and that others would be cleared. The quality of the government's evidence was spotty, which worked in favor of some of the traders. Thomas Donovan, president of the CBOT, coined a new phrase that he used throughout the ordeal: "Where there's smoke, there's not always fire, but where there's smoke, there's always smoke damage."[27] Clearly, the CBOT was worried about the fallout from what it thought were mostly frivolous charges brought by those unfamiliar with the inner workings of futures exchanges.

Two years following the initial indictments, the government's record was successful but not all the charges made against the traders resulted in guilty verdicts. In the first round of charges against the soybean traders, the government was very successful in obtaining guilty verdicts, including violations of the RICO law. In the case of the currency traders, however, the jury failed to return guilty verdicts and the defendants walked free of most of the charges. By 1991, the trials were mostly forgotten outside of Chicago. The prosecutions and the ensuing trials, having failed to produce a major defendant like Milken, Boesky, or Levine, eventually faded quietly into the background. The traders themselves became separated from the exchanges. They, too, were mostly forgotten within a short time period.

When the news was still dominated by the travails of the traders, some criticism was heard again from the heartland, where futures traders were never popular to begin with. "I've been flooded all day with calls from farmers who don't want more regulation," claimed Senator Bob Kerrey, Democrat of Nebraska. "They want to close the futures markets down." Senator Neal Smith, Democrat of Iowa, said that calls to his office reminded him that "there's a whole lot of people who just don't trust these markets."[28] Farmers could complain all they liked but the markets had moved far beyond their previous confines as grain pits. Now, despite all the bad publicity, even customers of the exchanges claimed they could not live without them.

The travails of the traders and the markets led one futures broker to do a survey of its customers to gauge the support for the markets in the wake of the scandal. Lind–Waldock of Chicago, one of the professional firms claiming to have been victimized in the scandal, mailed 4,353 of its customers a questionnaire. Of the 1,078 customers who responded, 63 percent believed that the exchanges did not do an adequate job policing themselves but they did not believe in further government regulation. Over 30 percent said that increased regulation was needed. Only 12 said that they would stop trading because of the scandal. Most telling, perhaps, was that 31 percent said that they did not believe the trading pits operate honestly and efficiently. Most did claim that the open-outcry method worked adequately, however.[29] In other words, they accepted the pits with all of their weaknesses but believed the exchanges could do a better job of regulating themselves.

The public took a somewhat dimmer view, however. In a Gallup poll conducted in October 1989, 1,007 people were asked whether they had lost faith in the honesty and integrity of the markets, given the insider trading scandal and the futures markets' problems. Twenty percent said that they had lost a great deal of faith; 30 percent said that they had lost some faith; and 28 percent responded that they had not lost any faith.[30] Fortunately for the markets, the bull market that would reemerge after 1991 would defuse future surveys as investors rushed to the markets in record numbers when the indices resumed an upward trend.

Separating the guilty and the innocent at the exchanges was never an easy task. After ADM sought FBI assistance for what it alleged were abuses of the markets that led to the investigation in the first place, the company attempted a market coup of its own in soybeans. After selling short a significant number of soybean oil contracts, ADM registered a large quantity of actual soybean oil for delivery the next day. By showing ample supply for the sales, the company demonstrated that its actions were not intended to be a bear raid. The visible supply effectively drove futures prices down, however. The company then covered its contracts, netting a large profit. When summoned before the CBOT Business Conduct Committee shortly thereafter, the company failed to appear, sending its attorneys instead. The penalty was light—only a $50,000 fine—which later was reduced.[31] Apparently, even critics of the CBOT and its monitoring procedures had no qualms in using the exchange as long as they could net a fast profit.

The four FBI agents had mixed reviews among the futures traders after their identities were divulged. One got high marks for his performance, two were considered adequate, and one was considered incompetent. On balance, they all lost money but there was some good news concerning the seats that the government purchased for them. The two seats on the IMM were sold for $52,000 in profit. The proceeds of one seat on the CBOT were not disclosed whereas the other netted a profit of only $3,000.

The revelations had one negative effect on Chicago commodities brokers. By the end of the 1980s, the top commodities brokers operating in Chicago were all subsidiaries or offices of New York brokers. The top 5 were Shearson Lehman Hutton, Merrill Lynch, Dean Witter, Goldman Sachs, and Prudential–Bache. Of the top 25, only 7 were Chicago-based, and their capital was much smaller than their New York–based counterparts.[32] The firms traded for customers and also actively traded for the house account. The brokers continued to prosper in the bull market, especially for financial futures. All of the bad publicity did not have much of an effect on the two major Chicago exchanges. During the first six months of 1989, volume was up at the CBOT by about 2 percent over the previous year. The CME had far greater success, with volume increasing by 39 percent. Although the CBOT was well diversified, the CME had a record of innovation that would help it attract orders at the expense of its older counterpart. The scandal and the constant corners and mini bear raids hurt the older exchange at a sensitive time. Another poorly timed incident involving the CBOT clearly tarnished its reputation even more.

## NOT AGAIN

Troubles on the futures exchanges never deterred traders from attempting to take advantage despite increased regulatory scrutiny. During summer 1989, another potential corner was discovered at the CBOT just before the indictments were handed down against the traders accused of illegal behavior. The incident raised more questions about the integrity of the exchanges at a pivotal moment. Was this latest incident a bold attempt to take advantage of the exchange at a weak moment or just another heavy-handed mess created by an unsuspecting party? Even a cursory view of the incident suggests the former.

The last scandal of the 1980s involved the CBOT and the CFTC against one of Europe's largest grain traders and food processors, Ferruzzi Finanziera of Italy. The company typically handled about half of the European Community's exports to the Soviet Union and Eastern Europe each year and had annual revenues of about $30 billion equivalents. The company bought futures contracts representing 23 million bushels of July soybeans on the CBOT. The problem was that only about 4 million bushels were in the visible supply of soybeans available for delivery. If no more soybeans could be produced quickly, the demand would overwhelm supply. The CBOT realized its predicament and claimed that the company was attempting a corner. The CFTC reacted first, ordering the company to reduce its positions to 3 million bushels by July 18. Then, the CBOT told the company to reduce its per-day holdings by 20 percent. As a result, soybeans prices tumbled.

The fallout from the affair extended in all directions, as would be expected. Ferruzzi had become much more aggressive in the American markets over the previous three years because of its deliberate expansion. Therefore, its aggressive stance did not surprise many industry insiders. It had little choice but to comply with the directives but it then launched its own counterattack on the CBOT. Taking square aim at the exchange, the company attacked its effectiveness in the face of large orders, suggesting that it was more of a trading den than an actual marketing mechanism for soybeans. The president of its American subsidiary spoke to a large gathering of farmers at the American Soybean Association annual convention. Turning the CBOT directive on its head, he stated that "on July 11, Ferruzzi received direct instructions from the Commodity Futures Trading Commission, to reduce our contracts in an orderly manner. Before we could do that, however, in fact, on the same day, we received an order from the Chicago Board of Trade. This highly publicized order forced us to exit from our contracts in a completely and different manner and caused heavy losses for us and for many others, including farmers. . . .We don't believe this order was necessary. It disrupted the market and prevented it from performing its function."[33]

Many farmers understood the remarks as they had many times in the past—the CBOT was dealing for itself and its members first. Several months later, the American Agriculture Movement, a lobbying group representing farmers, filed a lawsuit against the CBOT for $100 million. The suit alleged that the exchange's order to liquidate the Ferruzzi soybean contracts was, according to a spokesperson, "a bad faith and self-serving action initiated by the CBOT's dominant grain merchants and futures traders to create profits for their accounts and for their clients."[34] The group estimated that farmers, rural bankers, and farm-equipment dealers lost more than $1 billion from the 20 percent drop in soybean prices that followed the action. Karsten Mahlman of the CBOT responded by calling the suit frivolous but it was clear that over a century of friction between farmers and the exchange was again surfacing.

Considerations about the fallout of collapsing prices on farmers did not appear to be a factor in the exchange's rapidly prepared directive. Specifically, in the speech, the Ferruzzi executive called for improved delivery systems for the CBOT, which it claimed was out of step with international grain dealing. He cited the fact that the exchange had only two delivery points—Chicago and Toledo—for physical soybeans, although its business was truly international. Did this mean that the exchange did not expect most customers to be interested in delivery? That was the clear implication although the forced sell-off eventually cost Ferruzzi about $100 million in losses. If the affair was a corner, it certainly was one of the most unsuccessful.

The CBOT and the CFTC both had to react to Ferruzzi's actions in light of the trading scandal. After the initial liquidation of the company's positions, the battle would continue in the courts during the 1990s.

The 1980s ended in almost the same way the 1970s had ended—with a scandal that tarnished the futures markets' reputation and a host of lawsuits. The 1980s witnessed many innovations in new financial products and proved that many financial derivatives had a valid place in hedging and funds management. For the first time, a wide panoply of derivatives existed across the financial spectrum, appealing not only to small speculators and businesses but also to large corporations and governments. Nevertheless, the old problem of effective regulation was still not settled. The futures markets were still primarily self-regulating and the CFTC was not yet so securely established that it could be considered a serious force. In the larger swap market, regulation by outside sources effectively did not exist and only internal risk management by banks protected against serious problems. Both sides of the derivatives markets had to adjust to a volatile marketplace and hope for the best. Rogue traders still loomed on the horizon and trading scandals did not abate despite the markets' best efforts. The 1990s would prove to be more of the same.

## *NOTES*

1. *Commodity Journal*, May/June 1980.
2. *Fortune*, July 28, 1980.
3. *Commodities*, November 1980.

4. Leo Melamed & Bob Tamarkin, *Escape to the Futures* (New York: John Wiley & Sons, 1996), p. 309.
5. Some early swaps including interest rate swaps employing fixed-, floating-, and zero-coupon interest payments, along with different benchmarks such as eurodollar interest, Treasury bill rates, and certificate of deposit (CD) rates. Adding to the complexity was the fact that interest could be calculated on an annual, semiannual, quarterly or monthly basis.
6. *The Economist,* October 30, 1982.
7. *Commodity Journal,* January/February 1982.
8. *New York Times,* December 27, 1985.
9. *Securities Week,* April 15, 1985.
10. *Wall Street Journal,* November 17, 1989.
11. *Business Week,* September 29, 1986.
12. *New York Times,* September 18, 1986.
13. *Financial Times,* October 29, 1987.
14. Melamed, *Escape to the Futures,* p. 376.
15. *New York Times,* January 17, 1988.
16. Melamed, *Escape to the Futures,* p. 382.
17. *Wall Street Journal,* February 4, 1988.
18. *Chicago Tribune,* February 12, 1988.
19. *The Economist,* May 28, 1988.
20. *Financial World,* June 1988.
21. *Toronto Star,* April 2, 1989.
22. David Greising & Laurie Morse, *Brokers, Bagmen, and Moles: Fraud and Corruption in the Chicago Futures Markets* (New York: John Wiley & Sons, 1991), p. 182.
23. *Los Angeles Times,* August 4, 1989.
24. Ibid.
25. *Washington Post,* May 5, 1989.
26. *Los Angeles Times,* May 6, 1989.
27. Greising & Morse, *Brokers,* p. 267.
28. Ibid.
29. *Chicago Tribune,* October 27, 1989 and *Los Angeles Times,* April 26, 1989.
30. Gallup poll conducted for the "Nightly Business Report" and Reuters, October 27–29, 1989.

31. Greising & Morse, *Brokers*, p. 186.
32. *Crain's Chicago Business*, December 26, 1989.
33. Transcript of a speech by David H. Swanson of the Ferruzzi Group to the American Soybean Association, July 24, 1989.
34. *St. Louis Post-Dispatch*, November 15, 1989.

# CHAPTER 7
# ROGUES' GALLERY

T HE FUTURES AND DERIVATIVES MARKETS WERE MORE aggressive during the closing years of the twentieth century than at any other time in their history. New product development continued at a brisk pace and the inevitable scandals accompanied it, proving that good ideas often engender increased business and opportunists at the same time. The markets defended their respective turfs against encroachment and the ambitious grasp of regulators. As the 1980s ended and the 1990s began, the new decade appeared to be a repeat of the old. The 1990s seemed poised to repeat the previous years' record of innovation, scandal, and ambivalence toward regulators. In that respect, they did not disappoint.

The decade also witnessed a new bout of speculation. Gambling had been made legal in many states and state lotteries, developed since the mid-1970s, were becoming quite common. Lottery payouts sometimes exceeded $100 million and captured news headlines. The stock market recovered from the 1987 collapse and the recession in 1991 to begin an historic climb to almost 12,000 on the Dow Jones Industrial Average before finally falling. The decade of greed extended for yet another decade and paper millionaires abounded. Despite all of the publicity surrounding stock market gains and get-rich dreams coming true, the real news of the decade was found in the derivatives markets. Excluding Hammersmith and Fulham, over $7 billion in trading losses were recorded through either deceit or plain ineptness in the 1990s. The decade became known for the rogue trader and investment mangers easily deceived by their investment bankers.

Most of the staggering losses were recorded in the OTC derivatives markets. The problem truly was international. Several Japanese banks and trading companies lost several billion through surreptitious trading that only surfaced when the losses could not be contained. Futures traders in Europe, South America, and the United States also suffered heavily. The most publicized loss originated in an unlikely quarter of California, following on the heels of an even more unlikely loss in a West Virginia municipal investment pool. Suddenly, it seemed as if Ross Perot's dire prophesy about a futures meltdown made in the 1992 presidential campaign was about to come true.

As the decade progressed, it became obvious that the markets were able to defy tight regulation. The markets became filled with too many products, all of which had substantial variations and nuances. In addition to the exchange-traded futures and options, the OTC markets among the banks offered a bewildering array of swaps, options, and swaptions on dozens of commodities and financial instruments. When their features were crossed, the number of possible permutations became staggering. A simple plain-vanilla swap—swapping fixed for floating rates—produced thousands of variations. When compared to derivatives, the securities markets seemed almost simple.

No regulator could be expected to keep abreast of this development and the markets were able to keep one step ahead of their gamekeepers. By the mid-1990s, the United States futures exchanges were trading half of the world's futures turnover. On the exchanges, that amounted to over 400 million contracts. When OTC derivatives problems arose, the SEC and the CFTC always announced that they were looking into the problems, knowing full well that their jurisdiction did not extend into the unregulated arena. Derivatives originating from the banks were a banking-regulation problem, not a matter for securities or commodities regulators unless a major line of demarcation was crossed. Clients would also suffer because only the best-informed cash-and-risk managers at the major corporations, municipalities, and government agencies using derivatives knew how to employ them properly. When scandal erupted, it usually was accompanied by either fundamental mistakes or simple ignorance. Those who should have known better made mistakes that retail investors often made in bull markets—they either listened too closely to their commission brokers or they put all their eggs into one basket. The results often were catastrophic for the companies involved and their shareholders.

When compared to the securities markets, the product development was impressive and often contributed to the problem. Clients often purchased derivatives packages that they really did not understand. When things went wrong, they were not fully aware of their own predicament. The municipal government of Orange County, California, and several well-known companies were perfect examples of how not to manage risk. Most of the major Wall Street and Chicago houses specializing in derivatives hired well-known academic researchers to help build their presence in the market, the result of which was sophistication beyond the reach of many. Myron Scholes became cohead of derivatives at Salomon Brothers, Merton Miller joined the board of the CME, and a host of other academic specialists joined other exchanges and investment banks to help develop products and client business. Mathematical models became the norm for pricing and computers provided simulations and alternative scenarios that left many clients and market participants with less-quantitative sophistication bewildered. Before the decade was finished, however, even the mighty "quant jocks" would be humbled by a major financial fiasco.

The new emphasis on mathematical modeling was also used in the securities markets. The bond markets in particular began to experiment with features differing from traditional bonds and often used futures market-inspired concepts to design fixed-income instruments with unique features. The area of financial design was originally known as "financial architecture" and quickly became known as "financial engineering." Small-scale boutique firms sprang up around the country to design financial instruments on a specialty basis for clients. Sometimes, the designs had a wider appeal. The firm of Leland O'Brien Rubinstein in Los Angeles designed several notable financial instruments in the 1990s, including a basket of exchange-related stocks known as SuperShares. Others specialized in futures or bonds. Often, institutional investors purchased packages of synthetics and securities that were designed to react to different sorts of market scenarios.

Futures and other derivatives also had an unanticipated effect. They helped to internationalize the markets in the early 1990s. By the end of the decade, the term "globalize" would replace it, suggesting that the world's financial markets had become integrated to a large degree. Futures and options exchanges were operating in Europe and in the Far East and the London International Financial Futures Exchange (LIFFE) was vying with the Chicago exchanges for the distinction of being the world's largest market in terms of volume. The success of LIFFE was attributed mainly to the explosion of financial futures in Europe. While the contracts were not fungible with American contracts, they did provide a round-the-clock market of sorts for interest rate instruments.

Trading in stock index futures, both in Europe and the United States, provided domestic market watchers with a way to anticipate the opening of American markets before the fact. Basing their daily market predictions on the way S&P or other index futures were trading in Europe, market prognosticators would then anticipate the opening of the American market. Although not necessarily accurate, the method demonstrates how the book on index futures moved around the world before finally arriving back in the United States for a day's trading.

In the 1990s, the derivatives markets finally became accepted. Their functions and advantages for institutional investors were no longer questioned. The same could not be said for the CFTC, however. The agency still faced renewal every four years, setting up jurisdictional squabbles with the SEC and Congress. Any time the question of renewal was raised, old arguments were often dusted off and used again to either attack or defend the usefulness of the markets. Strong attempts were made to include swaps under the CFTC's auspices as well, but the huge OTC market—primarily conducted between banks and their customers—continued to escape the commodities regulators. After the United States and other industrialized countries agreed to a set of banking regulations prescribed by the Bank for International Settlements (BIS) in 1988, many central bankers, including those at the Fed, rested easier because banks were forced to have more equity capital on their balance sheets. More equity meant stronger banks able to withstand greater financial shocks. Although not totally reassuring, the measure showed that the banking regulators were attempting to come to grips with the new financial environment as quickly as possible without giving away their jurisdiction to other regulators.

The BIS agreement demonstrated that regulation of the huge swap market, like the forward market, could be maintained adequately on an international scale. Since the market was spread among banks around the world, a single regulator was impractical. By requiring the banks to monitor their own businesses closely, however, the agreement was able to enforce a general uniformity. Simply put, if a bank wanted to avoid the wrath of its own central bank, then it would make certain that its swap and forex positions were well managed. The system of loose self-regulation would not prevent future losses or trading abuses but it worked well most of the time. When it did not work, rogue traders and wild casino trading made the front pages of newspapers around the world.

## *MELTDOWN?*

The explosion of new financial products worried some analysts and commentators as volume increased in the 1990s. Swap dealers in particular assumed large nominal amounts of dollar risk by entering into contracts with clients. The swap market's professional association—the International Swap Dealers' Association (ISDA)—worked with accounting bodies to determine equitable ways of accounting for the risk on balance sheets without making it look like their bank clients had assumed mountains of debt.

Untrained observers would have been alarmed by what they discovered. Large-scale money-center banks routinely had hundreds of billions of dollars of contingent liabilities on their books as a result of swaps. These amounts often dwarfed the banks' combined capital and assets. Traders knew that these contingents would only become real liabilities if they were forced to assume the entire principal amounts of their swap partners, which was an extremely unlikely possibility. However, the sheer numbers bothered many in Congress. Regulators were dismayed by the fact that a bank with $20 billion of equity capital could have swap liabilities running into the hundreds of billions, even though technically they were booked as contingent liabilities on the balance sheet.[1] The innate fear would not completely disappear through explanation of the technicalities.

The futures exchanges' rush to create new contracts kept the CFTC busy as the 1990s began. In 1991, the CFTC broke its own five-year record by approving 38 new contracts, exceeding its 1986 record of 36. During the 1990s, the commission approved a bewildering array of contracts, ranging from futures on air pollution and shipping rates to major market indices. One of the new contracts represented an area the futures exchanges had been watching with envy since the 1980s—a contract on interest rate swaps. The CBOT applied for the contracts, hoping that it would be able to attract business from major commercial and investment banks and the multinational corporations that were the swap markets' primary customers. Mindful of past problems, the position limit was set at 5,000 contracts for speculators so that manipulation was discouraged.

The popularity of swaps also drew the attention of Congress. The Hammersmith and Fulham affair and the explosion of new futures contracts led some in Congress to believe that derivatives contracts in general posed substantial systemic risks to the financial system. Agricultural futures had been eclipsed in complexity by financial futures and now interest rates and stocks were being traded in rapid fashion, suggesting that they had become commoditized. Swaps had become the most notorious derivatives so naturally they drew the most attention. Representative Glenn English, Democrat of Oklahoma and member of a House subcommittee on conservation, credit and rural development, wanted to include swaps in pending legislation that would place them under the auspices of the CFTC. "It's highly unlikely that they are going to continue to be unregulated," he said, "as these instruments multiply, we're simply playing with fire."[2]

The markets did not need to be reminded that English was a Democrat from an agricultural state. His subcommittee was not attached to a major financial committee but primarily represented agricultural interests. The century-old reputation of the futures markets again was threatening new financial products far removed from the wheat and soybean fields. The irony was not lost. By steadfastly opposing SEC regulation for years, the markets opted instead for the looser regulation of the CFTC and occasional probing by congressional committees, which politically dedicated themselves to finding fault with the futures regulator, especially when the committee's renewal was reviewed every four years. The exchanges effectively played the CFTC and Congress against each other, as they had done for years. The English subcommittee was one that would play a major role in renewing the CFTC's charter.

At the heart of English's proposal was a definition of all derivatives and hybrid instruments that would have classified them as futures contracts, subjecting them to the CFTC. Other members of Congress opposed the strict mathematical definition. Representative John Dingell, Democrat of Michigan, wrote to English, stating, "Regrettably, I must conclude that your suggested resolution is totally unacceptable." English, though, was not persuaded. His idea was to have the CFTC vet all new products to determine which of them might fall under its jurisdiction rather than wait for an exchange to apply for permission to trade them. "We'd like to see everything come in the front door and have the CFTC take a look at them and sort out those to keep and those to exempt," he stated upon reading Dingell's letter.[3]

English was the 1990s' embodiment of the Sons of the Wild Jackass. Born in Oklahoma in 1940, he had attended a local college before embarking on a career in the oil and gas business and, later, gravitating toward politics. First elected to the House in 1974, he served nine terms before resigning in

1994 to take a job with a rural electric cooperative. What he recognized was the need for rigorous definition in the markets, at least from the regulators' point of view. That often brought him into conflict with the CFTC itself. But the manner by which he made his points separated him from many of his colleagues because of his use of extremely blunt, confrontational language.

The battle over the definition of what constituted a futures contract continued until the CFTC renewal in late 1992. At the heart of the matter was an old issue dressed in contemporary clothing. A tight definition would include swaps and forwards, putting them under the commission, whereas a loose definition would leave them outside and might also include other products not yet highly developed or still in the planning stages. That would create the intolerable situation in which the exchanges themselves designed contracts purposely to be traded off the exchange floor—that is, in the OTC market. The affair was reminiscent of the off-floor activities of nineteenth-century CBOT traders.

One of those opposed to a strict definition of futures contracts for regulatory purposes was Wendy Gramm, chair of the CFTC. She and her husband, Senator Phil Gramm of Texas, were both in favor of strong market regulation but even though she favored more power for the CFTC in derivative securities and bank-created options, she did not want a constricting definition. More to the point, English's definition would still have to exclude some products while including others and that would cause a mountain of paperwork for the agency, forcing it to spend most of its time reviewing definitions in addition to the actual products. As in most years when the charter was up for renewal, the CFTC postured for a stronger role on its own terms.

As the CFTC renewal vote approached, Gramm told English that new swap products should continue to be traded

OTC, subject to the banking laws then in place to monitor the banks that traded them. The futures exchanges proposed that they set up subsidiary companies that would trade swaps without regulation but most regulators would not hear of it. Accepting the proposal would have been tantamount to throwing in the regulatory towel, allowing the exchanges to escape regulation. When the CFTC was finally renewed, it proceeded as it had in the past. The exchanges and futures contracts were included, whereas swaps and forwards were excluded, as they always had been. Now, however, an element of campaign politics entered, illustrating how volatile the entire issue had become.

After Gramm's departure from the commission in 1992, William Albrecht became chair. In the wake of the CFTC's renewal, the commission began making decisions that infuriated English, and the commissioners were called before the agriculture subcommittee in May 1993 for addressing the issue of the CFTC's decision to exempt certain types of energy-forward contracts from its antifraud rules. Several weeks before, the agency effectively threw in the towel and exempted the swaps market from any potential jurisdiction. The agency maintained that the markets could not be adequately regulated and therefore that it would be more practical to free them from theoretical restraint. English did not endorse the action, responding to Albrecht by exclaiming, "Of the 18 years I've been in Congress, this is the most irresponsible decision I've come across." His target was the chair himself, for Albrecht revealed that the decision was not unanimous even though he personally supported it.

English was not mollified by Albrecht's assertion that it was within the agency's authority to make such decisions without interference. He snapped at the chair, "If you can't deal with fraud, Mr. Albrecht, there's no reason for you to be here." He considered the idea of markets monitoring themselves to be very naive. Finally, toward the end of the hearing, he shouted, "What in God's name is the CFTC all about?"[4] But any public interest that English was trying to arouse was negated by the fact that only 3 of the 24 subcommittee members bothered attending the fiery meeting.

In the 1992 presidential campaign, third party candidate Ross Perot included the prospect of a swaps meltdown in his campaign. Arguing for broad regulation of the swaps market, the claim was that the financial world was headed for a massive swaps default that would bring down banks and possibly the whole financial system. The notion certainly had all the earmarks of a drama. A meltdown could occur if a swap party reneged on its obligations, setting off a massive wave of other defaults. Because the market was already estimated in the trillions (nominal amounts), the argument seemed well placed. Several years before, in a highly unusual publicized transaction, J. P. Morgan & Co. described a swap it had done with New York City that required over 200 countervailing swaps before the risk to the bank was finally mitigated. Unfortunately for the campaign, the issue was too hypothetical. If the definition of futures still eluded the regulators after more than 100 years, there was little chance that they would prove to be a volatile campaign issue. The swap problems that had occurred were manageable and there was no reason to believe that Western civilization was a risk from some internal financial bug bearing the seeds of destruction. The near future would test the hypothesis, much to the chagrin of the banks and participants involved.

The Justice Department also pursued the charges brought against the Chicago traders in 1989. As the decade began, 10 soybean traders of the original 46 charged two years earlier were convicted of hundreds of charges of fraud and RICO violations. In 1991, a jury returned guilty verdicts against the 10 with potential sentences ranging to dozens if not hundreds of years in prison and hundreds of thousands of dollars in fines. The verdict was characterized as a "massacre" by one of the defense attorneys. Unfortunately for the traders, their defense backfired when their attorneys admitted that the charges were essentially true but trivial because the amounts involved in the fraud only came to $25 to $50 per trade. The jury saw it differently. "Most of the jurors figured that if it was dishonest, a penny or a million dollars is the same thing," remarked a juror spokesperson.[5] Not all of the traders were convicted of all charges, but the government's case had been made and the markets were on notice.

The CBOT reacted to the soybean traders' conviction by hiring Robert Bork, the former solicitor general and Supreme Court nominee, as counsel. The exchange wanted to challenge the conviction on the RICO charges, contending that the prosecution was a misapplication of the law. By charging the traders under the law, the government was equating commodities traders with members of organized crime for whom the law originally was written. The CBOT decided to file a brief on behalf of the traders, an action that elicited an angry response from the U.S. Attorney.

The FBI was not finished with the exchanges, however. In March 1991, agents attempted to infiltrate the floor of the New York commodities exchanges, searching for more trading floor violations. As in the past, the exchanges were not informed in advance, leading Robert Wilmouth of the NFA to wonder aloud about the FBI's intent. "Exchanges are just as eager to root out trading problems," he stated after hearing of the operation. He had to acknowledge, however, that the government still did not trust the exchanges to look after themselves. "There is a mistrust in the government over the exchanges' ability to clean house," he added, noting that over a century of suspicion about the pits still lingered.[6] Pit traders were livid about the FBI operation following indictments and successful prosecutions of many of their colleagues and Chicago traders were in full sympathy with their New York counterparts.

The exchanges reacted predictably to the new "sting" as they saw it. Executives of the COMEX and the New York Coffee, Sugar, and Cocoa Exchange denied applications by two clerks who wanted to become full trading members, remembering that two of the Chicago agents got their start in the pits by first becoming clerks. A trader on the COMEX exposed the operation when he recognized one of the agents posing as applicants. He remembered him from college, where the applicant had aspired to be an FBI agent. The sting was exposed before it got off the ground. Another trader sarcastically noted that the agents would have been detected before long in any event since the average COMEX trader did not wear wing-tip shoes and sport a crew cut.

The Chicago scandal changed the working lifestyle of futures traders. The futures exchanges adopted individual ethics-training courses, requiring pit traders to attend them in an effort to upgrade their image. Naturally, the courses were at odds with the pop Social Darwinism that many traders still espoused. The CBOT required members to attend courses beginning in 1992. All members, regardless of age or the time when they joined the exchange, had to attend a course given by either the CBOT or one by one of the other Chicago exchanges. Usually, the courses were taught by clinical-law professors rather than by ethics or philosophy professors, suggesting that ethics meant keeping out of legal trouble. The courses each were only two-hours long but most members begrudgingly attended.

The futures business remained a major Chicago industry in the 1990s, as it had for over a century. The exchanges employed over 100,000 people, although many were support staff and brokers. The CBOT had around 1,400 members by 1995, as compared to around 1,800 at the turn of the century.

There were many more brokers, commodities bankers, and clearinghouse employees, all accounting for a large portion of the industry. Within the CBOT ranks, women had made little progress, however. Of the 1,400 members, only 53 were women but the CME had a better showing, with 245 of its 2,725 members being women. The pit environment, although lucrative, still did not attract many women who wanted to roll up their sleeves and push the boys around all day to make a living.

## *KNOW YOUR CUSTOMER*

Despite the hyperbole and fear of imminent market collapse, the derivatives markets remained relatively calm in the wake of the Hammersmith and Fulham debacle. However, suspicions were beginning to grow that it was only a matter of time before a serious setback developed that would draw regulators into the swap and, possibly, futures markets as never before. The huge OTC market for swaps seemed primed for a problem for it was a truly international market with no single regulator setting the tone. Yet, the market remained in the background. Many in the financial world hardly knew of its existence.

The swap market was even more demure than the forex market. Although enormous, it was not reported in the financial newspapers with any regulatory. Even if it were, the bid-offer spreads were among the most confusing in the markets. Although many practical books appeared over the years explaining stock and bond tables and price quotations to laypersons, no one bothered to include swaps; the space would have been wasted. Swaps and other designer derivatives seemed a step apart from Wall Street and even LaSalle Street—until 1994.

Events in 1994 made the idea of a swap-related meltdown appear imminent. Since the late 1980s, many corporations had been using derivatives designed by banks to manage their assets and liabilities. When used cleverly, swaps and swaptions packages could help corporate treasurers minimize exposure to interest rates and currency fluctuations, but if not used cleverly, they could expose a company to as much risk as it sought to avoid. Banking was quickly adopting a Wall Street strategy at the time. Rather than simply making loans to companies, many big commercial banks were becoming transaction-oriented. They wanted to help their clients with trading operations as well, seeking to pick up trading fees which could be more profitable than loans. They had certain advantages over the traditionally smaller investment banks for most of the large commercial banks had higher credit ratings. Since swapping required corporate treasurers, as well as the banks, to know their clients' financial positions, strong credit ratings worked in favor of the banks. But no one thought that a bank would be accused of taking advantage of a client's inexperience or naivete by making inappropriate trades.

After a stinging loss in the derivatives markets, Procter & Gamble filed suit against Bankers Trust Co. in 1994. The company charged that some of the derivatives transactions that it entered at Bankers Trust's suggestion proved inappropriate, leading to losses estimated at $102 million. The consumer products company was not alone. A similar suit was filed against Bankers Trust by Gibson Greeting Cards. Another company, Air Products & Chemicals, also announced losses from derivatives as a result of adopting the bank's strategies and recommendations. Other companies announced losses as well, putting the New York bank under the spotlight for inappropriate trading of customer accounts.

When the losses were first announced, most knowledgeable bankers and traders thought that the threat of potential lawsuits was nothing more than sour grapes by companies that lost money. Most corporate treasurers were sophisticated enough to understand the risks involved with derivatives trading and if they got it wrong they had no one to blame but themselves. Derivatives should be used to hedge assets and liabilities that are vulnerable to interest rate changes so losses would indicate the adoption of speculative positions instead. Not so, claimed Gibson and Procter & Gamble. They claimed that Bankers Trust misled them, prompting them to begin legal proceedings.

Gibson Greeting Cards filed suit in September 1994, seeking damages for its $23 million in losses. The company claimed that Bankers Trust did not adequately inform it about the risks incurred. Procter & Gamble watched the suit carefully for its loss was incurred at about the same time. Both companies were hurt by the interest rate rises orchestrated by the Fed earlier in 1994, catching most of the market off guard. Procter & Gamble's chairman stated, "Derivatives are dangerous, and we were badly burned. We won't let this happen again" and added that "we are seriously considering our legal options relative to Bankers Trust."[7] For its part, the bank claimed that many of Procter & Gamble's derivative transactions made a profit and rejected the company's claims of being misled. It claimed that it officially told Procter & Gamble to unwind its positions before they did harm but that the company's "senior officials rejected these recommendations."

Revelations made later in Procter & Gamble's suit changed the complexion of the case. A common practice in most bank-dealing rooms involved taping all conversations made between traders and customers as a matter of course, to protect both customer and bank. The tapes began to trickle out when Gibson Greeting Cards sued Bankers Trust and became evidence as a result of the discovery process. Over 6,000 tapes eventually became part of the case. As lawyers listened to them, the tapes revealed a less-than-respectful attitude toward customers by bank traders and proved damning in the face of the charges.

Banks profited from swap dealing through the bid-offer spreads that dealers had made on the two sides of the deal. The spreads were calculated incorporating market conditions and the perceived risk of the client. Several tapes displayed almost total disregard of the client's needs by Bankers Trust's traders, who clearly appeared to be dealing for the bank and themselves. In a tape recorded on November 2, 1993, two employees of the bank were heard discussing a derivatives deal that the bank had just consummated for Procter & Gamble. "They would never be able to know how much money was taken out of that," one trader remarked to the other. "Never, no way, no way," the other affirmed. "That's the beauty of Bankers Trust."[8] They were referring to the amount of profit that traders had built into the spread on the deal. It was so complicated that Procter & Gamble employees were completely in the dark about its size.

Building unjustifiable spreads into deals was not the only problem uncovered. In another case, two bank employees discussed a client's loss on a trade. One remarked to the other, "Pad the number a little bit," to which the other replied, "Funny business, you know? Lure people into that calm and then just totally———— 'em."[9] Unfortunately for the bank, its customers were not amused. The bank claimed that many of the tapes were nothing more than traders letting off steam or bragging about a good deal. In the harsh light of potential legal proceedings, however, outside parties took a dimmer view. The bank's reputation as a major derivatives dealer was seriously tarnished.

As a result of the tapes, Procter & Gamble filed RICO charges against the bank in addition to its existing laundry list of fraud and deception. The bank fired or reassigned several employees as a result, although it initially fought the charges brought by Gibson Greeting Cards and Procter & Gamble. Most of the claims were settled out of court. Bankers Trust agreed to pay Gibson Greeting Cards $14 million, and it also compensated several other client claims almost $70 million. Initially, the future looked bleak for the bank, especially in light of the tapes. A court saw its problems less seriously, however. In 1996, it won two court battles in the Procter & Gamble suit, and the consumer product company's RICO suit was dismissed in the process. However, Bankers Trust suffered a crisis of confidence in its traders that was highlighted in a subsequent report ordered by several regulatory agencies—the CFTC, the Fed, the SEC, and the New York State Banking Department. The report, written by former U.S. Attorney Benjamin Civiletti and former New York State Banking Commissioner Derrick Cephas, criticized Bankers Trust for not maintaining strict controls over its traders, many of whom were described as "well-intentioned but inexperienced and undertrained for their positions. A few were venal and engaged in misconduct to further their self-interest." One trader "used his facility with mathematics to develop a formula for a leveraged derivative product that would conceal the amount of leverage that was embedded in such products."[10] The report was also critical of the bank's former president and chairman, both of whom had already left their posts. The bank was bloodied but unbowed by the incident, discovering that derivatives trading had both drawbacks and advantages.

## TOXIC WASTE

The popularity of swaps trading was in clear evidence by the early 1990s. The ability to change cash flows by entering into swaps proved a valuable corporate management tool and was widely adopted. The popularity also appealed to many new swap traders, who saw the rapidly growing market as a way to make huge salaries and bonuses based upon their clients' trading patterns. Bankers Trust already proved that greedy traders could cause widespread financial damage but proved to be small potatoes when compared with what was to follow.

Hammersmith and Fulham was not the only municipality involved in the swap market; it was just the best known to date. Many U.S. municipalities also used the market frequently to enhance their cash flows. The larger municipalities allowed smaller ones to participate in their portfolios through swap pools. The smaller municipalities could buy a small portion for themselves and assume the risk of its performance while the larger municipality earned a fee. Several large derivatives pools existed. One of the largest was the Orange County Investment Pool (OCIP), operated by the municipal government of Orange County, California, a wealthy suburban enclave located south of Los Angeles.

By any standard, the county had a formidable economy. It generated an annual gross domestic product of $74 billion in 1993, larger than the economies of Portugal, Israel, or Singapore. Standing alone, it was the 30th largest economic power in the world.[11] The county was an overwhelmingly Republican district—a fact repeated many times in the press, for events that enveloped the OCIP stemmed from local distrust of strong government combined with a paradoxically strong demand for high-quality municipal services. In that respect, it was no different from many other California counties except that it was the wealthiest.

The central figure in the county government was Robert Citron, the 69-year-old treasurer who had held the elected office for over 25 years. He ran unopposed in all elections except his last. A native Californian, Citron attended college for several years before dropping out and entering municipal government where he spent the balance of his career. Unlike many of the other traders and end-users of derivative products who led flamboyant lifestyles or considered themselves international jetsetters, Citron was an average middle-class suburbanite who apparently never benefited personally from the millions he made for his employer. However, the calm exterior belied a self-exaggerated sense of his financial acumen.

In the early 1990s, he began an aggressive series of investments with money the county borrowed through municipal bond offerings. Citron proved to be a good client for bond dealers. He purchased millions of government agency bonds of five years to maturity. In one particular deal, Merrill Lynch distributed a new issue for Sallie Mae, the student loan guarantee agency, for $600 million. Orange County bought the entire issue from Merrill at a slight premium to par. On the day the issue was announced, Bloomberg Financial Services calculated the price to be four full points lower. Citron had paid too much for the issue. Merrill Lynch pocketed between $2 million and $6 million on the trade.[12] In Wall Street terms, there was strong suspicion that Citron had been "stuffed" with agency paper at a high price.

The investment strategy was not finished; it was only beginning. Citron borrowed money against the bonds on margin and used the proceeds to assemble a derivatives portfolio. By doing so, he was able to triple the outstanding amount of investments under his control. The strategy was clever because investing in derivatives alone would have been prohibited but by parlaying them off the bonds the strategy appeared to be on a sound footing. Unfortunately, the strategy was not of investment quality but only a bet. By deploying the strategy, he was tripling his exposure, not limiting it.

On the surface, Citron appeared to be a financial wizard but the situation actually was much different. When questioned about the portfolio, he often appeared proud but confused. His comments about its composition and performance were often incoherent monologues, leaving county managers with the impression that he was either a genius or had no idea of what he was managing. As long as the portfolio continued to produce extraordinary returns no one cared so he safely occupied his office. The real brains behind the operation were to be found elsewhere.

Citron's main investment banker helping to assemble the deals was the San Francisco office of Merrill Lynch. His broker, Michael Stamenson, was the one who put together most of the deals for Orange County. The pending debacle was not the first in which the broker had been involved. Ten years earlier, he was broker to the San Jose, California, municipal government, which also assembled a derivatives portfolio during the early days of the swaps and derivatives craze. San Jose lost $60 million in 1984, employing a familiar leverage strategy using reverse repos—the same that would plague Orange County.[13] Both counties bought large amounts of agency bonds and then temporarily sold them to securities dealers in return for cash, with an agreement to buy them back on a specific date for a predetermined price. Leverage of that type only worked well when interest rates declined or remained stable. The dealers effectively were loaning the municipalities money, using the bonds as collateral.

The derivatives portion of the portfolio, when added to the bonds, gave it an enormous value estimated at $20 billion. Orange County was not the only local investor involved in the pool. In fact, its investment amounted to only to about 37 percent of the portfolio. Other investors included local school districts, transportation authorities, sanitation districts, and water districts. Over 200 local entities participated. Superficially, this fact seemed to diversify the ownership base adequately. The problem was that the fund was the only investment made by many of the smaller entities. Any default or serious loss had the potential to leave them with serious consequences.

The portfolio was closely tied to an interest rate formula based on the eurodollar interest rate—specifically, the London Interbank Offered Rate (LIBOR).[14] This was the standard method of pricing floating-rate notes and bonds. The **LIBOR** rate was used as a reference rate and the periodic interest rate was set at a specific percentage above it. Because the eurodollar rate constantly fluctuates, paying interest based upon this formula can be risky to the borrower for it normally changes twice a year for the life of the loan. Orange County was subject to fluctuating short-term interest rates but its exposure was more complicated. Being exposed to this type of payment is known as being subject to floating rates. However, the county took it one step further by arranging for exposure to what are known as "negative floaters."

Most of the OCIP portfolio was based on the formula of 15 or 10 **LIBOR**, meaning that its return was 15 or 10 percent minus the eurodollar rate, or twice the eurodollar rate. Therefore, 10 minus the rate meant that an exposure was 10 percent minus the rate; 15 minus the rate usually meant that an exposure was 15 percent minus twice the eurodollar rate. In either case, the formula was designed to expose an investor to the opposite of what normally was expected when short-term interest rates rose. Regardless of which formula was used, a rise in eurodollar rates would mean a lower rate of interest paid out, a condition that in a swap means that the payer would benefit but the recipient would lose.

When interest rates were low, the yield on the OCIP portfolio was high, sometimes reaching 8 percent when the market rates were only around 4 to 5 percent. However, the entire situation changed when the Fed raised interest rates in 1994, acting against market expectations. Much of the portfolio was based upon receiving payments using the negative **LIBOR** formula. The rise in short-term interest rates beginning in the winter of 1994 cut into the return on the portfolio and spelled eventual doom for Orange County's high return. Prior to its bankruptcy announcement, the return had fallen to around 5 to 6 percent. At those levels, the returns were too low for the sort of risk that the portfolio potentially posed. One municipal analyst remarked that "this is preposterous . . . these guys are out 'arbing' for a miniscule amount of money," referring to the lower level of returns created by the bond/derivatives arbitrage.[15]

The condition of the OCIP was not widely known but those who did understand it were dismayed by its exposure to rising interest rates. Citron's opponent in his last election in 1994 remarked that the pool was "a major bull market bet in the middle of a bear market . . . the incumbent has structured the portfolio . . . on the premise that interest rates would continue to decline."[16] That may have been something of an overstatement for his knowledge of the exposure was sketchy at best. However, politics in California had created a situation that made extraordinary returns for municipalities a godsend. In 1978, the state legislature passed Proposition 13, widely seen at the time as part of a nationwide revolt against higher taxes—in this case, higher property taxes. Because the law limited property tax increases, revenue shortfall had to be made up in some other way and investment pools such as OCIP fit the bill. Regardless of Citron's personal knowledge of derivatives finance, money was money and few questions were asked.

Another problem for municipalities was found in the Tax Reform Act of 1986, many which eliminated the arbitrage possibilities that municipalities exploited in the past by issuing their own bonds and buying tax-free (for them) U.S. Treasury bond obligations. As a result, more exotic types of arbitrage had to be found that did not involve Treasury bonds. The derivatives pool was a viable alternative although it was certainly more risky. Under the old strategy, municipalities borrowed and invested the money in a tax-free Treasury bond, pocketing the difference in yield. Quite often, the bonds were guaranteed by a third party government agency, keeping their coupons very low. The arbitrage was guaranteed by another governmental party until Congress finally closed the loophole.

The derivatives strategy employed the same idea except that the assets purchased with the money raised from bond issues were leveraged so that the derivatives, not the actual agency bonds purchased, would yield the high return, thereby avoiding potential problems with the law.

Orange County's fortunes clearly were built upon a derivatives foundation. The reverse floaters were not the only exotic instruments in the portfolio. A host of other strange and wonderful combinations could be found, including synthetic instruments such as zero-coupon bonds, diff swaps (where foreign short-term interest rates are used), and repurchase agreements, or repos. By themselves, the instruments were standard fare in the markets, but when combined the results could be puzzling and often unexpected. For instance, when the Fed raised short-term interest rates, repo rates increased, as did some foreign interest rates, and zero-coupon bonds declined sharply in value. What appeared to be a well-diversified portfolio to the casual observer was really a time bomb to the trained eye, waiting to explode. When the OCIP did decline sharply, no one in the markets who knew of its composition was surprised.

Problems started to surface in fall 1994 as rising interest rates began to take their toll. Prompted by Citron's assistant, Orange County hired a consulting firm to assess the portfolio, and the group examined the pool. It was discovered in November that rising interest rates had already caused the OCIP a loss on paper of $1.5 billion, with potential cash-flow problems not far behind. Then on December 1 the county officially acknowledged the loss at a press conference and Wall Street started to become very nervous. If the county had to declare bankruptcy, the loss would be the first substantial American derivatives fiasco in years caused by a customer.

Orange County unraveled quickly. At the meeting, the county announced its unanticipated loss. Officials tried to put on a brave face amid a desperate situation, partly intended to assuage Wall Street. At the meeting, as well as in meetings that followed, Citron was replaced by his assistant Matt Raabe as the treasurer's office spokesperson. Initially, they tried to brush off the loss as only momentary. "These are just paper losses," declared Raabe. The treasurer himself had some of the wind taken out of his sails as a financial genius able to produce cash and high returns. He was more defensive personally. "I have not done anything irresponsible in any manner, shape or form," he told reporters a few days after the announcement.[17] Technically, he appeared to be correct, but the roof soon fell in.

Many Wall Street houses having dealings with Orange County now wanted to be compensated for losses or demanded their securities back. Their rush to exit a bad situation turned the paper losses into very real ones. The portfolio had to be liquidated to satisfy their demands and Orange County hired Salomon Brothers to advise on the best exit strategy. When the smoke cleared, the loss totaled $1.7 billion. Although the investment banks were clearly in a great hurry to extricate themselves from the county, the timing was very poor. Credit market conditions pushed bond prices lower at the end of the year. If the liquidation had been postponed for six months, about $1 billion of the loss could have been recouped.[18] As Orange County discovered, its creditors did not have a six-month time frame in mind. They wanted to liquidate immediately and were entitled to do so. Bad timing plagued the pool and continued to do so until the end.

After the announcement, Citron resigned and the county's major bankers huddled to sort out the mess. Around the country, other investment pools came under scrutiny, several of which would later announce problems in their own portfolios, although of a lesser magnitude. Many of the bankers insisted on liquidating the portfolio so they could be paid back loans that they had made to the county. For its part, the county declared bankruptcy, for it was unable to meet its obligations in the wake of the loss. It was the largest municipal bankruptcy ever recorded and threw a damper on exotic financing techniques.

Within a few weeks, Orange County filed suit against Merrill Lynch, its main derivatives provider. The county sued for $2.4 billion, claiming that the portfolio was unsuitable for municipal needs. A major part of the argument was that parts of the portfolio were so unsuitable that they were actually illegal. This *ultra vires* claim was similar to the one made by Hammersmith and Fulham several years before. The county claimed that precedents over the years prevented a municipality from incurring debts that exceeded a year's revenues.[19] Beyond Hammersmith and Fulham, there was a U.S. case that also claimed the same defense. In 1987, a West Virginia investment pool also announced a $300 million loss in a derivatives portfolio caused by an interest rate spike at the time. West Virginia sued its brokers, including Merrill Lynch, and several of the investment banks settled out of court. However, Morgan Stanley, one of the pool's lead investment bankers, demurred and challenged the suit. A lower court originally ruled that the *ultra vires* defense was appropriate and that brokers had misled the state on the appropriateness of the investments.

Orange County's bankruptcy led to a serious reduction in municipal services until its finances could be sorted out. Garbage began to pile up in the streets and other municipal services were sharply curtailed in communities not accustomed to adversity of any kind. The suit against Merrill Lynch continued for several years before a settlement eventually was reached. Although Orange County was the most celebrated derivatives fiasco of the period, it was not alone. Several other corporate derivatives debacles also occurred, proving that municipal treasurers were not the only ones bewildered by the complexity of their portfolios. A smaller but nevertheless significant loss was also announced far from the sunny confines of southern California.

Two days after the Orange County announcement, the city manager of Auburn, Maine, announced a loss in the derivatives market amounting to more than 40 percent of the city's funds. The city had a portfolio of $16 million, of which almost $6.5 million was lost in the same interest rate rise that befell Citron. Auburn was not quite in the same league as Orange County, however. The city had 24,000 residents and a yearly budget of $44 million but the loss still was substantial. Even more disturbing was the claim by the city manager that the derivatives portfolio was never disclosed to the city council so the loss came out of the blue as a shock. "This problem was the result of a lack of oversight and an incompetent investment policy," she admitted when reporting the loss, adding, "part of the problem is that we were never invested in this way until 1993 and the markets have changed since then."[20] The admission was a breath of fresh air when compared with Orange County's reaction but Auburn's strategy was similar: it planned to sue its investment bankers. Unfortunately, its investment bankers were not all known at the time.

The fallout from the fiasco reverberated through southern California and the markets for years. Fear also spread through the country that more unforeseen bombshells like the one in Auburn, Maine, would be uncovered in unsuspecting places. The Cleveland *Plain Dealer* summed up the feelings of many when it attributed the problem not only to derivatives but to Citron as well. The newspaper said that "financial lunacy on the part of Robert Citron . . . the man abetted by commission-craving Wall Street trolls, behaved more like a go-go savings and loan instead of a prudent steward of taxpayers' money."[21]

Regulators and the courts saw it the same way. After the fiasco, Citron testified several times before state legislators and in the trial of his assistant Raabe. He changed his tune substantially since his days as treasurer. Humbled by the experience, he no longer portrayed himself as another master of the 1990s universe but as a humble victim of Merrill Lynch. Whether he was playing the role or simply did not understand the complexities of derivatives finance, he gave the impression of being slightly too old to understand the magnitude of the problem he created. As Citron admitted at his farewell board meeting with the county supervisors, "I don't know about you but I wish I had listened just a bit more, questioned just a bit more, and trusted just a bit less."[22] Being humble did not help, however, because both Citron and Raabe received short prison terms for securities violations for their actions. Merrill Lynch settled the case out of court for $437 million. When the final tally was reached, Orange County had not lost much out-of-pocket capital for Merrill Lynch's settlement, as well as other settlements, helped it regain much of the original trading loss. The entire affair did shine some light into the sleepy, provincial world of municipal finance and would help bring about greater monitoring by politicians of their treasurers and investment managers.

## BRINGING DOWN THE HOUSE

Because of market developments over the years, most banks and corporate treasurers became well-versed in risk-management techniques and knew how to limit their exposure. Problems arose when derivatives packaging was accompanied by high-pressure sales techniques, promoted by traders and salespeople more interested in their Christmas bonuses than meeting the needs of corporate clients. Most derivatives professionals were either bankers or traders conversant with the tools of their trade, learned in training courses at banks and brokerages, many of whom required their trainees to possess an MBA. Two of the notable fiascoes of the decade were per-

petrated by individuals who, somewhat incongruously, fell outside the profile of the trader of the 1990s. One was Robert Citron; the other, a novice trader in the far-flung office of a
venerable British merchant bank.

In the clubby world of British merchant banking, Baring
Brothers clearly was the best known and best-connected bank.
Since its founding in 1763, it had been the banker to British
nobility and emerging gentry, to the Crown, and to most major
British companies. During the nineteenth century, it was also a
major supplier of capital to the United States, which relied
heavily on investment from Britain. The bank stubbed its toe in
1890 when it had to be saved by the Bank of England and
other merchant banks after a series of losses on South American bonds left it almost bankrupt. In the post–World War II
period, the bank was less visible on the international scene but
was still considered the jewel of the City of London, especially
for its connections. However, it would not survive the twentieth
century intact.

The City of London, as Britain's financial district is known,
was relatively subdued by Wall Street standards. Many of the
merchant banks (investment banks that also took deposits) were
small and their stature was based upon reputations built up
over the years. Unlike their Wall Street counterparts, they were
not transaction-oriented. If a client needed a stock trade executed, it would use its traditional stock brokers rather than its
investment bankers. Many securities services, familiar and
taken for granted in the United States, were fractured in
Britain, with brokers, discount (money market) houses, and
merchant banks all fulfilling their traditional securities or banking services without much attempt at integration. By the mid-
1980s, that orientation changed significantly.

Parliament passed the Financial Services Act, better known
as "Big Bang," in 1986. With one deft stroke of the legislative
pen, Britain's financial services sector was changed overnight.

Many of the previous regulations were eliminated and transactions now became as important as the more traditional banking and corporate finance advice dispensed by merchant banks. Foreign firms, including those of the United States and Japan, had been moving to London for several years in anticipation of the change and were in a position to begin vying with British brokers and merchant banks for business. The Big Bang prompted many British institutions to quickly adapt to the new environment for fear of losing business to foreign firms. Even Baring Brothers responded to the challenge by adding trading operations, an area once considered anathema to traditional merchant bankers.

Adding trading operations also meant that Baring Brothers and other established merchant banks would need to add traders. In Britain, traders were drawn from the ranks of the "great unwashed" elements of the City of London, to use a traditional metaphor. These traders did not possess university degrees and did not attend public schools, which in Britain actually denotes private secondary schools. Most of them came from working-class or lower-middle-class backgrounds and formed a distinctly different group from the management of the banks and better brokerage firms. But after Big Bang was passed, many of the traders found themselves in great demand by financial institutions desperate to find staff to fill new positions that Big Bang had forced them to create.

The standard way that a trader was created was for him (women were almost never found in these ranks) to begin working in the back office of a bank or brokerage firm, doing account settlements. After learning the workings of the settlements process, which also included the basics of compliance, the more ambitious or talented would be offered a trader's position. These were jobs for which no particular education was required, only a measure of common sense and dedication to long hours. In mechanical terms, a young trader was versed in trading techniques, settlements procedures, and rudimentary securities law as it applied to the "do's and don'ts" of trading. Unlike their American counterparts on the futures exchanges and in the OTC derivatives markets, these traders were relatively uneducated and lucky to be able to read a balance sheet. They resembled Chicago traders of the 1920s more than pit traders of the 1980s.

Anachronisms like Citron were not uncommon in the markets in the 1980s and 1990s but only came into full view when financial problems arose from their trading patterns. The same was true, though in a slightly different sense, at Baring Brothers. The bank hired Nick Leeson, a 22-year-old trader who had spent the previous few years learning his trade at a British bank and later at Morgan Stanley in London, both in the settlements department. In its great rush to fill its ranks with experienced people, Baring Brothers violated the basic canons of financial practices that would lead it to its downfall. Also, the trader became something of an anachronism for being poorly trained for the high-speed environment that developed after Big Bang.

The bank hired Leeson to join its London staff to be a settlements clerk in its derivatives department. Leeson filled the bill for a settlements clerk perfectly. He was a "school leaver," meaning that he did not perform well enough on his secondary school exams to gain entrance to a British university. As a result, he gravitated toward the City of London searching for work and landed a job at Coutts, the private bank that was well-known as banker to the royal family. After spending a couple of years there, he took another settlements job at Morgan Stanley, where he learned derivatives settlements—mostly in options and futures. He was then hired by Baring Brothers which was impressed with his experience at two solid institutions. Unlike Morgan Stanley, Baring Brothers had a weak internal-management structure, and its derivatives trading was a mess. With hindsight, the bank should never have allowed Leeson to trade, for he had several outstanding legal proceedings pending against him for failing to pay off personal debts. In the fast-moving world of London finance, however, these proceedings were overlooked in favor of his "experience."

Leeson performed well during his initial assignments and was eventually assigned to the bank's newly opened Singapore office. The bank traded futures and options there, mainly with the Asian derivatives exchanges in Japan and in Singapore itself. Singapore's main exchange was the Singapore International Monetary Exchange (SIMEX). It was founded in 1984 and based upon the open-outcry method employed by the CME. In fact, the exchange was modeled closely after the CME with which it had developed capacities for trading similar sorts of contracts. Singapore's main contract was on the NIKKEI 225, representing the Japanese stock market index. As Leo Melamed stated, "Until the SIMEX began trading the NIKKEI 225 futures contract, a critical component of equity investing was missing: there existed no means by which portfolio managers could effectively and efficiently hedge risk in large portfolios of Japanese stock."[23] The CME considered the links with the SIMEX a feather in its cap for opening the Japanese market to outside investors but the bubble in the indices would prove the undoing of Baring Brothers.

When Leeson joined the newly formed subsidiary in Singapore in 1992, he admittedly was short of experience for a position in which he would have a great deal of autonomy. However, he filled the bill as a good settlements clerk and he was one of Baring Brothers' own, having received his most recent training from the bank's existing derivatives staff. Yet the bank allowed him to commit one of the cardinal sins of the futures markets. Originally sent as a settlements expert, Leeson also applied for a broker's license, allowing him to trade on the SIMEX. Traditionally, trading and clearing trades are two separate activities on all exchanges to protect against traders altering trading records. The safeguard was not followed, however, and Leeson found himself in the unique position of having accounting authority over his own market trades. Almost from the beginning, the stage was set for fraudulent activity if that was what the young trader had in mind.

While Leeson was settling into his new position in Singapore, Baring Brothers was suffering a crisis through losses incurred at its securities subsidiary and was making wholesale changes in personnel and reporting lines. The bank also enjoyed a cozy relationship with its regulators at the Bank of England and discovered methods of separating securities trading from the traditional banking business, taking pressure off its capital requirements. By deft maneuvering, Baring Brothers was able to deceive its regulators into thinking that it had adequate capital when, in fact, its capital base was surprisingly small given its activities in the markets. This would make the bank fragile, subject to wrenching change if the capital base fell under a cloud.

Leeson began trading options and futures as a floor trader on the SIMEX, using a catchall account, dubbed the "88888," to conceal trading losses. He was trading mostly on a proprietary basis for Baring's own account since the trading involved arbitrage. He managed to show a profit when he often lost heavily in the market. By booking fictitious trades and constantly switching balances, he appeared to be one of the bank's most savvy traders, ingratiating himself to senior management in London. More-seasoned floor traders in Singapore and Osaka, where the bulk of futures and options trading in eastern Asia took place, were amazed at how a relative newcomer to the pits could accomplish such results. By March 1994, when his position as a proprietary trader officially was recognized by the bank's management, he had already lost more than £50 million.[24] Baring's management in London set position limits for his trading but it was already too late.

Despite his apparent success and the bank's support of its new subsidiary, Baring Brothers did not have control over Leeson. Evidence suggests that management did not fully understand the nature of his business, either. The SIMEX pit environment was alien to his superiors. On a visit to Singapore, one of his London managers admitted, "It was clear to me from the minute I walked into the SIMEX pit that it was going to be very hard for anyone, let alone me, to make much of a value judgment about what was happening . . . or what the flow of information was. You are reliant on the people who are in it and doing it." As for Leeson's dual role in the process, similar doubts existed in 1994, but nothing was done about it. Another one of Leeson's London superiors admitted that "while he has no evidence to suggest that Nick Leeson has indeed abused his position, the potential for doing so needs examining."[25] The dual capacity that the young trader was fulfilling still bothered management but apparently not enough to do something about it. The profits eased their doubts considerably.

Much of the private skepticism surrounding Leeson's trading abilities proved correct. He continued trading but was losing substantial amounts. Many of the derivatives he traded were based upon the Japanese market indices, all of which were heading down after hitting historic highs earlier in the decade. Events started to percolate in early 1995 when losses continued to mount and became too difficult to hide. In January, he reported a profit of £5 million from arbitrage when, in reality, losses had amounted to almost £50 million.[26] Matters intensified when auditors from the SIMEX began questioning his accounts. Even his accounts showing a profit were beginning to dwindle as the NIKKEI index continued to decline. At one time, one of his trading accounts contained 65,000 options on the NIKKEI index, equivalent to £1.8 billion worth of underlying shares.[27] The head office also became involved and Leeson decided that he could not bear the pressure any longer and finally resigned on February 24, 1995. Baring Brothers realized it had a problem but the extent was not yet clear. The trader soon disappeared from sight, leaving the bank to hold the bag for its own incompetence and asking "how bad is the damage?"

The Bank of England was informed of the debacle by Peter Baring, a family member and one of the company's senior executives. The bank then assembled the chief executives of Britain's commercial, investment, and merchant banks in an attempt to find a solution to an imminent collapse. As it met, the committee discovered the full extent of Leeson's trading foibles. Losses initially appeared to amount to over £400 million, wiping out the bank's capital entirely. Neither the bankers nor the Bank of England was inclined to provide public money to bail out the venerable institution. The committee's attempts to provide Baring Brothers with a loan also failed. Finally, it was sold to the ING insurance group of the Netherlands and now operates as a subsidiary of the financial services company. Although it seemed almost incomprehensible at the time, one person brought down the bank with no outside help. When the smoke finally cleared, the loss amounted to well over £800 million, or about $1.3 billion equivalents.

Leeson escaped Singapore with his wife, flying to Frankfurt in an attempt to reach Britain for fear of being subjected to the Singapore justice system. On his arrival in Frankfurt, he was arrested and extradited. He was sentenced to six years in prison in Singapore for deceiving auditors and the SIMEX. Shortly after his sentencing, he signed a book deal to recount his version of the story and upon his release he returned to Britain. The long, arduous story of his massive positions and his habit of crossing client accounts with phony trades at fictitious prices to show profits only clouded the real issue behind the entire affair. A 200-year-old banking institution had been brought to its knees by a 25-year-old who was an incompetent trader but a genius at back-office deception. Chicanery in the markets had hit its zenith.

Part of the problem was that like many of its counterparts around the world, the bank did not understand derivatives and especially the pit system used by SIMEX. Many investors and institutions were often befuddled by futures and Baring Brothers was no exception. The bank suffered problems from the equity markets in the early 1990s and because Leeson's "profits" came at the right moment, no one bothered to ask the obvious questions. The most startling part was that when the meeting was called at the Bank of England to sort out the mess, its senior bankers and regulators had no idea that a problem even existed until they were informed of it. The unsettling feeling that the event had on regulators was incalculable. However, given the history of the markets in general, one thing was certain. Before long, another fiasco would arise, making those in the past look tame by comparison. Others were destined to copy Leeson's actions.

## COMING OF AGE

The timing of the Baring Brothers collapse came at an inauspicious time for the derivatives markets for it neatly dovetailed with the Orange County debacle. American bankers and regulators routinely claimed that the U.S. markets were the best-monitored and best-regulated in the world and Baring might have proved that point had the California debacle not occurred. The high-speed world of derivatives still had more surprises for the markets, however, despite the conscious efforts to clean up the previous mess.

Orange County's problems also sparked some activity at the CFTC. Since the last renewal of its mandate, the agency had all but relinquished control over nonexchange derivatives, but the publicity surrounding the Orange County debacle led its newly appointed chair, Mary Schapiro, to speak out. Schapiro said that she was willing to reconsider the earlier decision, which effectively exempted designer derivatives from federal regulation. "We did not give up the right to pursue anybody in that market for fraud," she stated in the aftermath of the Orange County debacle. As a former SEC commissioner, she also took her message to Chicago, where she gave one of the strongest speeches ever made by a CFTC commissioner to the exchanges. Even before Orange County's problems became known, she told a futures industry conference in Chicago that "you will see industry leaders degrade, denigrate and dismiss the CFTC. This perception is not in your best interests . . . if the regulator is weak then it follows that the industry must be inadequately regulated."[28] Criticizing the exchanges for not developing adequate controls to prevent trading floor abuses, it did not take long for the futures exchanges to give the sort of reply that was all too common with them. The CBOT president Thomas Donovan, after hearing Schapiro's remarks, commented that he would not "be intimidated by some 5-foot-2 blond girl," to which Schapiro, concealing her anger, simply replied, "I'm 5-foot-5."[29]

Schapiro became chair of the CFTC in October 1994. Previously, she served for six years as a commissioner of the SEC, including a short period as acting chair in 1993. However, her tenure at the CFTC was short; she left to become head of the enforcement division at NASD in early 1996. During her tenure, the CFTC was widely credited with limiting the effect of the Baring Brothers failure, particularly on U.S. firms that had significant financial exposure in Singapore and Japan. The agency also placed a renewed emphasis on its enforcement program by reorganizing the division, adding resources and pursuing a number of high-profile derivatives cases—including settlements with Bankers Trust Securities and two U.S. subsidiaries of the German metals firm, Metallgesellschaft, which previously incurred serious losses in the oil futures market.

One interesting sidelight during Schapiro's tenure was a small furor that arose when one of the CFTC's senior officials, Richard Klenja, was reassigned to a new job within the agency. Klenja was the CFTC's enforcement director when Schapiro asked him to head a newly opened office of the agency in New York. The move was seen by Senator Lauch Faircloth, a Republican from North Carolina, as punishment for a move Klenja had made two years before when he agreed to help the Whitewater special prosecutor investigate the activities of Hilary Clinton in the commodity futures market while she and the president still lived in Arkansas. According to Faircloth, the existing chair of the CFTC at the time had been replaced by a Clinton appointee when the Democrats won the White House in 1992 and the appointment, as well as Klenja's reassignment several years later, were political ploys to cover Hilary Clinton's activities. The first lady reputedly made about $100,000 on a $1,000 investment in futures over the course of a year with the help of friends in Arkansas and the deal became widely publicized.

The issue was raised many times in the press as an example of cronyism in Arkansas politics but it never amounted to more than a tempest in a teacup. After the revelations, an opinion poll asked the public whether the $100,000 return was the result of good advice and timing or was a result of preferential treatment of a politician's wife. Of those polled, 34 percent responded that it was good advice while 50 percent saw it as preferential treatment.[30] The affair did not generate much excitement in the futures markets where returns of that dollar size attracted little attention. However, the general skepticism surrounding the news of the trade only underlined the public's perception that the futures markets were places where the small investor could not get ahead without inside help.

Continued expansion of the futures exchanges also led many traders to study possible links among themselves. Several American and foreign exchanges offered similar contracts, drawing business away from each other. The CBOT and the LIFFE agreed to trade each other's bond contracts in 1995 while the New York Merc and the Sydney Futures Exchange linked up so that Sydney could trade the Merc's oil and gas contracts. The CME and the SIMEX continued their alliance after the Baring Brothers fiasco, where the SIMEX traded the CME's financial contracts. The Philadelphia Stock Exchange's derivatives unit hooked up with the Hong Kong Futures Exchange and several other exploratory relationships were established by the smaller exchanges. In addition to fostering easier and faster trading, such relationships also allowed the exchanges to share clearing data and trading patterns with their associates. The Baring Brothers affair made it clear that the exchanges needed a viable method of spotting excessive or questionable trading by members and clients.

Good intentions did not always prove successful. Within a couple years of their original announcement, the CBOT and the LIFFE truncated their trading relationship. The problem concerned not the contracts themselves but computer-based trading. The major American exchanges still maintained the pit system, but after-hours trading was done electronically with computers matching orders rather than traders directing the orders to the trading floors and pit traders. While LIFFE traded the CBOT contract, the Chicago exchange traded the German bund (long-term government bond) contract in return. However, when traders and investors realized that both contracts were available for after-hours electronic trading, the pit volume began to decline dramatically for each leading to the eventual dissolution of the relationship.

Computerized trading made great inroads during the 1990s but the exchanges still favored the pits. In winter 1997, the CBOT opened an expanded trading floor that could accommodate up to 8,000 traders and support staff. Although the new facility boasted the latest technology for trading and price reporting, most CBOT members did not use the innovations but remained faithful to their tried and true methods. An attempt in 1994 at linking the exchange with its rival the CME through Globex, a computer-based system, failed and the CBOT pulled out of the arrangement. The CBOT decided to adopt a slow approach to computer-based trading, which almost everyone on the industry expected to be the norm at some point in the future. The new CBOT floor was seen as a beginning, a way in which traders and brokers could be introduced to the new technology while still trading in the pits. "The new floor creates an environment to get people to think less defensively about technology," remarked CBOT Chairman Patrick Arbor in 1997.[31]

A strong motivation to keep the pits for as long as possible could be found in the stock market collapse of 1987. Futures traders remembered being blamed for helping to create a steadily declining market because of the computer programs that entered automatic sell orders. These orders created pandemonium for stock indices dropped quickly and futures followed suit, which only added to the problem. Keeping the order process in human hands was a process that the exchanges would not abandon quickly.

By the mid-1990s, the futures exchanges had made great strides in achieving an economic function that had been publicly disclaimed a century before. Nineteenth- and early-twentieth-century traders simply claimed that the purpose of a futures exchange was to provide a place to trade, nothing more. When questioned about the role exchanges had to play in determining cash and futures prices, traders always demurred, returning to their original point that the only function was to provide a physical location for trading. A century later that claim could no longer justifiably be made. Given the increased efficiency in trading and the enormous volume, it was now clear that cash prices affected futures prices and vice versa. The idea that exchanges now helped in the process of "price discovery" was fundamental to the markets; it was not a theory but an accepted practice. Only through the active trading of futures contracts could cash prices be tested, standing up to the forces of supply and demand endemic to each particular market.

The idea was given additional credence in the 1980s when the Fed began studying commodities prices and futures prices to better determine inflationary trends. Studying the relationships between cash and futures prices could help detect trends toward inflation or stable prices. Not all futures contracts could be used for price discovery, however. Many that were introduced in the 1980s and 1990s did not survive the trading pits and were eventually delisted. Only the most established could help detect future price trends for their trading volume was heavy enough to suggest that prices were not haphazard and, therefore, reflected a true market.

### EGG ON THE FACE

While futures exchanges made significant gains in the 1980s and 1990s—maturing into wide, full-fledged financial markets—OTC derivatives markets continued to capture the news headlines. The news was not good for derivatives in general. Supporters of the markets could point with pride at the wide array of additional hedging possibilities that the markets offered and the role that swaps could play in lowering interest rate and currency exposures. However, critics found many more fiascos, indicating weaknesses in the financial system as a whole.

The field became more crowded in the 1990s with the emergence of another new player in derivatives. Since the

1970s, hedge funds had become increasingly important as major buyers and sellers of securities and derivatives. The bull market in equities and bonds in the 1990s helped bring them to the forefront. Technically, they are investment partnerships, normally with fewer than 100 investors, able to avoid scrutiny by the SEC as a result. They operate offshore, although most keep their offices in the United States. Although their name implies that the funds hedge their market activities to limit risk, many of them are among the largest risk takers in their respective markets. As a result, their results often are impressive for their affluent investors, many of whom invested a minimum of $1 million to achieve results greater than those that could be found in traditional investment schemes.

A pure hedge fund arbitrages differences in prices between securities to take advantage of the discrepancies. If the difference between bonds in the United States and Britain is historically wide in yield terms, a hedge fund would buy the cheap one while selling the expensive one short. As yields converge again, the positions will reverse, resulting in a profit. However, these discrepancies are not usually large to begin with so an aggressive fund will borrow enormous amounts of money to buy as many bonds as possible, leveraging its holdings. The sheer size of the positions makes up for the small discrepancies, and when yields behave as expected, the profit is magnified by the size of the holdings.

Hedge funds and the OCIP had high degrees of leverage in common. If the strategy works well, the profit can be substantial but so can the loss. Citron's mistake with his portfolio was in tripling the size of his market exposure, which only exacerbated the eventual problems. A hedge fund manager seeks the exponential exposure because it means greater profits. Hedge funds rely largely on computer models used to predict price differences and the assumed behavior of securities. If the model makes a mistake, the fund can be headed for trouble. One thing is certain, however. The fund manager, not his broker, makes the assumptions for the fund and buys or sells accordingly. The fund manager does rely upon the good-will of bankers who lend the money needed for massive pur-chases.

Hedge funds can operate in any quarter of the financial markets and many often cross between them. The best known hedge funds are those able to make massive purchases of cur-rency or bonds and then ride out the market until profits emerge. Quantum Fund, founded by George Soros and heavily invested in the currency markets, took a massive position against the British pound in the early 1990s. Being exposed to high interest rates in the European Monetary Union (EMU), Britain decided to withdraw, opting for currency independ-ence. Betting that the pound would fall when it lost its link with the high-interest Deutsche mark and other European curren-cies, Quantum sold short a substantial amount and later cov-ered at a significantly lower price, netting the fund around a billion pounds in profit. Needless to say, the remarks about the gnomes of Zurich, which had not been heard in the currency markets for 20 years, were revived, blaming Soros and the Quantum Fund for the travails of sterling.

One of the largest funds was Long-Term Capital Manage-ment (LTCM), located in Connecticut. Founded in 1993, LTCM quickly became the apotheosis of what hedge funds tried to achieve. It was extremely profitable for its managers and clients and it was known for taking extremely large posi-tions in the markets. It played the hedge fund game in the tra-ditional manner. By taking extremely large positions in various bond markets, it waited for yield gaps to narrow to achieve profit. The technique was sound but the size of the positions was often staggering. The fund was Wall Street's equivalent of Sam Walton's Wal-Mart with a more impressive marquee. Because margins were thin, the only way to make a sizable profit was to do business in high volume. Even by Wall Street's standards, LTCM took the idea to dizzying heights.

The fund was the brainchild of John Merriwether, a former Salomon Brothers managing director. A native Chicagoan, he attended Northwestern and the University of Chicago business school before joining Salomon in 1974. A bond trader with a mathematics background, Merriwether opened a bond arbitrage department at Salomon in 1977. As he assumed more responsibility at the firm, he was responsible for bringing many of the mathematically oriented "quant jocks" into the firm before it became fashionable for academics to work on Wall Street. His acumen paid off when the department became one of the firm's most profitable. Quantitative techniques and bond arbitrage worked well together and before long many other firms copied Salomon Brothers and began assembling research and trading departments. Working hand in hand many produced stunning profits.

Merriwether left Salomon after being tainted by the government bond scandal in 1991 that exposed the firm's illegal attempts to control new issues of Treasury bonds. Generally acknowledged to be innocent of any wrongdoing, Merriwether was still forced out of Salomon. Ironically, before the scandal erupted he was considered to be in line for the top job at the firm; now, with his future wide open, he decided to open LTCM, a hedge fund where his former activities in the arbitrage department could be duplicated without having to fight in-house politics.

One element of Salomon Brothers' internal culture followed Merriwether to his new venture—the tendency of traders to constantly bet on all sorts of events and outcomes. Heavy betting had been a legend at Salomon, especially under chief executive John Gutfreund, and was endemic among traders in general. The tendency to make big bets within a hedge fund was understood by traders on Wall Street but did not play well on the outside when the press became aware of it. Eyebrows would be raised when it was discovered how much money LTCM had committed to the market.

The new hedge fund entered a field that had become somewhat crowded. Hedge funds were sprouting during the bull market of the 1990s, offering their wealthy clients all sorts of variations, just as mutual funds did for the average investor. Merriwether's new fund offered the basic Salomon Brothers package of previous years—arbitraging yield discrepancies on a relative value basis, then closing the trades when the market eventually reacted to the differences in yields. The marketing claim that LTCM would make was that it was a smart investing strategy, neither flashy nor particularly risky. However, Merriwether added more risk by planning to leverage the firm's holdings 20 or more times to maximize the thin yield discrepancies he planned to exploit.[32] For the fund's managers—and investors—to feel comfortable with high levels of borrowing, they would have to be assured that the fund was indeed smart, not just another planned roller-coaster ride in which they could lose heavily.

Merriwether added marquee names when he announced that Robert Merton and Myron Scholes were joining the firm. Scholes was a legendary name in finance because of the options pricing model that bore his name. Merton, a finance professor at Harvard, was equally famous for refining the original Black–Scholes model and was also famous for his work in developing the efficient-market hypotheses, one of the cornerstones of modern finance theory. In addition, David Mullins, a former vice chair of the Fed under Alan Greenspan, joined the firm in 1994. In LTCM were three of the best known individuals in finance, none having achieved his status by actually working on Wall Street or LaSalle Street. The blue-chip names brought dozens of blue-chip clients to the firm.

Investors needed a minimum of $10 million to invest in the

fund and, after a somewhat slow start, showed no reluctance in writing checks. Many banks and investment banks subscribed to the fund, as well as senior Wall Street officials. The client roster of LTCM was as impressive as its partners, and the program soon became highly successful. Scores of celebrities, universities, pension funds, and insurance companies signed up for what appeared to be the most sophisticated and highly regarded investment institution to develop in years.

The fund was still a relatively small institution despite all the interest in it. It had 11 partners and about two-dozen traders to oversee its enormous positions. Within a few years, its capital had increased to over $5 billion through successful bond arbitrage and it quickly acquired the reputation as the savviest hedge fund. The success began to bring unanticipated problems, however. Many other funds and investment firms began imitating LTCM, seeking to make similar sorts of arbitrage profits in the bond markets. Opportunities began to disappear and consequently the fund began making investments outside its original sphere of expertise. It began trading derivatives on equity investments, called equity swaps. By entering into swaps with banks, an action resembling interest rate swaps, LTCM could potentially benefit if equity prices rose. It would agree to pay a bank a fixed interest rate in return for payments based upon a stock's performance. If the stock price rose, the payment it received would exceed the fixed payments it had made; therefore LTCM would profit. This was also a clever but well-used method of avoiding the Fed's margin requirements on common stocks.[33] Although LTCM understood derivatives well, stock swaps still required knowledge of the companies involved and LTCM was weaker in that respect than it was with yield curves and futures trading.

The fund engaged in all sorts of derivatives trades. By 1997, its derivative book was valued at a nominal $1.3 trillion, twice the amount of the year before.[34] Extraordinary numbers of that nature put it in the category of a financial institution such as a bank, not simply a fund. Banks often accumulated swaps worth that much as off-balance-sheet liabilities but their capital was usually more than $5 billion. Generous loans from the banking system and large investments made by investors had given LTCM the aura of a bank in its own right. It was emerging as the 1990s' bull market version of a new-economy financial institution. It did not do much for a living. No customers were served and no banking functions were performed. All it did was borrow and make money by taking advantage of esoteric yield spreads and risk arbitrage in equities. How long could it last?

Because arbitrage spreads narrowed, LTCM was faced with a dilemma. At the end of 1997, it decided to start returning profits and to return all the money it invested after 1994 to its investors. It returned $2.7 billion at the end of 1997 while recording a 25 percent rate of return that year, the worst year in its short history. Investors got back $1.82 for each $1 invested.[35] The firm charged a hefty annual fee to investors along with a substantial portion of the annual profit as part of its return, so its own profit was therefore quite healthy. In the same year, the fund's public relations were bolstered again when Merton and Scholes were awarded the Nobel Prize in economics for their previous academic work. Clearly, LTCM was highly successful but the degrees of leverage that the firm acquired were beginning to concern some of its partners.

## COLLAPSING

All financial markets are governed by one axiom invoked in times of crisis. When market conditions become uncertain, investors quickly sell risky investments and buy U.S. Treasury securities instead. The Treasury market becomes a haven for "flight to quality" for investors seeking safety until a crisis ebbs.

The flight may be short but it cannot be interrupted and attempting to disregard it or stand in its way is futile.

Problems in LTCM began in 1998 when credit market conditions began to change. In autumn 1997, many Asian economies began to suffer economic problems and a flight of capital as the "Asian contagion" gripped the world economy. Then in August 1998, an international financial crisis was fueled when Russia announced that it would not honor its debt and devalued its currency. The situation was catastrophic for LTCM because Russian bonds were among those from developing countries that the fund had bought while selling short Treasuries of comparable maturities. The idea of converging yields evaporated overnight as the Russian obligations fell precipitously in price and the Treasuries gained as a result of the flight to quality.

Many other positions on LTCM's books declined precipitously as a result. Swaps, equity positions, and bond trades all went sour and LTCM's capital began to erode. Moreover, the markets did not correct themselves quickly. Russia's problems exacerbated an already tenuous position in the developing world and poor-quality less-liquid debt declined and did not recover quickly. Merriwether and his partners found themselves between a rock and a hard place. Their assumption about the behavior of markets was one important problem, for it was based upon models that did not use history as part of their calculations. Efficient-market theory held that knowledge of the past was no indicator of future price performance. Many of LTCM's models were based upon what were considered ineluctable forces that caused yields to converge over time. Flights to quality and the subsequent poor liquidity found in poor-quality bonds were not part of the consideration.

Attributing LTCM's problems solely to faulty risk management does not present the entire picture, however. Its positions were simply too large to manage and the traders' assumptions about placing a clever bet may well have superseded the best intentions of prudent risk management. The models did not take the past into account but the traders' assumptions apparently did. Accumulating large positions seemed a good bet since they had always worked in the past without major losses. Based upon such emotive evidence, the future could only be rosy, for the risk appeared to have been conquered. The situation was aptly summed up by another academic, Eugene Fama of the University of Chicago, who stated, "I don't think hedge funds have anything to do with the options-pricing model, I think they're just about betting."[36]

The distortions in the marketplace only were exacerbated by the disclosure that LTCM was in bad shape. The solution to the problem was unusual by Wall Street standards. Although a private investment fund, LTCM was bailed out by a consortium of 50 commercial and investment banks in a deal orchestrated by Alan Greenspan at the Fed. Although hedge funds technically are unregulated, the Fed had to step in to prevent damage to the banks themselves rather than the fund. The commercial banks in particular had loaned so much money that had a satisfactory arrangement not been worked out, their own capital could have been jeopardized by the losses. Some of the investment banks—notably Goldman Sachs—had been major trading partners with LTCM and could not afford to see trades simply die because their counterparty was insolvent. As a result, a deal was worked out allowing LTCM to remain in business but with severe restrictions on its trading activities.

Former Salomon Brothers' partner Henry Kaufman, an erstwhile colleague of Merriwether, remarked that "LTCM nevertheless got into deep trouble. Surprisingly the firm's analytical wizards apparently did not take into account some financial market fundamentals . . . that sizeable positions in individual securities cannot always be liquidated quickly, especially when the obligations are of weaker credit quality. And they misconstrued the complexities of convergence trade."[37] Simply put, they assumed that the yields on their different holdings would narrow, presenting them with a profit. However, the combination of strong analytics and the traders' penchant for gambling proved too combustible. The cocky attitude of LTCM cast long shadows over the markets and revived debates about the role of regulators in the derivatives markets.

The fund's collapse put a damper on the entire market. Kaufman ran a fund similar to LTCM called Strategic Partners. It, too, ran into difficulties but on a much smaller scale. When a similar bet on yield discrepancies failed, Kaufman and his partner decided to close the fund rather than forge ahead. When the Russian securities it purchased failed to respond in a predictable manner, Kaufman remarked that "this lack of convergence doesn't surprise me in a sense. This was credit without a guardian. There's the illusion that it has a market, that you can sell it and pass the risk to someone else."[38]

After the $3.65 billion rescue package was complete, the Toronto *Globe & Mail* had a little fun with LTCM, naming it as the winner of its "Too Big to Fail Award." Citing the well-known principle in banking that some institutions are too large to be allowed to fail, the paper noted that regulators enlisted others to put it back on its feet. It was possible to lose several billion dollars and still be allowed back in business. "Don't expect the same treatment from your friendly neighborhood banker if you fall behind on your mortgage payments," the newspaper warned its readers.[39] The reputation of Scholes and Merton also brought the inevitable barrage of comments about the role of academic models in real-world finance. A reader from Oxford wrote in *The Guardian* that they "precipitated a world financial crisis. Previous distinguished economists have only managed to destabilize individual economies."[40]

Larger investors who insisted on remaining after LTCM began returning money also suffered—at least temporarily.

Over 100 Merrill Lynch executives had a total of $22 million invested in the fund at the time of the bailout package. The news hit Goldman Sachs so hard that its highly publicized initial public offering had to be postponed to allow investors to assess the impact of the losses on the bank's bottom line. The Union Bank of Switzerland (UBS), which was LTCM's largest bank investor also lost a substantial amount. Repercussions were heard long after the initial five-week period of crisis that led to the bailout. The fund itself continued in business on a diminished scale, now subject to limits on its positions and activities. Critics naturally questioned the role of the Fed in the affair. Many failed to recognize that LTCM had created a major problem for the banks that would require a strong regulatory hand to correct. However, the overriding concern that emerged was the absence of a viable derivatives regulator. The fund was a unique institution and its star-studded banner of partners and traders should have provided some internal controls over risk. However, external regulation over the unique institution was sorely lacking. A scandal had erupted with apparently no one at the controls and the fund was allowed to continue operating after the fact.

The fund was the center of attention when Congress considered the fate of the financial services industry in 1998. A flurry of legislative activity revamped many of the existing securities and banking regulations passed during the 1930s. In late 1998, Congress passed the Financial Services Modernization Act, superseding parts of the Glass–Steagall Act of 1933 that had separated investment and commercial banking. The futures markets received a similar uplift from the Commodity Futures Modernization Act (CFMA) passed a year later in 1999. The new law actually was the four-year renewal of the agency.

The new law sought to add flexibility to the structure of the CFTC. It sought to identify parts of the derivatives industry where glaring oversights existed and attempted to provide some regulation before a new LTCM-type fund emerged. The proposals were drafted by CFTC Chairman William Rainer. Broadly, the new emphasis of the agency was shifted from enforcement to oversight. The prevailing philosophy emphasized compliance with, rather than enforcement of, the rules, which in the past had normally meant doing so after a crisis occurred. The problems caused by the traders at LTCM and by Nick Leeson at Baring Brothers were clearly in the forefront of the new operating procedures. The law also gave regulatory approval to a new product jointly approved by the CFTC and the SEC.

Critics of the derivatives markets raised their eyebrows when the two agencies lifted a ban on the introduction of individual stock futures. Although the new contracts did not begin trading immediately, even the idea was repugnant to many who remembered previous battles between the two agencies and the SEC's insistence on keeping a lid on equities derivatives. Individual stock futures seemed to be a capitulation to the notion that increased trading in derivatives did not fundamentally harm the market for the underlying securities. The role of options was openly discussed 25 years before. At the time, there was concern about puts and calls draining funds away from new issues of stock and diminishing secondary market trading. Would individual stock futures signify that stock trading had finally become commoditized, as critics had feared for years? Or was it simply the culmination of the 1990s' bull market when all sorts of ideas were bandied around without much regard for their implications when markets would be weaker in the future.

As the 1990s ended, the markets certainly remained one step ahead of regulators and committed to financial innovation. Given the derivatives markets' entrepreneurial spirit and dislike of outside intervention, the old tradition born in the nineteenth century could be expected to survive into the twenty-first. The markets will innovate, experiment, and resist attempts to interfere in their affairs. Some traditions die hard.

## NOTES

1. The face value of swaps was listed on company balance sheets as contingent liabilities, usually found in a footnote on the balance sheet. Although it was understood that only the actual interest payments were actually being swapped between two parties, the total amount was listed in the event that one party had to assume the other's liability. When taken in aggregate, the numbers could be quite large.
2. *Investment Dealers' Digest*, November 25, 1991.
3. Ibid.
4. *Securities Week*, May 3, 1993.
5. *Journal of Commerce*, January 11, 1991.
6. Ibid., March 28, 1991.
7. *Washington Post*, April 13, 1994.
8. Kelley Holland, Linda Himelstein, & Zachary Schiller, "The Bankers Trust Tapes," *Business Week*, October 16, 1995.
9. Ibid.
10. *New York Times*, July 2, 1996.
11. Philippe Joiron, *Big Bets Gone Bad: Derivatives and Bankruptcy in Orange County* (San Diego: Academic Press, 1995), p. 2.
12. Ibid., p. 102.
13. *Washington Post*, December 10, 1994.
14. The LIBOR is a rate set by the largest banks in London and quotes what interest rate the banks are willing to loan money to other banks. Nonbank customers pay a spread over LIBOR, based upon their credit ratings. The rate at which banks are willing to accept deposits is the bid rate, or the London Interbank bid rate (LIBID). The difference between LIBID and LIBOR is the bank's margin of profit.
15. *Bond Buyer*, December 6, 1994.
16. Jorion, *Big Bets*, p. 9.
17. *Barron's*, December 5, 1994.

18. Jorion *Big Bets*, p. 105.
19. Ibid., p. 100.
20. *Bond Buyer*, December 9, 1994.
21. Allan Sloan, "Financial Lunacy Comes Home to Roost," *Plain Dealer*, December 11, 1994.
22. *Los Angeles Times*, June 5, 1998.
23. Leo Melamed, *Leo Melamed on the Markets* (New York: John Wiley & Sons, 1993), p. 91.
24. Stephen Fay, *The Collapse of Barings* (New York: Norton, 1996), p. 122.
25. Ibid., pp. 123, 124.
26. Ibid., p. 155.
27. John Gapper & Nicholas Denton, *All That Glitters: The Fall of Barings* (London: Hamish Hamilton, 1996), p. 281.
28. *Washington Post*, December 7, 1994.
29. Ibid.
30. Hart and Teeter Research Companies poll for NBC News and the *Wall Street Journal*, April 30, 1994.
31. *New York Times*, February 17, 1997.
32. Roger Lowenstein, *When Genius Failed: The Rise and Fall of Long-Term Capital Management* (New York: Random House, 2000), p. 26.
33. Ibid., p. 103.
34. Ibid., p. 104.
35. Ibid., p. 120.
36. *Plain Dealer*, February 3, 1999.
37. Henry Kaufman, *On Money and Markets: A Wall Street Memoir* (New York: McGraw-Hill, 2000), p. 283.
38. *Dow Jones Newswires*, "Capital Markets Report," October 31, 1998.
39. *Globe and Mail*, December 31, 1998.
40. *The Guardian*, April 7, 1999.

# Postscript

FTER 150 YEARS OF DEVELOPMENT, IT IS CLEAR THAT cowboy capitalism still survived at the end of the twentieth century. The rogues of the 1880s made the original case for it, and their counterparts in the 1990s carried on the tradition. Benjamin Hutchinson cornered wheat in the nineteenth century and LTCM applied a variation of the same concept to bonds. Both did so while ingenuously pleading their innocence. Hutchinson studied the price and travels of gold to predict wheat prices, while LTCM used complex quantitative models which could not manage the tendency to leverage trading positions. Like any good Wild West show, the boundaries were limitless and success was measured by achieving what others could not.

Both Hutchinson and LTCM discovered that models and risk-management techniques cannot fight a basic fact of market history. When futures contracts become commoditized, no one is interested in playing the game with the same vigor that existed in the past. Profits disappear and what was once considered novel becomes passé as price discrepancies and the vagaries of supply and demand disappear. If history is any guide, the problem for regulators becomes obvious. Something new will come through the pipeline that is equally clever and will do serious financial harm unless regulators are able to detect it in advance. Although that sounds reasonable, the record to date is not encouraging. The ingenuity of the derivatives markets is far ahead of the understaffed agencies trying to direct traffic on the corner.

The derivatives markets have displayed market capitalism with all of its blemishes and warts. They have also displayed flashes of brilliance in which genuine economic benefits have been derived from trading in futures and swaps. The economic boom of the 1990s owes much of its impetus to the adroit use of swaps and futures, helping many companies to reduce their costs of capital. The result was low inflation and a general sense of prosperity. Unfortunately, the same decade and the same markets helped produced some of the largest fiascoes ever seen in financial markets. Public reaction can be sharp, becoming more so when the sums of money involved in such fiascoes become enormous. The markets run the risk of a strong reaction from the government. Usually, stringent financial regulations in the United States are imposed only after a financial crisis. One of the casualties of potent regulation can be the very innovation that the derivatives markets have demonstrated over the years, especially since the early 1970s. As the markets become more sophisticated, tension between the two sides of the markets will become obvious. Is the innovation worth the spotty regulation and the inevitable crisis?

While some would argue that the occasional financial fiasco is simply the price of innovation, the sums of money involved in the derivatives markets cannot be written off easily. The amount of money lost in derivatives fiascoes in the 1980s and 1990s alone equals the gross national product (GNP) of the United States in 1890. The lesson that the history of derivatives markets makes clear is that regulators need to be as clever and quick as the markets before another inevitable attempt at cowboy capitalism causes more harm.

# Bibliography

Frederick Lewis Allen, *Only Yesterday: An Informal History of the 1920s* (New York: Harper & Row, 1931).

Albert W. Atwood, *The Stock and Produce Exchanges* (New York: Alexander Hamilton Institute, 1921).

Julius B. Baer & George Woodruff, *Commodity Exchanges* (New York: Harper & Bros., 1935).

Neil Baldwin, *Henry Ford and the Jews: The Mass Production of Hate* (New York: Public Affairs, 2001).

Bernard Baruch, *My Own Story* (New York: Holt, Rinehart & Winston, 1957).

Peter L. Bernstein, *The Power of Gold: The History of an Obsession* (New York: John Wiley & Sons, 2000).

Fischer Black & Myron Scholes, "The Pricing of Options and Corporate Liabilities," *Journal of Political Economy*, vol. 81 (May-June 1973).

James E. Boyle, *Speculation and the Chicago Board of Trade* (New York: Macmillan, 1921).

Nicholas Brady et al., *Report of the Presidential Task Force on Market Mechanisms* (Washington, DC: U.S. Government Printing Office, 1988).

Harold Brayman, *The President Speaks Off-the-Record: Historic Evenings with America's Leaders, the Press, and Other Men of Power at Washington's Exclusive Gridiron Club* (Princeton, NJ: Dow Jones Books, 1976).

John Brooks, *Once in Golconda: A True Drama of Wall Street 1920–1938* (New York: Harper & Row, 1969).

————, *The Go-Go Years* (New York: Weybright & Talley, 1973).

Brendan Brown & Charles R. Geisst, *Financial Futures Markets* (New York: St. Martin's Press, 1983).

D. Bruner, *Short-Selling the USA: An Opinion in the Form of Analysis of the System of Short Selling and Its Influence in the Creation of the Depression* (Philadelphia: John C. Winston Co., 1933).

Willard W. Cochrane, *The Development of American Agriculture* (Minneapolis: University of Minnesota Press, 1979).

Kinahan Cornwallis, *The Gold Room* (New York: A. S. Barnes & Co., 1879).

Cedric B. Cowing, *Populists, Plungers, and Progressives: A Social History of Stock and Commodity Speculation 1890–1936* (Princeton, NJ: Princeton University Press, 1965).

Kenneth S. Davis, *FDR: The New Deal Years 1933–1937* (New York: Random House, 1979).

T. Henry Dewey, *Legislation Against Speculation and Gambling in Futures* (New York: Baker, Voorhis & Co., 1905).

Edward Jerome Dies, *The Plunger* (New York: Covici-Friede, 1929).

Patricia A. Dreyfus, "Commodities Futures for the Small Investor," *Money* (May 1979).

Henry C. Emery, *Speculation on the Stock and Produce Markets* (New York: Columbia University Press, 1896).

Stephen Fay, *Beyond Greed* (New York: Viking Press, 1982).

————, *The Collapse of Barings* (New York: Norton, 1996).

Federal Trade Commission, *Report on the Grain Trade* (Washington, DC: U.S. Government Printing Office, 1920–1926).

————, *Economic Report of the Investigation of Coffee Prices* (Washington, DC: U.S. Government Printing Office, 1954).

William G. Ferris, *The Grain Traders: The Story of the Chicago Board of Trade* (East Lansing: Michigan State University Press, 1988).

John M. Findlay, *People of Chance: Gambling in American Society from Jamestown to Las Vegas* (New York: Oxford University Press, 1986).

Milton Friedman, *Essays in Positive Economics* (Chicago: University of Chicago Press, 1953).

George H. Gallup, *The Gallup Poll: Public Opinion 1935–1971* (New York: Random House, 1972).

John Gapper & Nicholas Denton, *All That Glitters: The Fall of Barings* (London: Hamish Hamilton, 1996).

356

Charles R. Geisst, *Wall Street: A History* (New York: Oxford University Press, 1997).

———, *Monopolies in America: Empire Builders and Their Enemies from Jay Gould to Bill Gates* (New York: Oxford University Press, 2000).

———, *The Last Partnerships: Inside the Great Wall Street Money Dynasties* (New York: McGraw-Hill, 2001).

[Clinton Gilbert], *The Mirrors of Wall Street* (New York: Putnam, 1933). (The book was published anonymously.)

B. A. Goss & Basil Yamey, *The Economics of Futures Trading*, 2nd ed. (London: Macmillan, 1978).

Leslie Gould, *The Manipulators* (New York: David McKay, 1966).

R. W. Gray, "Onions Revisited," *Journal of Farm Economics*, vol. 45 (1963).

David Greising & Laurie Morse, *Brokers, Bagmen and Moles: Fraud and Corruption in the Chicago Futures Markets* (New York: John Wiley & Sons, 1991).

Kurt W. Hemr, "Commodity Litigation Update," *Standard & Poor's Review of Securities and Commodities Regulation* (June 5, 1996).

John Hicks, *Value and Capital* (Oxford: Oxford University Press, 1978).

John Hill Jr., *Gold Bricks of Speculation* (Chicago: Lincoln Book Concern, 1904).

G. W. Hoffman, *Futures Trading upon Organized Commodity Markets in the United States* (Philadelphia: University of Pennsylvania Press, 1932).

Richard Hofstadter, *The Age of Reform: From Bryan to F.D.R.* (New York: Alfred A. Knopf, 1955).

Kelley Holland, Linda Himelstein, & Zachary Schiller, "The Bankers Trust Tapes," *Business Week* (October 16, 1995).

Edwin P. Hoyt, *The Goulds* (New York: Weybright & Talley, 1969).

Jesse Jones, *Fifty Billion Dollars: My Thirteen Years with the RFC* (New York: Macmillan, 1951).

Philippe Jorion, *Big Bets Gone Bad: Derivatives and Bankruptcy in Orange County* (San Diego: Academic Press, 1995).

Henry Kaufman, *On Money and Markets: A Wall Street Memoir* (New York: McGraw-Hill, 2000).

Philip Kinsley, *The Chicago Tribune: Its First Hundred Years*, 3 vols. (Chicago: The Chicago Tribune, 1946).

T. A. Kofi, "A Framework for Comparing the Efficiency of Futures Markets," *American Journal of Agricultural Economics*, vol. 55 (1973).

BIBLIOGRAPHY

Thomas L. Lawson, *Frenzied Finance* (1905; reprint, New York: Greenwood Press, 1968).

Walter Lippmann, *Interpretations, 1931–1932* (New York: Macmillan, 1932).

Roger Lowenstein, *When Genius Failed: The Rise and Fall of Long-Term Capital Management* (New York: Random House, 2000).

Jonathan Lurie, *The Chicago Board of Trade 1859–1905: The Dynamics of Self-Regulation* (Urbana: University of Illinois Press, 1979).

Mary Jane Matz, *The Many Lives of Otto Kahn* (New York: Macmillan, 1963).

Wesley McCune, *The Farm Bloc* (Garden City, NY: Doubleday, Doran & Co., 1943).

Robert S. McElvaine, *The Great Depression* (New York: Times Books, 1984).

J. C. McMath, *Speculation and Gambling in Options, Futures and Stocks in Illinois* (Chicago: G. I. Jones & Co., 1921).

James E. Meeker, *Short Selling* (New York: Harper & Bros., 1932).

Leo Melamed, *Leo Melamed on the Markets* (New York: John Wiley & Sons, 1993).

Leo Melamed & Bob Tamarkin, *Escape to the Futures* (New York: John Wiley & Sons, 1996).

Merchants' Exchange of St. Louis, *Articles of Association, Rules, By-Laws and Regulations* (St. Louis, 1903).

Norman C. Miller, *The Great Salad Oil Swindle* (Baltimore: Penguin Books, 1965).

New York Stock & Exchange Board, *Report of the Committee of the Gold Board* (June 3, 1865).

New York Stock Exchange, *Demand and Supply of Equity Capital* (New York: New York Stock Exchange, 1975).

———, *Fact Book* (various issues).

Victor Niederhoffer, *The Education of a Speculator* (New York: John Wiley & Sons, 1997).

James L. Orr (ed.), *Grange Melodies* (Philadelphia: Geo. S. Ferguson Co., 1912).

Frank Partnoy, *FIASCO: The Inside Story of a Wall Street Trader* (New York: Penguin Putnam, 1999).

Mark J. Powers, "Does Futures Trading Reduce Price Fluctuations in the Cash Markets?" *American Economic Review,* vol. 60 (1970).

Mark J. Powers & David Vogel, *Inside the Financial Futures Markets* (New York: John Wiley & Sons, 1981).

358

# BIBLIOGRAPHY

John M. Quitmeyer, "Fiduciary Obligations in the Derivatives Marketplace," *Standard & Poor's Review of Securities and Commodities Regulation* (October 25, 1995).

Donald T. Regan, *A View from the Street* (New York: New American Library, 1972).

C. E. Russell, *The Greatest Trust in the World* (Chicago: Ridgway-Thayer, 1905).

Paul A. Samuelson, "Economic Problems Concerning a Futures Market in Foreign Exchange," *The Futures Market in Foreign Currencies* (Chicago: Chicago Mercantile Exchange, 1972).

Alfred E. Smith, *Campaign Addresses of Governor Alfred E. Smith* (Washington, DC: Democratic National Committee, 1929).

Robert Solomon, *The International Monetary System, 1945–1976* (New York: Harper & Row, 1977).

Karl Sparling, *Mystery Men of Wall Street* (New York: Blue Ribbon Books, 1930).

George Sullivan, *By Chance a Winner: The History of Lotteries* (New York: Dodd Mead, 1972).

Bob Tamarkin, *The New Gatsbys: Fortunes and Misfortunes of Commodity Traders* (New York: William Morrow, 1985).

———, *The MERC: The Emergence of a Global Financial Powerhouse* (New York: HarperBusiness, 1993).

C. H. Taylor, *History of the Board of Trade of the City of Chicago* (Chicago: Robert O. Law Co., 1917).

Owen Taylor, *Short Selling: Theory and Practice* (New York: Stock Market Publications, 1933).

Richard J. Teweles & Frank Jones, *The Futures Game*, 2nd ed. (New York: McGraw-Hill, 1987).

Ray Tucker & Frederick R. Barkley, *Sons of the Wild Jackass*, 1932, reprint (Seattle: University of Washington Press, 1970).

Report of the Committee on Banking and Currency. *Gold Panic Investigation*, 41st Cong., 2nd sess., Feb. 28, 1870, Rept. 32.

U.S. Department of Commerce, *Historical Statistics of the United States: Colonial Times to 1957* (Washington, DC: 1961).

T. H. Watkins, *The Great Depression: America in the 1930s* (Boston: Little Brown, 1993).

Lloyd Wendt, *Chicago Tribune: The Rise of a Great American Newspaper* (Chicago: Rand McNally, 1979).

Daniel Yergin, *The Prize: The Epic Quest for Oil, Money and Power* (New York: Simon & Schuster, 1991).

# Index

# INDEX

# INDEX

# INDEX